WITHDRAWN

CHABOT COLLEGE-HAYWARD

2 555 000 064426 $

S0-ALB-112

CAMARGUE

Karl Weber / Lukas Hoffmann

Translated by Ewald Osers

CAMARGUE

The Soul of a Wilderness

Joseph J. Binns
Publisher
Washington – New York

QH
147
W413
1977

This publication
is recommended by the

WORLD
WILDLIFE FUND

The photographs were produced with its support and in collaboration with the
SOCIÉTÉ NATIONALE DE PROTECTION DE LA NATURE, France.

Published in the United States 1977
ISBN 0-88331-092-9

All rights reserved, including the right to reproduce this book, or parts thereof,
in any form except for the inclusion of brief quotations in a review

Library of Congress Card Catalog Number 77-71399

Graphical presentation: Kümmerly & Frey, Geographical Publishers, Berne
Printing and binding by Stæmpfli + Cie Ltd, Berne
© 1968 Kümmerly & Frey, Geographical Publishers, Berne
English translation © Kümmerly & Frey, Berne 1970
Printed in Switzerland
ISBN 0 245 50467 2

Contents

Scientific collaborator and consultant

Dr. Lukas Hoffmann

Technical collaborators and members of the expedition

Heinz Hafner, Peter Horner, Edith Stöhr

Photographs

Heinz Hafner   Nos 21, 22, 101
Peter Horner   Nos 5, 8, 13, 17, 20, 43, 66
George K. Yeates   No 23

All others by Karl Weber

All photographic work on KODAK films

123899

Preface

These pictures of the Camargue take me back a few decades, to those far-off days of the first of my many visits. The memory of that early morning when I first entered my promised land by the waterway is as fresh as if I had only just returned from that kayak trip down the Rhône. We had paddled all through the night because the midges on the banks of the Lesser Rhône would not leave us alone. But how richly we were rewarded by the miracle of the rising day! From the trees on the bank the herons flew up, rose-coloured in the first early light, and round a big bend in the river the rising sun lit up the white horses and the dark cattle of the Camargue. And then the unforgettable picture which opened before us as we drifted out from the estuary into the sea, into the white surf, into the blinding light dancing on the waves, and then to our rest on the sunny beach.

This was the Camargue before its rapid industrial development, the Camargue which I have since revisited time and again and which, happily, continues to exist amidst an environment fundamentally changed by man's economy, a change which is increasingly affecting also that vast region of the Rhône estuary. But this book, born of love for the more hidden life of the Camargue, testifies that what delighted me so long ago lives on. This book leads us into wild nature away from the busy tourist routes. Naturally, the visitor will not get such a close and comprehensive view of all forms of life as is provided by these pictures. Such observation requires patience and luck—and anyone who has taken the time and trouble to observe nature for himself will soon begin to understand the degree of dedication and patience, as well as the amount of knowledge of the secret life of the vast plains, that were necessary before the present wealth of pictures could be spread out before us in book form. It is hoped therefore that the book will inspire the reader and viewer to go out, stay awhile, and see for himself. That is why biologists with many years of experience of the region teamed up with the photographer to capture not only the more conspicuous and larger forms of life, but to reveal to him also the less obvious riches which the Camargue has to offer at all times of the year—in early spring when the water buttercups spread out their white carpet across the sheets of water, when the rich life of dragonflies begins to unfold and countless birds settle down to breed, in the closing months of the year when the life of the dragonflies reaches one more climax, and in winter when thousands of birds inhabit the vast sheets of water.

The Camargue is not, properly speaking, a primeval landscape. Too many changes have been wrought by the taming of the Greater Rhône, by the utilization of the coastal areas for salt production and, more recently, by rice cultivation, which again meant an entirely different kind of interference from that of the salt-pan industry. But it shows us that, in spite of technological progress, a great wealth and variety of flourishing life can continue—so much, in fact, that we seem to be feeling the mighty breath of the wilderness. Travelling south under the blue sky of Provence and seeing the witnesses of a great past, the traces of the Mediterranean civilization which has so powerfully shaped our Western world, one is struck by the contrast when, on entering the Camargue, one comes face to face with timeless nature, with an overpowering impression of a primeval world. It is to be hoped that the present colourful testimony to this life, collected between the covers of this book, will not only help a great many friends of nature to gain a deeper understanding of this wild nature but also arouse in us a sense of responsibility without which the preservation of this natural life will not be possible in future. Surely the riches which still surround us today and which belong to everybody must be preserved for the future, to give the same pleasure to all those who love nature.

PROF. DR. ADOLF PORTMANN
Zoological Institute of Basle University

Introduction

Camargue—a name full of magic and legendary romance. A frontier of Europe—a mysterious wilderness on the coasts of the Mediterranean—realm of white horses and wild bulls—home of the *gardians,* of gipsies, of flamingos. Camargue—a vast primeval landscape stretched out between sky and water, born of the Rhône over thousands of years, reconquered by the sea, risen up again in the ceaseless battle of the elements. The name of the Camargue has always conjured up gipsies, horses, and flamingos. Whether it was at the end of the last and the beginning of the present century, or in the years between the two World Wars, or more recently, the stranger invariably carried these concepts with him when he first entered the Rhône delta. This mental image has remained unaffected by present-day reality. An almost infinite number of newspaper and magazine reports, books, films, television programmes, and publicity slogans of wideawake travel agencies have praised the virginity of the Camargue soil, the unspoilt character of its men and beasts. Thus they have all helped to keep alive to the present time a picture of days gone by, a picture that has crystallized into a virtually unchangeable pattern.

It is a questionable, an outdated, and a frequently misleading and incorrect picture. There is talk of herds of wild horses, of full-blooded bull-fighting contests, and of swarms of birds darkening the sun. Gipsy pilgrimages, competitions of horsemanship, and the silhouettes of flamingos against a purple night sky continue to supply the background for romantic accounts. Hardly ever does anyone mention the fact that, alongside with idyllic landscapes and enchanting birds, alongside cowherds and gipsies, the modern age with its technical achievements has long taken possession of large tracts of this remote region. It has done so suddenly, ruthlessly, and accompanied by not invariably welcome consequences. As a result, the new arrival is frequently disappointed to find reality far less paradisial than his mental picture. He came to see vast unspoilt steppes —and he finds surfaced roads, giant high-voltage pylons and barbed-wire fences stretching for mile after mile. He hoped to get a view of flocks of rare birds—and instead he finds his road lined with rice paddies and vineyards. He looks for the legendary horses and bulls—and all he sees are brightly painted bulldozers. The peace and solitude which he hoped to find here are lost in the engine roar of long columns of lorries and in the scream of jet aircraft streaking overhead. He seeks, perhaps without realizing it,

that Camargue which the lonely wanderer a quarter of a century ago might still have found. But what he finds today is the new, modern face of a landscape whose still intact nucleus is trying to pit its natural strength and a deep-rooted tradition against the destructive influences of the outside world. This is a fact which comes as a surprise and as somewhat of a shock to all those who remember the Camargue in a less hectic age. And many a newcomer, lacking both the time and the leisure to make the acquaintance of the delta in all its different forms and shapes, finds himself disillusioned and turns back home.

The face of the Rhône delta has changed a great deal over the past few decades. It is criss-crossed by roads, tracks and artificial dikes. Soil-moving machines have torn many a gaping wound in its body; along its borders tourism bursts into astonishing flowers during the summer months. The scars left behind by the stream of visitors, a stream which grows from year to year, cannot be concealed; even folklore and custom suffer heavily from it. To shut one's eyes to these facts would be short-sighted; it would be putting one's head in the sand. To disguise them would be a service to no-one—least of all to the Camargue itself. For thanks to all those who have for years struggled for the protection of the Rhône delta, the vast wilderness which the Camarguais loves as his home is not dead. Life still throbs in every watery ditch, in every clump of bulrushes, in every tamarisk grove. Its wonders are still revealed to him who looks for them in the flooded rice paddy or on the wind-swept salt grass steppe; in the twilight of the tall reeds as much as along the fringe of shallow lagoons; in ponds and swamps as much as on the beach and in the troughs of the dunes. But they do not force themselves upon the beholder. On the contrary, they want to be sought out and discovered. The land, by nature hostile to man, guards its secrets more jealously than ever. Let no-one who spends a few hours dashing in a car along one of the main roads from Arles to the sea and back claim that he knows the Camargue. A man hurrying across the delta according to a carefully fixed timetable, from north to south and from east to west, and at the same time visiting the near-by sites with their famous monuments of antiquity, may see a great deal but will probably not experience anything. And anyone driving from Les Saintes-Maries to Salin-de-Giraud along the *Digue de la Mer,* with barely two or three short stops, can never feel even the slightest breath of this magnificent landscape. He will never understand why others, in spite of rice paddies and high-voltage pylons, in spite of hard roads and artificial dikes, to this day succumb to the magic of the Rhône delta and, wherever they find themselves, feel an unassuageable nostalgia for this region. There is too much beauty hidden in the Camargue and in its border regions for much of it to be seen in a few hours or days, or even in weeks or months. Years would be needed to acquire even a modest idea of the variety of its great and small miracles. Yet few are fortunate enough to be able to devote such years to the Camargue. Most visitors come for a few days or weeks of vacation. Naturally they want to see as much as possible of what they have heard or read about. In spite of this understandable desire, or perhaps just because of it, one feels one should warn them: To see less is to see more! It may sound like a cliché, but it is still valid for this unique landscape. Its most precious features are not revealed on a random exhausting cross-country race. A person stopping quietly and unobtrusively by a pond or inland lake will gain a deeper insight into the harsh beauty of the land than one restlessly chasing after botanical or zoological rarities. A person walking through the steppe for half a day or a whole day will return richer in experiences and more satisfied than one who drives his car this way and that through the landscape, without ever leaving his wheeled strait-jacket.

Access to certain parts of the delta, in particular to the reserve proper, must be barred to the tourist for obvious reasons. The flood of visitors reaches its first peak at the very time when many rare and shy birds are breeding—at a time, therefore, when they require particular quiet and security. Moreover, the structure of the landscape prevents the exploration of large tracts of the middle and lower Camargue by any special tracks. Instead, steppe, salt mud-flats, ditches of brackish water, and lagoons intermingle suddenly in the most varied way. Ignorance or thoughtlessness on the part of a visitor could cause a great deal of irreparable damage.

But these inevitable restrictions scarcely affect the possibilities of observation. Most of the birds breeding in the reserve also nest outside its boundaries, and birds flying out in search of food circulate with great regularity between the zones barred to tourists and those open to them both as pedestrians and motorists. Indeed, in these boundary areas, where the animals are more or less used to the presence of man, it is usually possible to approach them at a lesser distance and observe them more closely.

No-one who is interested in such things will ever be disappointed in a stay in the Camargue, no matter how short. Whether he comes in the spring at blossom-time, or in the summer when the land groans under a parching heat, or in the autumn when heavy rains fill the dried-up ponds and swamps, or even in the winter—he will always leave with unforgettable impressions of the Rhône delta. And he will realize and understand that no effort can be too great to protect and preserve this landscape which is so unique in Europe.

KARL WEBER

The Camargue—a European National Park

Wild Nature, Ancient Culture, and a Long History

The Camargue is the area of the Rhône estuary. Bounded by the two arms of the Rhône, which divides above Arles, and by the Mediterranean coast, it forms a triangular island. The visitor who enters the totally flat region of about 800 square kilometres (300 square miles) first of all passes through rich farmland, where vines, rice paddies, corn-fields, orchards, and pastureland are cultivated on large farms with the most up-to-date machinery. Only when he has penetrated a good distance towards the centre of the Camargue, towards the areas nearer the sea, do the fields gradually give way to a mosaic of lakes, reed-beds, pools, and salt steppes with a sparse growth of tamarisks, until eventually he crosses the dunes to reach a magnificent fifty-kilometre-long beach (thirty miles) of finest sand. This is the wild Camargue of the flamingos, of the herds of black cattle and white horses, of graceful avocets, black-winged stilts, and little egrets—of those vast numbers of birds of the most varied species which have made the area so famous among ornithologists and nature preservers throughout the world. Nowhere else in industrialized Western Europe has such a rich fauna been preserved in such an original natural habitat. One would have to travel to Andalusia or to the Danube delta, or perhaps to Africa and Asia, in order to experience wild nature in a similarly impressive way.

The Camargue was created by the Rhône. Starting as a violent torrent among the glaciers of Switzerland, the river soon reaches the plain, is joined on its right and left banks by streams and other rivers, and reaches the Camargue as a slow majestic river. Lyons, 310 kilometres (193 miles) up-river from its estuary, lies at an altitude of only 169 metres (555 feet) above sea-level. As a result, by the time it reaches the Camargue, the Rhône has long deposited all heavy detritus and gravel, and even all coarse sand. All it carries is fine silt, and it is from this silt that the delta has been built up in the course of hundreds of thousands of years. This building process, however, was not continuous; it was a perpetual struggle in which, owing to floods and gales, advances of the land alternated with inroads of the sea, and during which the Rhône's arms continually changed their course. Even though, in the end, the Rhône continued to gain more and more land, this land still bore the imprint of the sea which, during its retreat, had left its salt in the soil. This salt has been a decisive factor in shaping the peculiar vegetation and fauna of the Camargue. It was relatively late that man, as a third power, intervened in this struggle between river and sea. True, there was a first flourishing in Gallo-Roman days. Even then horses and bulls were bred in the Camargue and used for sport—but no-one knows whether these were the ancestors of today's *taureaux* and white horses, or indeed whether they were anything like them. In the Middle Ages large parts of the Camargue were the property of monasteries, but the soil was not used agriculturally to any considerable extent. Indeed, this would have been scarcely possible so long as the island was apt to be flooded again as the arms of the Rhône kept changing their course, or as southerly gales caused the sea to inundate large parts of the delta. Although there were some dikes along the Rhône in the early Middle Ages, these were in no way equal to the major disasters which occurred time and again. In spite of these unfavourable circumstances nearly all the farmsteads *(mas)* existing today were set up during the sixteenth to eighteenth centuries. At that time the Camargue was regarded as the granary of Provence, but the fields nevertheless remained small enclaves amidst its vast steppes and marshes grazed by large herds of sheep, bulls, and horses. Over the years the dikes against the Rhône were improved and new defences built against the sea. The present *Digue de la Mer* was built only in 1857/58, and the definitive Rhône dikes were built between 1858 and 1869. The Camargue peasants were then, at last, safe from floods, and the next few decades saw the construction of a network of irrigation and drainage canals which carried fresh water from the Rhône to the fields and in turn drained these towards the lower-lying salt lakes at the centre of the Camargue. These developments not only promoted rice cultivation, grass and lucerne grazing, and cereal growing, but also enabled the farmers to plant vines on a large scale when the French vineyards were ravaged by phylloxera towards the end of the last century. It had been discovered that this parasite, which in winter withdraws to the roots of the vines, perished in irrigated vineyards and caused no damage in the Camargue.

In spite of all this development and progress, the area under cultivation in the Camargue, strangely enough, had not risen above 18,000 hectares (44,480 acres) by the time of the Second World War, with more than 50,000 hectares (123,550 acres) remaining as steppes, marshes, and lakes. There has been no shortage of cultivation plans. Ever since the late eighteenth century large-scale projects for the cultivation of the whole region have been put forward by engineers working for the public authorities or by outstanding individuals from the near-by towns. The money for the realization of these projects could have been raised easily enough, but all proposals were invariably shelved after endless discussions, simply because landowners and peasants in the Camargue were never able to agree. It is not the hostility of nature that has saved the wild character of the Camargue for the twentieth century, but the individualism of its inhabitants. These have always struggled hard, each for himself or perhaps just with his immediate neighbour, and achieved outstanding results in maintaining and enlarging their farms—but they have always refused to listen to any plans involving interference by the authorities or a large-scale amalgamation of those who owned and worked the land.

Since the Second World War, however, progress has accelerated. Rice, until then grown only on a small acreage, was a commodity in great demand at the end of the war, and within a few years between 10,000 and 12,000 hectares (25,000 to 30,000 acres) of new land were put under this crop. The same period also saw an upsurge in salt production. The salt is extracted from the seawater by pumping it or letting it flow into lagoons where, under the heat of the sun, the water evaporates and increases its salt content until the salt crystallizes out. Salt production has been practised in small salt-pans for several centuries. It has been expanding ever since the end of the last century and by the end of the Second World War accounted for roughly 2500 hectares (6000 acres). Since then the importance of common salt for the chemical industry, and in particular for the manufacture of synthetic materials, has greatly increased, and the salt-pans of the Camargue, which are all grouped around Salin-de-Giraud and belong to the *Cie des Salins du Midi,* now cover an area of about 11,000 hectares (28,000 acres). Thus the agriculturally and industrially used area of the Camargue, after thousands of years of slow and fitful development, has very nearly doubled in little more than twenty years. We shall see later what problems arise for the future from this development. For the present, however, the realm of unspoilt nature—the steppes, reed-beds, lakes and pools with their flamingos, little egrets, *taureaux,* and horses —still covers some 35,000 hectares (86,000 acres), or very nearly half the Camargue. It is to this part that this book is dedicated.

Favourable and Hostile Elements

The character of the Camargue's flora and fauna is determined chiefly by four factors—the Mediterranean climate, the water, the salt, and the wind. The first two are the basis of its wealth, the last two limit its fertility. A Mediterranean climate means a lot of sunshine, warm dry summers, and mild and rather damp winters. Although the winter temperature in the Camargue can be substantially lower than on the Riviera—sometimes all stagnant water freezes solid—the January average of 6 °C (43 °F) is a good 5 °C (9 °F) above the average of the Central European plains. The highest temperatures are found in July, with an average of 23 °C (73 °F); this is rather warm but not really hot. Total precipitation, at an average of 564 millimetres (22.2 inches), is considerably less than in Central or Northern Europe, but more than in true arid regions. Most of the rain falls in the autumn and winter, whereas the summer is very dry. This means that the water is lacking at the time when warmth and sunshine would make for great fertility. For that reason, also, most Mediterranean areas exhibit only a sparse, dry vegetation. In the Camargue, on the other hand, the Rhône supplies ever new quantities of fresh water even during the summer, and, thanks to the impermeability of the soil, the water brought by the winter rains frequently remains in many pools and marshes until spring or summer. Here, therefore, the Mediterranean climate coincides with ample supplies of water and this provides the basis for exceptional fertility. For that reason, also, life in the Camargue is concentrated on and around all moving and stagnant water, while the remaining areas exhibit an almost desert-like poverty. The third decisive factor is the salt (see map 3). Left behind by the retreating sea, it occurs in solution in surface and ground water, as well as crystallized and absorbed in the soil. For a long time it was the main obstacle to the expansion of agriculture. Only when extensive installations for

12

irrigation and drainage had been built did it become possible to wash the salt out of the surface layers of the soil. Nevertheless, it remains present in the ground water and will rise to the surface wherever irrigation and drainage are inadequate. For that reason even the vines in the Camargue are flooded twice a year.

The two arms of the Rhône, as well as ditches and swamps in their vicinity and in the northern part of the Camargue, contain fresh or nearly fresh water. In the Vaccarès lake there are already a few grams of salt to every litre of water. In the *étangs* south of the Vaccarès the salt content is higher and in summer can exceed that of the Mediterranean. In the salt-pans, finally, the water is always more salty than in the sea and is further concentrated to saturation point. A similar graduation is found also in the soils. In the north of the delta, and also in areas more than three feet above sea-level in the south, the topmost layers of the soil are usually fairly free of salt. They support a vegetation appropriate to dry conditions and consisting chiefly of grasses and hard-leaf scrub. In the lower-lying parts of the Camargue, on the other hand, the salt content sometimes rises so high that no plants are able to thrive and vast tracts remain entirely bare.

The salt exercises a decisive influence on flora and fauna. On dry land, life gets increasingly sparse as the salt content rises, until only sporadic salicornia plants, which are particularly well adapted, remain on an otherwise bare soil. By way of contrast, we find a great variety of life in sweet, brackish, and salt water everywhere. The types of plants, worms, insects, crabs, frogs, and birds occurring in fresh water, however, are totally different from those found at the various concentrations of brackish water, and these again are different from those found in salt water. The fine graduation of the salt content of the water is responsible for the great variety of wildlife in the Camargue. Thus the salt, which on land operates as a limiting factor, is a differentiating factor in the water.

Finally, a word about the wind. With the exception of the summer months from June to August, there are few days in the Camargue without wind. The prevailing wind, the mistral, which comes from the north-west, blows for nearly half of the year. Sometimes it is very strong for days on end, increasing the evaporation of plants, drying out the soil, churning up the water, and impeding land and water animals in their freedom of movement. Without any doubt it is a markedly destructive factor, and one may safely assume that but for the mistral the wealth of varieties and individual samples in the Camargue's flora and fauna would be considerably greater. The wind therefore is an important limiting factor.

The Human Pattern

The present-day extent of cultivated land, salt-pans, and wilderness is shown on map 1.

1. The zone of intensive agriculture covers the north of the delta, and along the present and former arms of the Rhône it thrusts far down to the south in several places. Here the whole land is ploughed, and irrigation and drainage systems make intensive farming possible. Rice, wine, fruit, grain, hay, and lucerne are the main products. There is also some sheep breeding. Rice is planted in water in April and partially replanted in May and June. Not until September or October, a short while before the harvest, is the water run off again. The grape harvest is from the beginning to the middle of September. The farming estates are for the most part extensive, and employ modern equipment.

2. The salt-pans are in the south-east of the Camargue, around Salin-de-Giraud. They consist of strings of shallow lagoons. Seawater is pumped in at one end, and this gradually evaporates in the lagoons under the action of sun and wind. Thus the salt content increases progressively from one lagoon to the next. The saturated solution is eventually pumped on to the 'harvesting areas', where the salt crystallizes. The crust of salt, which can be as much as ten centimetres (four inches) thick, is lifted off in the autumn with the most up-to-date machinery and is then crumbled, washed, and stacked into huge mountains of salt. The harvest, which depends a good deal on the weather, takes place in September. In good years up to a million tons of salt is produced in the Camargue. Salin-de-Giraud is the biggest salt-pan system in Europe. The lagoons into which the seawater is pumped are frequented especially by flamingos, avocets, and gulls. The salt-pans are enclosed and cannot be visited by tourists.

3. The natural zone occupies the central and coastal parts of the Camargue. Here the soil is not cultivated, nor is any salt produced. This is the world of the half-wild black Camargue cattle *(taureaux)*, the white horses, and sheep, the world of hunting, fishing, of birds and wild animals. This zone can be further sub-divided:

a) The nature protection area known as the Réserve de Camargue, founded in 1928 and administered by the Société Nationale de Protection de la Nature, a private organization. It covers some 100 square kilometres (forty square miles) and embraces the major part of the Etang de Vaccarès, the Bois des Rièges (a thicket of tree-forming Phoenician juniper), the salt steppes, and the brackish sheets of water between the Vaccarès and the sea. In this nature reserve neither hunting nor grazing is permitted; commercial fishing is allowed on a small scale in the Etang de Vaccarès. Apart from the two warden's lodges, the Réserve de Camargue contains no buildings, and access to it is barred. Permits are issued only to persons able to prove membership of scientific research or nature preservation bodies. Applications should be addressed to the Direction de la Réserve de Camargue, Rue Honoré-Nicolas, Arles. The nature reserve represents a unique landscape and contains special plant associations and a few important bird breeding places. In autumn, spring, and winter it is a resting place for huge flights of shore birds and wild duck.

b) Les Impériaux nature reserve of over thirty square kilometres (twelve square miles), bought from the State (the Département des Bouches-du-Rhône) in 1964 and now administered by the commune of Les Saintes-Maries-de-la-Mer. Access to this area is also prohibited, and so is hunting; fishing is permitted to a few professional fishermen from Les Saintes-Maries. The Impériaux includes some of the best breeding places in the Camargue for gulls, terns, avocets, and ducks.

c) The still natural areas lying between the nature reserves and the agricultural zone. Although these have shrunk over the past few decades, as a result of large parts being ploughed up or turned into salt-pans, they are still very extensive. They are privately-owned and are chiefly used for hunting or for the grazing of *taureaux* and horses. Their importance for the preservation of the Camargue's fauna and flora is equally great as that of the nature reserves, and many characteristic species are encountered most often, and sometimes exclusively, in this region.

The Natural Habitats

These wild parts of the Camargue consist of a variegated mosaic of different habitats, among which the following are the most important (see map 2).

1. Land

a) Deciduous woodland: Along the banks of the Rhône runs a strip of luxuriant deciduous forest, frequently flooded when the river is in spate and consisting chiefly of white poplar, elm, willow, alder, and ash. Lesser strips of the same kind of forest extend along the irrigation canals which as a rule follow the ancient courses of the Rhône. Here the salt has been washed out over the centuries; otherwise the trees could not thrive.

b) Dry grass lands: In the highest-situated areas, where only small amounts of salt penetrate to the surface layers of the soil, we encounter dry grass cover, consisting of various grasses, bulrushes, and sedges, with an admixture of many flowers which lend the grassland a colourful appearance in spring—daisies, whitlow grass, cranesbill, dandelion, various varieties of clover and bird's-foot trefoil, pimpernel, several orchids such as the spider orchid, blue flags, and wild gladioli. In late summer and autumn the violet sea-lavender is in bloom, known in the Camargue as *saladelles,* as well as yellow elecampane. Where these stretches of grass are not grazed too heavily, nor burnt down, mock privet with its dark, narrow, evergreen leaves gains a foothold. It can form fairly dense patches, with trees reaching a height of three to four metres (ten to fourteen feet).

c) Salt steppes: In the lower parts of the Camargue the soil contains so much salt that only a few specially adapted plant species can grow there. These are, above all, various kinds of salicornia, known in the Camargue as *enganes.* These plants form small lignified bushes. Where the salt content is not too high they stand close together like sheep in a flock. Where the salt content is higher, a good deal of bare dry soil remains between individual bushes. This salt steppe with its patches of salicornia is called *sansouïre* in the Camargue. During the winter a large part of the *sansouïre* is flooded by rain and is taken over by wild duck. The only tree or bush to advance as far as the *sansouïre* is the tamarisk with its fine-feathered top. In May this is covered with pink blossom. But even the tamarisk thrives only on the edge of the lakes or of ditches carrying fresh water during much of the year. However, it can be demonstrated quite easily that tamarisks can manage also on slightly salty water. If one licks a tamarisk leaf in the summer one will discover a salty taste. This comes from the crust of salt which remains on the leaf when the water taken up by the roots evaporates from it.

d) Dunes: Behind the beach rises a belt of dunes, occupying an appreciable area, especially in the Beauduc Peninsula and in the Little Camargue. Here we find marram grass, and in May and June also the blossoms of medick, chamomile, everlasting flowers, etc. In July and August we may occasionally encounter a fragrant short-stemmed white lily, the *Pancratium maritimum.* On some of the higher dunes grow umbrella pines whose cones, like those of the stone pine, contain edible kernels. There are also a few dunes a good distance away from the sea at the centre of the Camargue; the best known of these are the Bois des Rièges south of the Etang de Vaccarès, which carry a thick growth of Phoenician juniper which here grows to a height of up to six metres (twenty feet). In the spring narcissi bloom here, as well as asphodel, rock-roses, rosemary, and gladioli. The Bois des Rièges, at the very centre of the nature reserve, are difficult of access; admission, moreover, is subject to a special permit.

2. Water

a) Ditches and canals: These carry fresh water from the Rhône to the irrigated fields or else drain the fields into the Etang de Vaccarès or back to the Rhône. The water they carry is fresh and they are frequently hemmed by reeds and yellow flags. They form a network which links nearly all the waters of the Camargue. They serve as migration routes for the fish and tortoises. The freshwater canals or ditches are called *roubines* in the Camargue.

b) Freshwater marshes: Most of the freshwater marshes are densely grown with reeds and reedmace; they dry out partially or completely during the summer. They are the nesting places of the bittern, the purple heron, water rail, and of many songsters. They also provide the best hiding-places for the wild boars. Whenever these marshes are heavily grazed by the *taureaux,* the reeds are thinned out and open sheets of water are formed with pondweeds and water buttercups. Clumps of bulrushes may also flourish under these conditions. Instead of bittern and water rail we then have whiskered tern and stilts breeding here, and many ducks and waders visit these waters during their migration and in winter; such waters are known in the Camargue as *baisses* or simply *marais.*

c) Brackish lakes: Where the salt content exceeds an average of about five to eight grams per litre no vegetation is found growing out of the water—but there are still agglomerations of floating plants whose leaves and seeds are a favourite food for many kinds of wild duck. Only in the salt-pans, and where the water is evaporated, do these plants disappear also. These brackish lakes, most of which are fairly large, are known in the Camargue as *étangs.*

1 The sea—cradle of all life.
   The element separating and uniting nations, countries, and continents

2 Shifting dune with wind ripples and sparse growth of marram grass *(Ammophila arenaria)*

3 Dung beetle *(Scarabaeus semipunctatus)* guarding a food pellet

4 Weightless elegance of pointed wings: Sandwich terns *(Sterna sandvicensis)*

5 Flat beach with jetsam in the
  Gulf of Beauduc

6 *Erianthus ravennae*

7 *Pancratium maritimum*

8 Jetsam—hidden beauty under the harsh light of the Midi coast

9 *Inula crithmoides,* an elecampane thriving on saline soil

10 Along the *Digue de la Mer* between Les Saintes-Maries and Salin-de-Giraud.
In the foreground the remains of an earlier dike reinforcement

12 *Argiope lobata,* an orb-web spider. The underparts of the spider seen through its web

13 Sun-cracked earth in the lower Camargue ▷

14 Kentish plover *(Charadrius alexandrinus)* ▷▷

15 Typical patchwork vegetation of the glasswort *Arthrocnemum glaucum* in summer

19 Black-headed gull *(Larus ridibundus)* in breeding plumage

21 Gull-billed tern *(Gelochelidon nilotica)* with newly hatched chick

23 Breeding colony of flamingos *(Phoenicopterus ruber)*

24 The firebirds rising into the sky from the lagoons *(Phoenicopterus ruber)*

25 Where the salt is won from the sea. Depressing, blinding white vastness of the salt-pan area

27 Brackish lagoon near the sea

Man the Hunter

It is obvious that in such an extensive and largely undeveloped region as the Camargue hunting and fishing are of considerable importance.

Many private owners, in line with the two reserves, lease their fishing rights to commercial fishermen. These use nets and fish traps and, according to the salt content, catch fairly considerable quantities of the most varied kind of fish, ranging from true sea fish such as sea bass *(Morone labrax)* and sole *(Solea vulgaris),* through many brackish-water types such as grey mullet *(Mugil spp.)* to typical freshwater species such as pike-perch *(Lucioperca lucioperca)* and pike *(Esox lucius).* Commercially the most important fish is the eel *(Anguilla anguilla),* which is caught in large quantities and for the most part shipped alive to Holland in tank wagons for smoking. Carp *(Cyprinus carpio)* are very numerous in fresh water but are not fished since there is no local demand for them. However, there are fish-breeding centres near Sylveréal and near Le Sambuc which breed carp and drain their ponds just before Christmas in order to ship their whole output alive to Germany and other Central European countries. In addition to commercial fishermen there are also some amateurs who cast their lines mainly along the canals and who are chiefly interested in pike-perch. Now and again they succeed in landing exceedingly large specimens.

Hunting, however, is more popular in the Camargue than fishing. There is a great wealth of all kinds of game, and the bags of wild boar, hare, rabbits, pheasant, and partridge are often very considerable. Far more important still is the shooting of game birds such as wild duck, coot, and shore birds. While the ground game season *(chasse de terre)* extends as a rule from mid-August to the first Sunday in January, water game may continue to be shot until March 31st. Only a few species—chiefly flamingos, little egrets, and avocets—are protected all the year round. Needless to say all shooting is prohibited in the two reserves. In one part of the salt-pan area and on certain privately owned pieces of land there is likewise a ban on shooting, so that a very rich wildlife can thrive in a protected area of about 200 square kilometres (seventy-seven square miles). In addition there are large estates which are being run by their proprietors, or by syndicates who have leased the shoot, for the purpose of more or less intensive shooting. In many of these areas there are only one to four shoots per month, so that in between those dates the waterfowl find ample food and the necessary quiet. On certain small properties and on public land, and this means mainly along the roads, anyone holding a licence may shoot. There are three types of duck shoots—the *passée,* the *affût* and the *battue. Passée* and *affût* are based on the observation that the duck, which during the day accumulate in vast numbers on large undisturbed sheets of water, the so-called *remises,* swarm out in all directions at nightfall and invade all small pools and flooded fields in search of food. Early in the morning, before dawn, they then fly back to the *remises.* The *passée* is the shoot of the impecunious sportsman who owns no property and is not a member of a syndicate. He places himself on public land, which means along the roads, under the flight routes used for decades by the duck when swarming out from the reserves into the neighbourhood. It is just possible that he may succeed in bagging a bird or two while they pass overhead. But the ducks adapt themselves exceedingly well to this form of hunting. Whereas before the opening of the season in August they will fly at an altitude of only about ten metres (thirty feet), within a few days of the start of the season their height of passage will be forty to fifty metres (150 to 180 feet)—*i.e.,* beyond shotgun range. Only rain, gales, or heavy fog may force them to fly at a lower level. Thus the sportsman practising the *passée* must bag his birds either as soon as the season opens or in exceptional weather. During the rest of the time he may loose off a lot of cartridges to amuse himself but he will not often succeed in killing a duck. This method of shooting, which is a surprise to the ornithologist unacquainted with local practice and frequently outrages him, is in fact fairly harmless as far as the duck are concerned.

For the *affût* the sportsman places himself by a sheet of water in the evening or early morning, and fires at the duck as they try to invade it. This method is practised by the impecunious holder of a hunting licence at flooded rice paddies or vineyards or along small pools, as well as by the members of private shooting syndicates along somewhat bigger sheets of water. In the *affût* the duck approach the guns at an easier angle and the sportsmen are usually more successful than with the *passée.*

The *battue* finally is practised only four or five times in the season on large privately owned shoots. A great number of sportsmen take up position before sunrise around a *remise* —i.e., a sheet of water on which large numbers of duck spend the day. As soon as it is light enough someone gets out on to the water among the reeds and the sportsmen then fire at the duck as they rise up in all directions. This rather crude and ostentatious form of shoot is looked down upon by many sportsmen who are also naturalists. It frequently turns into a veritable massacre with often more than 300 and occasionally more than 500 duck killed within two hours, not to mention the coots which are not included in these figures. No-one knows whether the wild birds can survive the present scale of shooting in the long run or whether it has already caused their numbers to decline. Certainly the popularity of gamebird shooting is increasing and the risk of overhunting in the future is very real.

Man the Cattle Breeder

Intensive hunting is a very new feature in the Camargue. For centuries the bull graziers (the *gardians*), together with a few poachers and fishermen, were the only humans roaming the *sansouïres* and *étangs*. They lived in the typical reed-thatched white-painted clay huts, which are open to the south and which turn their apse-shaped curved rear wall to the mistral. Quite a few genuine *cabanes de gardians* survive to this day, but more common are imitations with all kinds of variants of style which are inhabited by townspeople who spend their vacations in the Camargue. The herds of cattle *(manades)* today are as much a part of the wild Camargue as the natural fauna and flora. Although these herds of course contain bulls, cows, and calves, the animals are collectively referred to as *taureaux*.

There are plenty of theories and legends about the origin and early use of Camargue bulls and horses, but very little precise information. They are undoubtedly rather primitive breeds, hardy and independent of human attention. They were used for bullfights and contests even in Roman times. Nowadays there are basically two types of bullfights:

1. The *course provençale* or *course à la cocarde,* held in the ancient Roman amphitheatres of Arles and Nîmes or in one of the lesser bullfighting arenas which exist in very nearly every village of the hinterland. In these events the bullfighters *(razeteurs)* have to snatch from the pursuing *taureau* certain trophies (the *cocardes* and the *glands*) which are fixed between and beneath his horns. The bull afterwards returns to his grazing unscathed, whereas the *razeteurs* are frequently injured.

2. The *ferrade* (from *fer* = iron) was originally the branding of one-year-old calves *(anoubles)* with the brandmark of the *manade*. Nowadays it is the occasion for a fête to which a *Club Taurin* is usually invited from a neighbouring village. A mounted group of *gardians* singles out one *anouble* from the *manade* and chases him at a gallop among the public, who have to catch him. After that the *anouble* is branded with a red-hot iron and released. When several calves have been branded in this way a picnic is held and the afternoon passes in various games with cows and young bulls in a stockade. Anybody is allowed into the stockade. To avoid serious injury the *taureau* first has his horns covered by leather sheaths. *Ferrades* are held every Sunday from Easter until September in several *manades,* and frequently they even take place on working days. They are closed events, but many associations and *manadiers* raise no objection to the presence of foreign spectators. The Spanish bullfight, the *corrida,* is not practised with Camargue *taureaux*. For it, the bulls and matadors come from Spain. In the Camargue, however, there are a few herds of bulls of Spanish and Portuguese origin whose animals are used for *corridas*. The herds of bulls and horses can be watched very successfully from the roads and tracks of the Camargue. Particularly suitable are the roads from Albaron to Villeneuve and from Villeneuve to the south, along the Etang de Vaccarès to the *Digue de la Mer*. Access to the grazing grounds themselves is prohibited, unless one is admitted to a *ferrade*. The bulls and horses form part of the Camargue wildlife not only because they inhabit the *sansouïres* and the marshes, and because these black herds and white groups impart to the landscape one of its typical touches, but also because their grazing has an important effect on the habitats. In the freshwater marshes, for instance, they are in a position to wipe out the reed-beds and thereby to change the entire flora and fauna. Bird life, in particular, would be the poorer by several species if there were no *taureaux*.

18

Birds and Beasts

The Camargue is the home also of an original world of wild mammals, even though the visitor rarely glimpses more than a rabbit or a hare. All other species are shy or nocturnal. Beavers are still present in considerable numbers along both arms of the Rhône, but one has to spend many a night sitting in the open to hear, let alone to see, them. Only the gnawed trees and the collapsed trunks testify to their activity. Wild boars are fairly common; though a little smaller than their brothers in the Central and East European oak forests, boars nevertheless reach a weight of 150 kilos (330 pounds). During the day they usually hide out in reed-grown marshes and in winter also frequently in the Bois des Rièges. At night they roam far afield in search of tuberous roots, dead animals, or anything edible. After rainfall especially their fresh tracks are encountered everywhere, criss-crossing those of badgers and foxes which are also fairly numerous. The otter, on the other hand, survives only in small numbers.

The French tourists who come to the Camargue are attracted chiefly by the bulls, the horses, and the *gardians*. They come in search of the Wild West in their own country. Foreigners, on the other hand, usually come to see the birds which have given this region its international reputation. The most famous of the birds of the Camargue is undoubtedly the flamingo. A visitor travelling along the *étangs* near the coast, between Les Saintes-Maries, Salin-de-Giraud, and Salin-de-Badon, either along the *Digue de la Mer* or by other tracks, will soon spot a pale rose or nearly white band along the horizon shimmering in the hot air. If he waits long enough he will suddenly see deep red flames leaping up from it as the group of flamingos takes wing, revealing those red feathers which are hidden when the wings are folded. If he is lucky the red and black cloud will move towards him, and hundreds and thousands of noisily chattering, cross-shaped birds will pass over him at low altitude. The Camargue is the only spot in Europe where the flamingos propagate regularly—if indeed one may use the word 'regularly' at all in connection with these mysterious birds. It has long been known that the flamingos do not breed every year and that sometimes they skip a number of years. They are also thought to be among the birds reaching the greatest age in open nature, for they not only breed

irregularly but do not start breeding until they are about five years old. Only one egg is laid at a time, and usually a great many eggs and chicks are lost before they reach maturity. But for the fact that they reach a great age the species would have long died out. In spring there are usually some 15,000 flamingos in the Camargue, and in April frequently a breeding colony is formed which numbers some 4000 to 5000 nests. Since 1914 at least 39,000 flamingo chicks have been nursed to fully fledged age.

A list at the back of this volume contains information about the many other types of birds in the Camargue. Only a few of the most typical bird associations need therefore be listed here. The visitor in the late spring or in summer may think the solitude of the brackish lakes in the reserve, in the protection area of Les Saintes-Maries, or among the salt-pans, to be almost entirely dead—until he encounters one of the few islands on which all bird breeding is concentrated. Here, crowded together in the narrowest possible space, are the nests of thousands of gulls, terns, shore birds, and duck. The commonest species are herring gull, black-headed gull, common tern, Sandwich tern, gull-billed tern, little tern, avocet, Kentish plover, redshank, mallard, gadwall, and red-crested pochard. Species encountered less frequently or less regularly include slender-billed gull, Mediterranean gull, roseate tern, oystercatcher, shelduck, pintail, etc. All these birds are crowded together on the islands because here they are safe from their enemies. It may also be that mutual stimulation gets them into a more favourable mood for breeding. Many of them do not seek their food among the brackish lakes at all but undertake rather lengthy flights to forage for their young. The gull-billed terns, for instance, fly inland in the spring in search of insects and frogs among the paddy fields, irrigated meadows and freshwater marshes; later in the year they hunt for grasshoppers among the dry pastures and dunes. The Sandwich tern and common tern, on the other hand, fly out to sea and there catch small fish.

Another important group of birds are the herons: little egret, night heron, and Squacco heron breed in their hundreds and thousands in the deciduous and evergreen thickets which extend along the two arms of the Rhône. Their nests are several feet up in the trees, often a number of them in a single tree. To seek their food, the birds roam all over the Camargue, visiting principally all water-carrying ditches, paddy fields, and marshes of fresh or brackish water. Their diet consists mainly of water insects, small crabs, and frogs, with only occasionally small fish. The purple heron breeds apart from the other species in small colonies established in reed-grown marshes. This heron is fond of fish, and frequently, if one is disturbed in a ditch, it will be seen flying off with an eel in its beak. From the same patches of reeds where the purple heron breeds one may hear the dull boom of the bittern during spring nights.

The stilts and the whiskered terns like to build their nests along open freshwater marshes where the vegetation is cropped by the *taureaux*. The pratincoles visit these areas from the near-by dry *sansouïres* to hunt for insects. The whiskered tern builds a floating nest of bulrushes and sedge stems. However, it lacks the strength to pull the stems out itself and therefore follows the *taureaux* to pick up the ones dropped by them during grazing.

Finally, considerable bird populations are also encountered outside the breeding season. The Camargue acts as the winter quarters for some 150,000 to 200,000 wild duck, among which the most common are teal, wigeon, mallard, pochard, shoveller, gadwall, tufted duck, pintail, and red-crested pochard. Large numbers of these duck spend the day in the nature reserves and on a few sheets of water on neighbouring property, and at night swarm out to the flooded *sansouïres,* to brackish and freshwater marshes, rice paddies, and vineyards in search of grain, tubers, and other plant food. It is on their morning and evening flights that they come under often heavy fire from sportsmen along the best routes of passage outside the reserves.

In the spring and autumn large flights of shore birds also use the Camargue as a favourite resting place on their flight between tundra and tropics. Some species prefer the salt-pans and brackish lakes: the most numerous among these are ruff, dunlin, little stint, redshank, Kentish plover, ringed plover, grey plover, and whimbrel. Other species, as for instance wood sandpiper, green sandpiper, snipe, little ringed plover, Temminck's stint, etc., chiefly inhabit the freshwater marshes and rice paddies. A third group is encountered just as often in the vicinity of fresh as salt water. Prominent among these are black-tailed godwit, greenshank, spotted redshank, and common sandpiper.

Threatened Paradise?

Can the wild Camargue with its unique fauna and flora survive? We have seen that the area used for agriculture and salt production has roughly doubled over the past few years. If this trend were to continue at the present rate then what is left of the wild Camargue would disappear by about the end of the century. True, nearly 150 square kilometres (sixty square miles) are protected and cannot therefore be turned into either salt-pans or agricultural land. Will the survival of this area be enough to save the fauna and flora of the Camargue? The answer, unfortunately, is No. The Camargue is a mosaic of various habitats and only some of these are represented in the nature reserves. Many animals in the nature reserves, moreover—especially the birds—require several different habitats over the course of a year and cannot therefore survive in the nature reserves alone. If nothing except the present nature reserves were to remain, then only a section of today's fauna and flora would survive, and the Camargue in its present meaning would cease to exist.

What is necessary, therefore, is to preserve in its original state as much as possible of the land situated between the reserves and the agricultural zone, land which at present is used for hunting and as grazing for the *taureaux*. There can be no doubt that such a preservation would meet a universal demand. The Camargue is one of the most popular excursion areas for the Provençals, who go there to seek contact with nature and healthy and instructive recreation, no matter whether this is achieved by shooting, fishing, riding, or, increasingly, by observation of the rich fauna and flora. Les Saintes-Maries-de-la-Mer with its hotels and riding stables attracts a growing number of tourists, both French and foreign, who stimulate the economic development of the region. The region, finally, is of considerable scientific value, and this is utilized by the researchers of the Centre National de la Recherche Scientifique at their laboratory near Le Sambuc. It must be remembered, however, that the land between the nature reserves and the agricultural zone is largely privately owned. It is therefore thanks to a dozen landowners that the Camargue has so far continued to be the kind of paradise described in this book. The future destiny of the region lies very largely in the hands of these same people.

In the present economic situation there is little inducement to put any further land to agricultural use. Those areas which could be put under profitable crops at small expense have come under the plough over the past twenty years. Further reclamation would be expensive, with little prospect of a financial return. Matters are different, however, where salt production is concerned. Common salt today is a raw material in great demand by the chemical industry, chiefly for the manufacture of synthetics. There is therefore a considerable demand for land to be turned into salt-pans. However, there are other methods of salt production, for instance by extraction of the salt accumulated in the Provençal soil.

At present the still wild parts of the Camargue are being utilized by their proprietors in a manner agreed with the nature protection authorities, though not perhaps very profitably—the keeping of *taureaux* and hunting. It is quite possible that this utilization will prove more profitable in the future. The various forms of bull fighting are enjoying increasing popularity, and the demand for Camargue horses, especially for tourists, has driven up prices; the charges for hunting and shooting rights have also gone up a great deal.

Conditions for the preservation of the Camargue are not therefore too bad at the moment. However, economic circumstances are subject to sudden change and new losses might easily occur.

One threat to the wild Camargue at present arises from the rice paddies themselves. These are largely drained into the Etang de Vaccarès which, as a result, rises to such a level that it overflows to the sea through the flood-gates in the *Digue de la Mer*. This results in the salt being washed out, and the Vaccarès lake as well as the *étangs inférieurs* could eventually become reed-grown marshes if this trend continued. In consequence, the Camargue landscape would lose its entire beauty and uniqueness, and the most interesting birds and animals would disappear. Another point is that the effluent from the agriculturally used areas contains increasing quantities of chemicals which could do grave harm to the plants and animals of the wild Camargue.

Tourism, finally, brings with it its own dangers since fauna and flora must be allowed to remain undisturbed over large areas if they are to continue to thrive.

In this situation a number of the inhabitants of the Camargue have themselves voiced the desire to co-ordinate the efforts of landowners, authorities, and interested associations to preserve the region. This wish was taken up by the authorities, and negotiations are at present taking place with a view to setting up a Parc Naturel Régional de Camargue. The programme includes four major points:

1. Prevention of any further northward or westward spread of the salt-pans.
2. Subsidies for the traditional management of still natural parts of the Camargue, provided that the owners undertake to preserve these areas.
3. Drainage of agricultural areas into the Rhône instead of into the Etang de Vaccarès, with a view to preventing the further desalination and chemical contamination of the nature preservation areas.
4. Organization of tourism to enable visitors to see the scenery, the fauna, and the flora without causing damage through interference.

This programme no doubt would ensure the future of the unspoilt Camargue.

The next few years will show whether it can be realized. A great deal has changed since the last century. Then it seemed to be in the interests of the *Camarguais* to transform their region into an agricultural area; today it seems to be in their interests to keep it in its natural state. Then their individualism prevented the execution of concerted plans; will it now be possible to safeguard the future of this paradise?

Profile of the Rhône Delta

The diagram below exhibits the succession of the various types of land and water vegetation from the sea to the Rhône through the higher parts of the Camargue. The flat, bare, sandy beach gives way, first of all, to dunes carrying a vegetation dominated by marram grass with sporadic appearances of pines and various flower species, such as *Anthemis, Medicago,* everlasting flowers, and the lily *Pancratium maritimum.* Behind the dunes are sparsely grown salt steppes with the glasswort *Arthrocnemum glaucum* and highly salty brackish lakes in which, apart from algae, the thread-shaped submersed *Ruppia maritima* are able to maintain themselves as the only flowering plant. A little further inland the salt content of soil and water diminishes rapidly and the sparse growth of *Arthrocnemum* gives way to dense heaths of the more luxuriant glasswort *Salicornia*

fruticosa; these areas are often flooded during the winter. In this zone we also find ancient dunes carrying vegetation, with the juniper *Juniperus phoenicea* predominating (Bois de Rièges). In the sheets of water, which include also the vast Etang de Vaccarès, the salt-loving *Ruppia* are replaced by pondweeds and water buttercups better adapted to fresh water, while sedges, reeds, and bulrushes appear along the shores. Where only small amounts of salt are left in the soil a dry grass cover *(Thero-Brachypodion)* is found which contains a great variety of xerophilous grasses, and in which salt-loving plants such as sea-lavender *(Statice)* at first still hold an important place, but nearer the Rhône yield entirely to xerophilous plants. Here the hardy mock privets thrive. It is chiefly in this last zone that agriculture has gained ground and changed the original environment. Directly alongside the Rhône and its ancient courses grows luxuriant and frequently flooded deciduous woodland in which white poplar, elm, ash, alder, willow, etc., predominate.

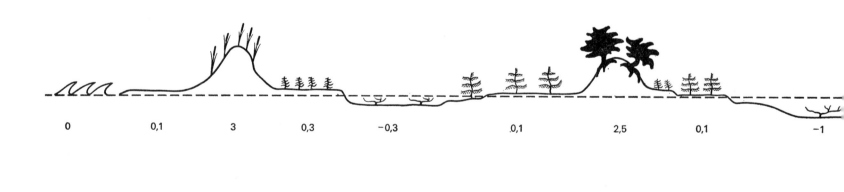

| 0 | 0,1 | 3 | 0,3 | −0,3 | ,0,1 | 2,5 | 0,1 | −1 |

| 1 | 2 | 3 | 4 | 5 | 6 | 7 | 8 | 9 |

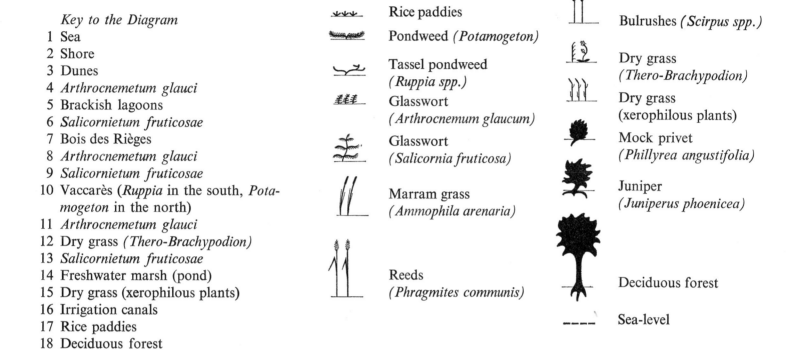

Key to the Diagram

1 Sea
2 Shore
3 Dunes
4 *Arthrocnemetum glauci*
5 Brackish lagoons
6 *Salicornietum fruticosae*
7 Bois des Rièges
8 *Arthrocnemetum glauci*
9 *Salicornietum fruticosae*
10 Vaccarès (*Ruppia* in the south, *Potamogeton* in the north)
11 *Arthrocnemetum glauci*
12 Dry grass *(Thero-Brachypodion)*
13 *Salicornietum fruticosae*
14 Freshwater marsh (pond)
15 Dry grass (xerophilous plants)
16 Irrigation canals
17 Rice paddies
18 Deciduous forest
19 Rhône

Rice paddies

Pondweed *(Potamogeton)*

Tassel pondweed *(Ruppia spp.)*

Glasswort *(Arthrocnemum glaucum)*

Glasswort *(Salicornia fruticosa)*

Marram grass *(Ammophila arenaria)*

Reeds *(Phragmites communis)*

Bulrushes *(Scirpus spp.)*

Dry grass *(Thero-Brachypodion)*

Dry grass (xerophilous plants)

Mock privet *(Phillyrea angustifolia)*

Juniper *(Juniperus phoenicea)*

Deciduous forest

- - - - Sea-level

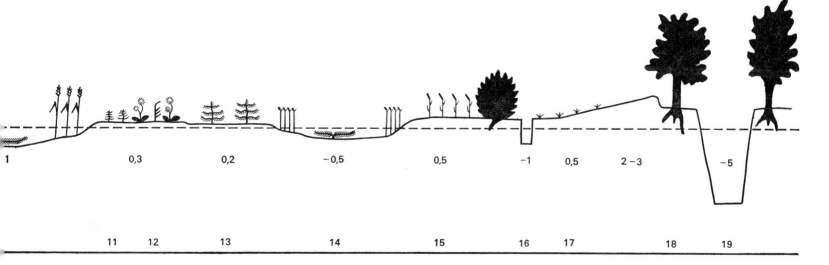

| 1 | 0,3 | 0,2 | -0,5 | 0,5 | -1 | 0,5 | 2 - 3 | -5 |

| 11 | 12 | 13 | 14 | 15 | 16 | 17 | 18 | 19 |

Ornithologist's Itinerary through the Camargue and Crau

(Sketch map 4)

The Camargue has long been a favourite excursion and holiday area for birdlovers and ornithologists from all over the world. The Rhône floodlands are known as an area where, especially in the spring and summer, large numbers of birds, including flamingos, many different species of herons, gulls, terns, wading birds, and birds of prey are found. Even a number of almost exotic 'land birds', such as bee-eaters and rollers, are at home here. Anyone wishing to study these birds thoroughly should equip himself with a pair of good field-glasses; a light portable telescope could often be even better. What is more, he must be prepared to spend several days roaming through marshes and steppes.

It should be pointed out, of course, that the visitor usually encounters difficulties in trying to leave the roads. Part of the delta landscape is a nature protection area to which access is subject to a permit from the Direction de la Réserve de Camargue in Arles (see page 4). Such permits, however, are issued only to persons who can prove membership of a nature preservation society or a scientific research organization. The land outside the reserve is privately owned, and most of the landowners prohibit access to strangers. Fortunately, the most typical bird species of the Camargue can be well observed also from roads and tracks. The ornithologist's itinerary marked on the map is designed to facilitate for the visitor the spotting of some of the most interesting species; this applies particularly to the months from April to August.

Naturally, the visitor will not always immediately find what he wants; the birds are highly mobile and do not settle at exactly the same spot each year. But with a little patience there are reasonable prospects of spotting many varieties in the places shown on the map. From April until early June it is, moreover, advisable to search the rice paddies, especially those close to the boundaries of the reserve. Various marsh and water birds can frequently be observed here. These include terns (especially the gull-billed, black, and whiskered terns), stilts, herons (especially the purple heron, the little egret, the night heron, and the Squacco heron) as well as numerous Nordic species of wading birds; the latter stop here on their spring migration. Generally speaking, the bird-watcher will see most in the early morning, up to about two hours after sunrise. Later in the day traffic on the roads is so heavy that the birds withdraw to more remote areas.

Flamingos—the birds most in demand from visitors—can be seen regularly at the spots shown throughout the whole day, but nearly always at a great distance. For better observation the early morning or the evening are recommended. During the day these birds keep to the enclosed salt-pans and fly into the nature reserve at night. Anyone keeping watch near Clos Desclaux (Point 11 in the Camargue) before sunrise and staying there for the next two hours, or anyone going there in the evening two hours before sunset and waiting there till dusk, will almost invariably get an impressive close-up view of the flamingos in flight.

(Legend for map 4 appears on page 25)

Natural areas outside the reserves

Zone of intensive agriculture

Salt-pans

Réserve de Camargue

Réserve des Impériaux

0   2   4   6km

Scale 1 : 180,000

© KÜMMERLY & FREY, BERN

Fresh water, average 0–2 g NaCl per litre

Slightly brackish water, average 3–6 g NaCl per litre

Brackish water, average 7–30 g NaCl per litre

Salt water, average over 30 g NaCl per litre

Canals and irrigation ditches

Boundaries of undeveloped areas

0   2   4   6km

Scale 1 : 180,000

© KÜMMERLY & FREY, BERN

Deciduous woodlands

Dry grassland with or without shrubs

Salt steppes (Sansouires)

Dunes

Pinewoods

Bois des Rièges

Densely grown freshwater marshes

Open fresh, brackish or salt water (étangs)

Sporadic thickets

Individual deciduous trees

Canals and irrigation ditches (roubines)

Boundaries of undeveloped areas

0   2   4   6km

Scale 1 : 180,000

© KÜMMERLY & FREY, BERN

ORNITHOLOGY OF THE CAMARGUE AND THE CRAU

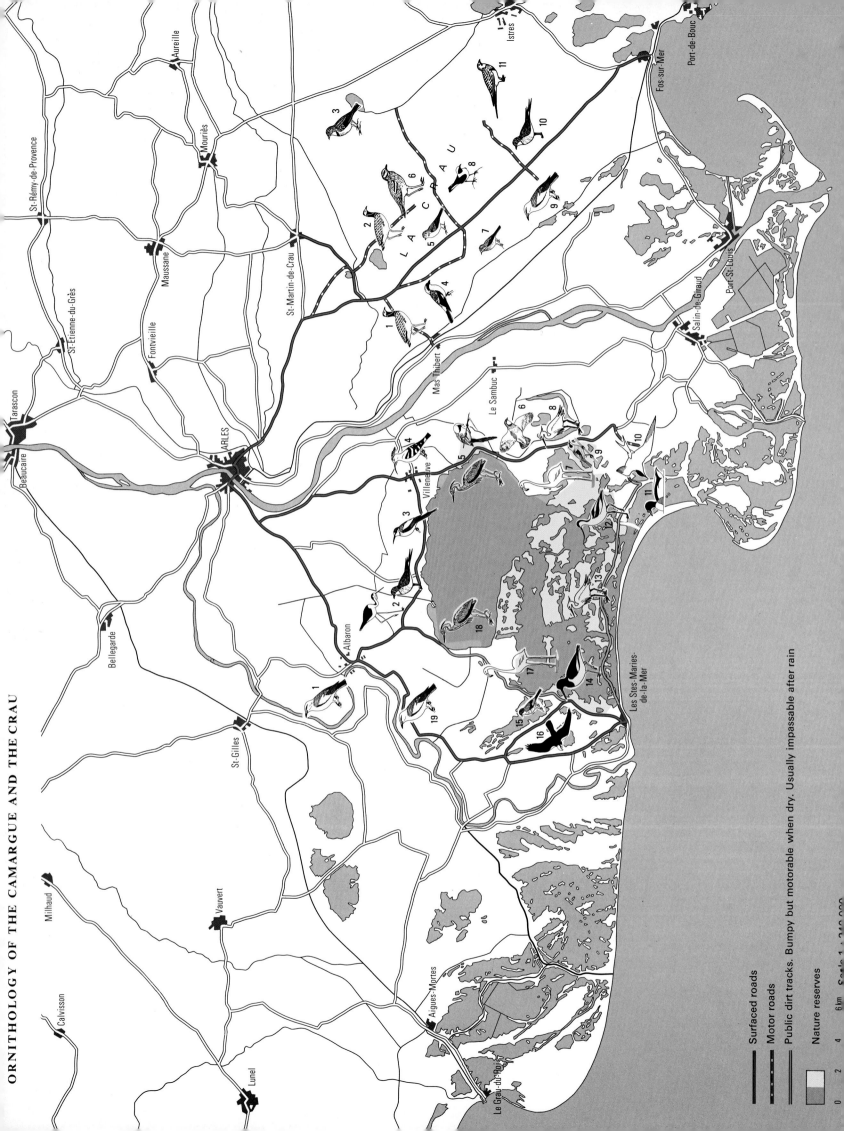

Surfaced roads

Motor roads

Public dirt tracks. Bumpy but motorable when dry. Usually impassable after rain

Nature reserves

Camargue Bird List

1 **Roller** *Coracias garrulus*
2 **Black-winged stilt** *Himantopus himantopus;* Pratincole *Glareola pratincola;* also Little egret *Egretta garzetta* and various wading birds
3 **Bee-eater** *Merops apiaster;* from early May to mid-August
4 **Hoopoe** *Upupa epops*
5 **Purple heron** *Ardea purpurea;* Bearded tit *Panurus biarmicus;* also Marsh harrier *Circus aeruginosus;* Moustached warbler *Lusciniola melanopogon;* and Savi's warbler *Locustella luscinioides*
6 **Red-legged partridge** *Alectoris rufa;* Stone curlew *Burhinus oedicnemus*
7–8 **Flamingo** *Phoenicopterus ruber;* Little egret *Egretta garzetta;* also Kentish plover *Charadrius alexandrinus;* Lapwing *Vanellus vanellus;* Red-crested pochard *Netta rufina;* and Night heron *Nycticorax nycticorax* (overflights at dusk)
9 **Penduline tit** *Remiz pendulinus*
10–14 **Terns,** in particular Common, Little and Sandwich tern (*Sterna hirundo, S. albifrons, S. sandvicensis*); Shelduck *Tadorna tadorna;* Avocet *Recurvirostra avosetta;* Little egret *Egretta garzetta;* Oystercatcher *Haematopus ostralegus.* All these species can be seen along the *Digue de la Mer,* as also Kentish plover *Charadrius alexandrinus,* and Flamingo *Phoenicopterus ruber,* especially at Point 11 in the early morning and in the evening in flight; also numerous species of wading birds on their spring migration in April and May
15 **Spectacled warbler** *Sylvia conspicillata*
16 **Marsh harrier** *Circus aeruginosus*
17 **Flamingo** *Phoenicopterus ruber*
18 **Purple heron** *Ardea purpurea;* also Stone curlew *Burhinus oedicnemus* and Kentish plover *Charadrius alexandrinus*
19 **Roller** *Coracias garrulus*

Crau Bird List

Between the Camargue, the Alpilles, and the Etang de Berre the stone desert of the Crau provides a suitable habitat for several unusual bird species. Large parts of the Crau are quite accessible; indeed, at the risk of a broken spring, much of it can be explored by car.

The map shows the spots in the Crau where some of the most interesting species may be observed:

1–2 **Little bustard** *Otis tetrax;* also, in the near-by almond and olive groves, Great spotted cuckoo *Clamator glandarius*
3 **Calandra lark** *Melanocorypha calandra*
4 **Lesser grey shrike** *Lanius minor;* also Roller *Coracias garrulus* and Hoopoe *Upupa epops*
5–6 **Short-toed lark** *Calandrella brachydactyla;* Stone curlew *Burhinus oedicnemus*—both anywhere in the Crau. The Scops owl, *Otus scops,* can be heard in the near-by clumps of trees at nightfall
7 **Subalpine warbler** *Sylvia cantillans*
8 **Black-eared wheatear** *Oenanthe hispanica*
9 **Roller** *Coracias garrulus*
10 **Pratincole** *Glareola pratincola*
11 **Pin-tailed sandgrouse** *Pterocles alchata*

Wilderness Experienced

The mistral had been raging for several days, sweeping the sky clean over the delta. As so often in springtime, the cold north-westerly wind seemed to have an inexhaustible capacity for making life difficult and miserable for man and beast. It burst in massively across the arms of the Rhône. Its fierce gusts pushed on far into the flat plain. On the marshes groups of bulrushes and reed-beds were like a choppy sea, with silvery reflections flitting over the deep green crests of the waves. The *étangs* were churned up, with dirty white spume crests flecking the dull brown water. Whenever the waves struck the bank they would burst into a spray of a thousand drops as the water bit deeper and deeper into the soil. On the beach the wind drove before it long white veils of sand. The foreshore dunes seemed to lie under a ground mist, under a haze gliding along smoothly and regularly until a whim of the wind would snatch it up and carry it far out to sea. Trails were wiped out. Cracks and crevices were filled with sand. Behind empty shells of mussels and snails and other jetsam the drifting sand piled up into bizarre shapes. Wherever deciduous trees surrounded farm buildings or freshwater canals, either singly or in groups, the gusts would encounter their only real obstacles. Furiously they would strike the tops of poplars and elms, tug at branches, and shake their trunks until a loud groan rang through their ranks. Dry branches crashed into the undergrowth. From time to time a rotten tree-trunk would snap and strike the ground with a dull thud.

Out there, over the open steppe, the gale was producing a veritable witches' sabbath. Here it was able to unfold its force to the full. It howled across the wide, sparsely covered landscape, carrying with it whatever was not bolted down. It seemed virtually impossible to stand up to its force. A kestrel in a bare tamarisk was desperately trying to keep its balance. Wings raised and tail fanned out, it tried to stand up to the gusts of wind. But the very next gust swept it from its branch, and heavily it flew off close to the ground. Scarcely a creature would venture out, from its shelter. The grating call of the partridges had ceased. The small grey rabbits stayed in their warrens. Here and there a curious head could be seen peeping out of a hole but almost immediately it would disappear again. Even the marsh harrier, which came sailing over every day from the nearby marsh to pounce on a young rabbit, had failed to appear. It probably felt that this was no day for hunting. Where the salicornia steppe fades into the dry sea-lavender steppe two stone curlews were flattening themselves against the sparse vegetation. One of the two birds was sitting on two dark-spotted eggs while its partner kept watch. Their large sulphur-yellow eyes identified them as crepuscular birds which would not come to life properly until the late afternoon or early evening. A few yards further on, in a gnarled salicornia shrub, a spectacled warbler had its nest. It seemed a miracle that its carelessly built home had not long been blown down by the wind.

The gale did not abate during the night. Its howling seemed eerie and almost menacing in the dark. Somehow the ear noticed the groaning of branches rubbing against each other or the snapping and crashing of split trunks more clearly than in the daytime. Our tents were flapping in the most alarming manner. The nylon loops were see-sawing in the eyelets and the poles were bending under the pull of the guy-lines. There could be no question of sleep. The ceaseless cracking of the canvas kept one awake or, if one had dropped off for a few moments, tore one out of unquiet dreams. The sounds of the stormy night, at first experienced as an adventure, were becoming torture. In spite of the raging of the elements the nightingales were singing in the nearby undergrowth. Oblivious of the mistral's violence among the branches above them, they went on producing their exhilarating song. But their voices were audible at a short range only against the loud background noise. Beyond that short distance they were drowned in the roar of the treetops. Even the croaking of a thousand frogs was swallowed up by the storm.

For twelve days and nights the mistral raged through the lower Rhône valley and across the Camargue. The following night, at long last, its force seemed to have spent itself. The next morning dawned pale and calm. In the warm spring sun men and beasts soon recovered from the uncomfortable boisterous days behind them. Everybody was happy and relieved to find that the cold wind had blown itself out. Hardly anyone has a good word to say for the mistral: it is a really troublesome wind, wrecking the farmers' crops, tangling up the fishermen's nets, and alarming the black *taureaux* of the *gardians*. It has only one good point —and that mainly in summer. Then the mistral brings a welcome coolness and keeps the mosquitoes at bay in a few sheltered spots. And anyone who has made the acquaintance of these insects knows that that is worth a lot. The calm after the storm tempts the rabbits out of their warrens and brings the ducks and coots from their reed thickets on to the open ponds. From the poplar grove comes the monotonous mating cry of the hoopoe. A flight of bee-eaters chases across the tamarisk avenues, hunting for warmth-intoxicated insects. These elegant birds have only recently returned from their African winter quarters. The red-legged partridges, too, now venture out from the shelter of the mock privet shrubs and roam through the *sansouïre,* scrabbling and pecking. Jealous cockerels trumpet their raucous "chuck-chuck-err" into the warm sunshine. Nature, held in thrall by the mistral for days and nights on end, is again taking its normal course.

No other season in the Camargue throbs with life to the same extent or is so lavish with dazzling colour as the short spring. True, the late autumn sees the steppe ablaze with red salicornia and the ponds edged with the bright yellow of sear reeds. But that season lacks the life-giving touches of whole fields of blooming narcissi, irises, and water buttercups. The air then is no longer filled with the calls of many voices, with the song of birds or the whirr and buzz of millions of various insects. But now, at the end of April, as we were getting down to our filming, matters were different. Everywhere the newly opened blossoms lent brilliant patches of colour to the landscape. In an almost ceaseless stream vast flights of birds arrived from their winter quarters, either to stop here, disband their formations, and get down to breeding, or merely to rest for a few days, gain new strength, and carry on towards more northerly breeding grounds. The nights were still chilly and the approach of summer was not yet entirely credible. But the moment the sun rose above the ground mist, sending its first probing rays across the awakening land, a pleasant warmth would spread everywhere. This is the moment when a great, almost physically perceptible tranquillity lies over steppes and marshes. Not a bird sound to betray the presence of life in the bush, not the least rustling of silver dragonfly wings. The roaring of the bulls in the marshy fields has fallen silent, even the croaking of the frogs has ceased for once. A deep and reverent waiting, with only the shadows of grasses and leaves shifting noiselessly as the sun rises in the sky. Minutes pass. It is as if no-one wanted to break the silence.

Then, abruptly, the soft and tentative cooing of a turtle dove from a tall bramble thicket. Timidly, almost shyly, its "trurr-turrturr-trurr-trurr" rings out. Immediately it is taken up by a second and a third bird, other voices join in, louder now and more self-assured, and a moment later the most magnificent chorus is in full voice. Other songsters join in with their tunes; the noise of the frogs in the ponds swells mightily; pheasants cackle; a green woodpecker chuckles somewhere in the poplar-trees. Life has woken up, the day is under way.

A few early breeders are already feeding their young. The young tawny owls in the rotten elm behind our tent left their hollow tree-trunk a day after our arrival. Since then they have been sitting among the branches—grey sleepy balls of wool blinking in the sun. They are scarcely able to fly yet, but they are excellent at climbing. At nightfall, when we make our last inspection tour round our camp, we often hear them urgently calling their parents. Sometimes, when they are perched on low branches, we even succeed in approaching them carefully or luring one of the parent birds into our vicinity by imitating the begging cry of the young. All through the night, right until daybreak, the screeching of the insatiable young flock continues.

The tweet of perpetually hungry beaks also comes from concealed nests in the vast reed thickets. The brood of bearded tits is almost fully fledged; soon the young birds will leave their increasingly constricting nurseries. Like acrobats the old birds climb up and down the stems of the reeds in their search for food, skilfully flitting through the yellow-green labyrinth of stems, picking up a dragonfly larva here and a caterpillar there, and suddenly streaking off with a glassy "jing-jing". Their magnificently camouflaged nests are exceedingly difficult to find in the dense sea of reeds. Almost without exception they are only a few centimetres above water-level, in a tangle of dry snapped stalks and leaves. Their colour and texture make them blend perfectly with their surroundings. The fact that the parent birds returning to their nests with fodder rarely dive down on them direct but approach them unobtrusively, close to the water, through the reeds, and that after feeding their young they sneak off again in the same surreptitious way, does not make the search any easier. Yet otherwise these feathered clowns seem quite trusting. Their natural curiosity frequently makes them approach man to within arm's length, and they can then be observed at leisure. For their part, they examine any strange object with painstaking thoroughness. If one happens to be the object of their curiosity it can at times be rather uncomfortable. Standing motionless in a marsh, knee-deep in stinking decaying matter, one presents an easy target to bloodthirsty mosquitoes. And there is no shortage of those at this time of the year. Conditions were favourable for setting up our base camp, which was to be our home for the next five months or so. The vegetation had not yet grown to any great height, and the soil, even here at this higher part of the delta, still showed the traces of the heavy winter precipitations. It was damp, soft and deep. Thus we had no difficulty in digging a widely ramified system of drainage ditches, some nearly two feet deep, all round our living and storage tents. Having experienced the devastating effects of midsummer rainstorms the year before, we were determined this year to take all necessary precautions. Later in the season, once the soil was dried out and bone hard, the same measures would have required much more time and labour.

In the *sansouïre,* the vast flat salicornia steppe, the water was still several inches deep in places, and even knee-high boots were not always sufficient for crossing these marshy lowlands without getting one's feet wet. Yet only a few weeks earlier, after the last heavy rainfalls, the scene would have been totally different. Then the shoots of salicornia would have only just shown above the water. And where now the lapwings were keeping their eggs warm on small clumps of grass surrounded by water, there would have been nothing but vast lakes ruffled by the wind. Since then the sun and the mistral had done their work. The water-level had dropped markedly everywhere. The dry patches of land were already covered with a carpet of small white marguerites. Before long the glittering pools of water would disappear from the rest of the *sansouïre* and the earth would slowly but inexorably begin to dry out.

Masterpieces of Nest Building

Along the two arms of the Rhône and wherever nearby irrigation canals carry precious water to the crops, one finds forest-like patches of deciduous trees, with a thick undergrowth between them. Along ditches no longer in operation but still carrying water these patches of woodland sometimes reach the density of a jungle. Any attempt to penetrate these thorny green strongholds involves sweat, blood, and bruises.

The nest of the penduline tit which we chose for our filming was in just such a thicket. Not that we could not have found a nest elsewhere—that was not the problem. Indeed, the characteristic wooing call of the small, agile birds was to be heard almost everywhere. And whenever their high-pitched drawn-out "sich-sich" is heard, only a little perseverance is needed to find also their elaborate suspended pouches woven from animal fur and plant fibres. They dangle in elms and poplars, willows and tamarisks—now high up among the tree-tops, now low down among the bushy vegetation, but invariably among the extreme thin points of the boughs, and frequently above pools and ditches. The reason why we picked on the nest in the inaccessible thicket was its uniquely favourable position. It was hanging free above an irrigation canal, only six feet from the ground, protected from its feathered and furry enemies and secure also from being flung against neighbouring branches by a raging mistral.

With seemingly furious haste a still unpaired cock bird was working away at the bottom of the nest which had only just begun to take on the shape of a basket with handles. At short intervals its protracted wooing call would be heard close by, and a moment later it would appear, its beak full of nest material. Its small head with its black cheeks was totally hidden behind the white or brownish bundles of fluff whenever a load was particularly large. Sheep's wool and horsehair, reed fibres and the tangled seeds of last year's reed-mace were carted up by the cock bird and woven and stuffed into the rapidly growing pouch with indefatigible activity. Long hairs and fibres were used with particular care for securing the suspension of the nest. First a loose loop was laid round the bearing bough, then one end of the fibre was guided through with the beak, gripped on the far side, and made fast with a vigorous jerk. Thereupon the bird, still holding the fibre in its beak, performed a few elegant rotations around the bough—just like a gymnast on a horizontal bar—so that a proper winding was achieved. Finally, the loose end was thrust deep into the side of the nest until nothing stuck out. In this way the pouch-shaped nest gradually achieved its high elastic strength. Foot after foot of film passed behind the lenses of our cameras. We were able to shoot the growth of this elaborate structure in every detail. And to watch the tit building it was pure joy. A mere five days later the nest was nearing completion. Now there were two birds arriving with nest material in an almost continuous succession. The cock bird had found himself a female, and by the look of it the hen bird could not get her home finished quickly enough. The walls of the nest had grown to more than three-quarters. Only at two diametrically opposite points, close below the dome, two oval openings had been left. One of these would later become the entrance to the nest. Both birds were now chiefly engaged on finishing the inside and most of the time disappeared from view. The hollow of the nest must be soft and warm, and only the finest material was used for this upholstery. So vigorously were the birds working inside that the large pouch rocked and shook, occasionally causing the whole bough to swing. But as the pair's home approached completion, the keenness of the cock bird flagged. More and more frequently he would just sit among the branches of the willow, performing his short harsh snatches of song. And the hen bird, as if driven on by some inner urge, would work away at roofing over the entrance. A few days later, when the nest was complete but for the extreme end of the entrance tube, and when there were already two eggs in the pouch, the cock bird failed to return altogether. Restless, without another thought for his future brood, he would be roaming somewhere about the neighbourhood. Not much time would elapse before he started building another nest and finding himself a second, and later perhaps a third, mate.

Encounter with Horses

Who does not know the white horses of the Camargue? Who has not heard of them, read about them, or perhaps even hoped to ride them across the wide steppes of the Rhône delta? The horses are inseparably linked with the name of the Camargue; they belong to it just as the sea and the Rhône itself, they are one element in the triad upon which the present fame of the alluvial region is founded—horses, bulls, and flamingos.

But what are the real facts? Do the legendary herds still exist? Do they still live free and wild in marshes and steppes, or are those more or less groomed animals which one sees standing, saddled, outside the trekking hotels of Les Saintes-Maries, Albaron, and the other villages of the neighbourhood, waiting for their more or less skilled riders—are these perhaps the last descendants of that ancient free race?

A great many books have been written by competent authors on the history of the Camargue horse in the past and present. The sons of the land itself, *gardians* and *manadiers,* have recorded and written down their lore and extensively discussed the type of the Camargue horse. Many of these books contain a sensitive and all-embracing account of the *cheval blanc de la Camargue.* The present author—quite apart from the fact that he does not regard himself as an expert—has no intention of retelling what can be found elsewhere; this chapter, as its title suggests, is intended to be an account of his encounter with genuine Camargue horses. Yes, certainly, those white herds of horses still exist, even though their number has dropped considerably over the past few decades and even though their habitat has been greatly reduced. For the moment, however, the future existence of the Camargue horse is not threatened. At the same time, especially since the end of the Second World War, a development has been taking place which has a detrimental effect on the type of this semi-wild race—the attempts at crossbreeding. Many horse breeders deliberately cross-breed the Camargue horses with animals of predominantly Arab strains. Opinions may differ about the value of the mixed breeds in which the characteristics and properties of the Camargue race are increasingly lost. There is no doubt that these mixed breeds are at times faster but always substantially less hardy than the true Camargue horses. Such cross-breeds are found in many herds, and the riding horses offered to tourists are chiefly recruited from among them or are indeed pure Arabs imported from North Africa. A genuine Camargue horse is probably the exception among those promenade mounts. Truly pure-bred herds—the term 'pure-bred' to be taken relatively since no absolutely pure race exists—are rare enough, and only a few major breeders endeavour to preserve the pure breed.

We were lucky enough to know that one such herd was quite close to our camp. Every morning, on our way to the nest of the penduline tits, we had to cross a tamarisk thicket on the edge of a freshwater marsh. The thicket, together with the stretch of dry grass beyond, was part of the grazing of a herd of roughly thirty horses. Although the animals had at their disposal an area of several square miles, complete with marsh, reed-beds, deciduous forests, and open steppes, and although no restrictions were placed on their movements, the tamarisk thicket appeared to be their favourite spot. Thus it happened that we encountered the herd regularly, whenever we went to observe the penduline tit. During the weeks in question the animals were far more cautious and shy than usual and avoided humans whenever possible. Stallion and mares would throw up their heads, on guard, as soon as one of us appeared in the distance. It was the time when the mares were due to foal. Many of them were heavy with foal, others had already given birth and their young were making their first tentative, unsteady steps under the protection of the herd. On their far too long and spindly legs they stalked about amidst the adult animals; fortunately there was always its mother or some other mare close by for a foal to lean against for rest. Most of the foals were clothed in a thick, pitch-black, woolly coat with a white patch on their foreheads. There was an occasional rust-coloured or fawn foal. At about eight months old they lose this youthful coat. By the time they are about four years old their colouring will have changed to a pale grey; subsequently it turns to its final white or whitish grey hue.

The closer we approached the herd the more restless and nervous the animals became. They closed up to form a serried white front—head to head, nostrils flared, ears pricked up and in continuous motion. In their large expressive eyes was the ever-present mute question which we believed we could read in the eyes of every wild animal: What do you want, human? The mute and accusing question of the wild creature addressed to 'the pinnacle of creation' who has so often proved unworthy of this title.

To see the powerfully built horses crowded together in suppressed excitement is an unforgettable experience. Their muscles can be seen twitching under their gleaming white and grey coats. All necks are taut, all legs pressed firmly against the ground. A slight movement and the big bodies would be flung back for escape. For even though the horses of the Camargue have long ceased to be ownerless, they must still, in a sense, be regarded as wild animals. The herds of the horse-breeders mostly know neither stable nor saddle. Summer or winter they are left to their own devices, out in the open, exposed to heat and cold, rain and snow, thunderstorm and mistral. Without human help the mares give birth to their foals, protecting the young life against the inclement weather with their own bodies. The stallion, the master of the herd, watches jealously to make sure his animals remain undisturbed. Especially at foaling time, towards the end of winter or in early spring, it is not advisable to approach these

horses too unconcernedly. One might all too easily make the acquaintance of the powerful jaw or the massive kick of an angry stallion. I shall never forget an experience when, together with a friend, I had crept up near to the mares in order to take some close-up shots of newly born foals. Of course we kept our eyes on the stallion all the time—or at least we thought we did—and we were also continuously watching our line of retreat. And yet, suddenly, the stallion was behind us. With head stretched forward and bared teeth he was coming at us at a gallop. We dropped our cameras and ran like rabbits. If I ever described the Camargue horses as not particularly fast runners I regretted my judgment at that moment. And although, until that day, we had both seen irrigation canals only from their banks, we now got an unexpectedly good fish's-eye view of them.

In fact, the wide, deep canal was our only salvation. The stallion was only a few yards behind us as we reached the low bank by the ditch and with a desperate dive plunged in. I should love to have a picture of that scene—two photographers yapping and snorting in the water, and on the bank, contemptuously surveying the situation, a majestic stallion.

That was in the spring of last year. Later in the season, towards the end of the summer, when the foals were quite steady on their legs and capable also of fairly fast movement, we shot sequences of the herd in full gallop. Only in movement, in a full trot or gallop, is the primeval strength and beauty of these animals truly appreciated.

The idea was that a few *gardians* should drive the herd along a prearranged route to a pasture two miles further along and—on the following day or the day after that—drive it back to its old grazing. That was the simple plan for shooting that sequence. For the best part of a week, therefore, three sweating figures could be seen trudging through steppes and marshes in the noontide heat, carrying picks, spades, planks, and other impedimenta, digging holes, suspending observation cradles from trees, and building hides of the most various types. The horses had to be driven past the cameras as closely as possible, and this would work the more successfully the less the animals saw of the cameras and, more importantly, the cameramen. A great deal of work had to be done before each post was ready for operation. In particular, the digging of holes in the rock-hard dry soil was torture. But eventually all hides were completed, camera settings worked out and rehearsed—and everything was ready for action.

28 The Bois des Rièges, a chain of bushy forests, an ancient isolated dune formation

29 In the green maze of the Bois des Rièges.

A clump of *Juniperus phoenicea,* the rare species of juniper found only here ▷

30 Rock-roses *(Cistus albidus)* of the Mediterranean Garrigue ▷▷

On the eve of the first day's shooting we once more rode down the route with René, the chief *gardian*. We knew very well that in this virtually boundless space it would take a great deal of time to round up a herd of stampeding horses and drive it back to the intended route. Everything possible had therefore to be done to prevent that kind of accident. At all danger points, where escape was possible or even probable, sticks and lines with brightly coloured scraps of material were placed in position to scare the horses off. The idea was to prevent a break-out and stampede and to keep the horses along the planned track. To make doubly sure, the *gardian* was going to send out mounted men to watch all danger spots provided the course of events made this possible.

Our filming the following morning went perfectly. The horsemen drove the herd with an accuracy almost beyond our expectations, and the horses ran as if they had practised the scene for days—the trot along the irrigation ditch, crossing it in front of the clump of elms, bursting through the tamarisk hedge, and then full gallop across the open steppe. Only by the high earth dam did things very nearly go wrong. The animals had to climb up one side and immediately run down the steep embankment on the other. We were concealed at the foot of the slope in a narrow dug-out, hoping that the herd would chase past it quite close or, better still, right over it. But just as the first mare appeared on the dam she suddenly shied. For a second she hesitated and then broke away to the side, storming along the dam and sweeping the whole herd with her. It looked as if our sequence was ruined. But now the *gardians* showed that their reputation for horsemanship was justified. The drivers raced over the top of the dam, in pursuit of the horses fleeing along its ridge, and forced them back down the side from which they had only just come. In a wide circle they then brought them back for another charge. An outrider placed himself at the head of the herd, the other drivers followed closer and faster than on the first attempt—and now the crossing was accomplished to everybody's satisfaction.

In the early morning of the next day we were in position again. The various scenes were discussed at length with the drivers concerned, since especially on the way back a number of delicate sequences were planned, requiring the utmost attention and wholehearted co-operation of the horsemen. Shortly after eight the *gardians* had rounded up the herd. Slowly it got moving. For the first kilometre—a stretch of sparse salicornia steppe as flat as a pancake—no shots were planned. But after that came three camera emplacements in quick succession. The approach to them was to be taken at a very steady pace. But things worked out differently. The horses, probably sensing that they were approaching familiar ground, put on a turn of speed which made it difficult for the *gardians* to keep them together and steer them in the right direction. The mare which had led the herd the day before—it was interesting that the stallion throughout kept to the tail of the herd—again headed the group this morning. Her caprices gave us a lot of trouble. The first sequence was a complete failure. The horses were to have turned through a clump of tamarisks into a dry trough of swampland, next to have turned at a right angle beyond a line of shrubs, and then to have covered the 400 metres between cameras one and two along a flat trough. Instead, they broke through the three lines of scare barriers we had erected there, chased across the dry ford, and within seconds had disappeared among the tamarisks. The second sequence did not work out much better. According to the scenario the animals, in a long-drawn-out file, were to pass left of a camera mounted close to the ground. But they preferred to form two groups, one of which passed the camera hide-out on the left and the other on the right. But the third sequence went according to plan. The trickiest scene, however, still lay ahead—the crossing of a pond. This sequence was to be taken in a particularly effective way, and for that reason we had envisaged the galloping herd being driven straight at the camera and over it. We had done a similar thing with a herd of *taureaux,* and then, of course, the risk of the cameraman being trampled down was far more serious than with the horses. I believe experts will agree with me if I say that horses never run a human down deliberately. One can without risk throw oneself in front of a galloping horse's hooves and it will always try to avoid one or to jump over one. But this very reaction made the shooting of our sequence very difficult. The galloping animals must not see the cameraman until the very last moment, when there would be no time left for evasive action. A hide-out was out of the question because it would have kept the herd too far away from the camera. And it was vital that they should pass close—the nearest animal within less than a metre. Success depended on the lead horses being taken by surprise.

31 Milk thistle *(Silybum marianum)*

32 Asphodel *(Asphodelus cerasifer)*

33 Yellow flag *(Iris pseudacorus)*   34 Wild gladiolus *(Gladiolus communis)*

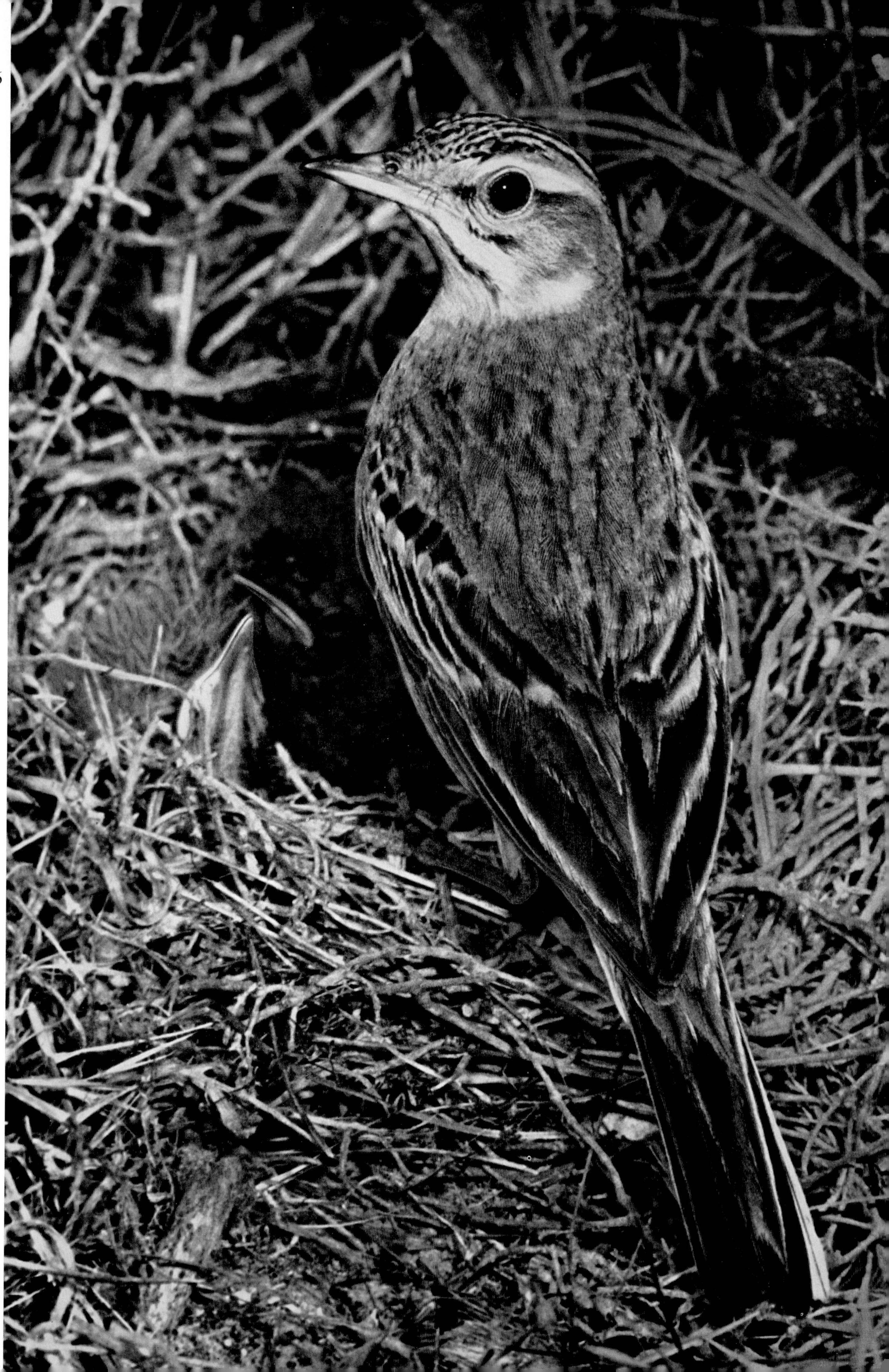

35 Jewelled lacerta *(Lacerta lepida)* in menacing posture
36 Tawny pipit *(Anthus campestris)*
37 Spectacled warbler *(Sylvia conspicillata)*

As the most suitable spot for this sequence we chose a slightly elevated stretch of shore running diagonally out into the lake and covered with a tall, bushy thicket. There was just one gap in that line of shrubs and through this the herd was to be driven into the water at a full gallop; there a number of *gardians* would be waiting to hem the herd in on its two flanks and force it towards the cameraman, who was in position about thirty metres from the bank. Once more the main points of the drive were recapitulated—a fast gallop in close order, the herd to be contained in the water and the animals kept together until they were level with the camera. The horsemen then rode off to their appointed stations and we took up position behind our cameras. We had three of them, arranged in an acute triangle aligned on the expected route of the horses; the two lateral cameras at normal eye-level but the middle one barely twenty centimetres (eight inches) above the surface of the water. This one was to be 'overrun' by the herd. As he passed me the protective helmet I was going to wear during the shooting, my colleague muttered something about 'hair-brained recklessness'. He was not far wrong. But there was no time for reflection. A few moments later we were ready for the herd.

Five minutes passed. No sign yet of the outrider who was to signal to us the imminent arrival of the horses. There must have been some hitch. From where we were we could not see what was happening on the far side of the tamarisk thicket. It was a tense wait. To both sides of me, slightly forward, my two colleagues were crouching behind their cameras, intent, their nervousness ill-concealed. Again and again they tested their cameras by panning them across, checking the settings. Their task was to get an over-all picture of the horses and then take them again in semi-close-up—less spectacular shots perhaps but at least as important as my extreme close-ups. There was quite a lot at stake that brilliant late summer morning—and we all knew it. The four *gardians* in front of us among the tamarisks also knew what importance we attached to the sequences of the crossing of the pond. True, they were not personally involved and tended to regard the whole business as a huge joke. They were looking across towards us now, grinning, and with all kinds of mute gestures conveying how they thought this sequence would end. And their gestures clearly included a chopped-off head and a crushed camera. But they were not being serious—one could see

the impish humour in their eyes—and we could be quite sure that they would do their utmost to make our enterprise succeed.

More minutes passed and nothing happened. I felt suddenly shivery. Fear? Nonsense—what could happen to me? We would be glad if those horses did not break away before reaching us. No, it was probably just the temperature of the water and my rather uncomfortable crouching position behind the camera. Only my head and neck and part of my shoulders were now showing above the surface of the water. I was hoping the horses would come soon.

Two minutes later I caught myself estimating how many horses would pass in single file between my colleagues and me and come galloping straight up at me. Perhaps I was nervous after all? Just then one of the horsemen on the bank raised his arm: the herd was approaching. An instant later came the first calls of the *gardians,* and the dull thud of hooves pounding the hard steppe floor grew into a rapid crescendo. A glance at my colleagues—a nod to indicate that they were ready. The pounding of hooves grew louder still and the calls of the drivers seemed closer. There was a snorting and whinnying as the herd came galloping along the tamarisk hedge.

A white flash behind the shrubs—the outrider! Now he was wheeling into the narrow gap and approaching the edge of the pond at a short gallop. A red-and-black checked shirt, a black broad-brimmed hat above a gaunt face. That was Jacques, *"Jacky le maigre"*, as the locals called him. A short, wiry lad who had the handling of the bulls and horses in his blood. He called out something to the waiting *gardians,* something I could not quite catch but which sounded like *"Ils sont fous, ces bestiaux"*. Then he rode into the water. His mount's skin was sticky with sweat and a froth of saliva hung about its mouth. The voices of the drivers now came across shrill and loud. Dust was whirled up. Excited neighing. Grey-white bodies piled up into a solid wall—and then, bursting from the thicket in a broad front, the herd raced down into the shallow trough so that the water and algae were thrown up high. A wall of spray rose in front of the pounding horses and closed over the heads of the foals. White manes waved. Mud smacked against the animals' flanks. The serried phalanx was coming straight at the camera. The white, grey, and black bodies burst out of the silvery spray, tall and powerful against the sky. Suddenly all my misgivings were gone—the wild primordial force of the scene held me spellbound. All around me was forgotten—the magnificent picture in the ground-glass viewer of the camera was the only reality.

Seconds later, when the voices of my friends and the assembled *gardians* snatched me from my exciting dream, I knew that I had just been fortunate enough to shoot one of the most magnificent scenes of our film. Caked with mud and soaked to the skin, I rose from the water. Only then did I notice that my finger was still on the trigger of my camera, now running empty. A hundred feet of film had been shot, full of pictures about which, a few minutes earlier, I had been worried. One of the scenes still stands as fresh in my memory as if no more than a few hours had passed, and not over nine months. It was the moment when, out of the thick haze of spray which surrounded me, there emerged a young foal, wedged in between the bodies of fully grown animals, unable to avoid me and making two attempts to jump over me and my camera. Only then did a gap open to the side and the frightened young animal sprint away.

The Heart of the Wilderness

On the southern edge of the Etang de Vaccarès, in the middle of the treeless and shrubless wide open space of the salicornia steppe, the chain of bush forest known as the Bois des Rièges rises from the monotonous landscape. It is here, where on a hot day the horizon disappears in the blinding haze, where the air shimmers over the dry hard ground, conjuring up flickering mirages, that the heart of the Camargue beats. Far from all human habitation and activity, this magnificent piece of wild nature is enclosed and sealed off on all sides by the network of brackish lagoons near the sea. Wherever the eye roams, it finds nothing but water, salicornia, and salt-encrusted stretches of dry ground. The latter do not exist in the winter. Then only the red, yellow, and brown branches of the salicornia plants show above a boundless waste of water. Once a striking range of dunes along the Mediterranean shore, the sandhills of the Bois des Rièges, now flattened and thickly covered with vegetation, are a long way from the sea. Only

on very clear days can they be made out from the *Digue de la Mer,* the terminal dyke running along the coast, as distant dark silhouettes in a pathless plain.

Only in hot, dry summers, when the sun and wind have dried out the *étangs* with the exception of a few deep ditches, can this remote spot be reached without getting one's feet wet. But even then one might too readily trust the crust of soil, only to find oneself suddenly breaking into pitch-black salty mud. And it is by no means always easy to get out of this stinking and ever-yielding morass. By far the pleasantest and probably also the most impressive way of seeing this patch of virgin nature is on horseback.

It was an early morning in May, with the air crisp and clear. The sky, deep blue and infinitely high, promised a warm summer's day. We had been riding for half an hour. Our animals were well rested and moving at a brisk pace. They had spent the night out on the pasture, and only at daybreak had the *gardian* rounded them up and brought them to the stable for saddling. We set out shortly before four. No sooner had we left the *mas* behind us than men and horses had to run the gauntlet of the clouds of mosquitoes and gadflies which rose from the dewy foliage. A brisk gallop seemed the only way to save us from the black plague. But not until we had crossed the tamarisk thickets enclosing the vineyards did we leave our tormentors behind.

There was no doubt that the warm weather of the past fortnight had greatly advanced the growth of all plants. After a cold early spring the year's display of blossom had been rather late and, to begin with, a little half-hearted. But by now the buds were pushing out everywhere. The *sansouïre* was brilliant with the fresh green of salicornia. Yellow flags lined the banks of the irrigation ditches and the shallow edges of freshwater swamps. The ponds were covered with the delicate star-shaped blossoms of water buttercup. The whitish-yellow flowers covered the water like a carpet—so much so that hardly any water was visible. Only where the grazing *taureaux* had trodden their tracks into the swamp did their dark wavy trails snake through the white surface. Even the delicate tamarisks now seemed to be in a hurry to thrust their first bud clusters towards the warming sun. Here and there sporadic pools of water still glistened in the steppe—but their number had greatly diminished over the past few weeks. The most persistent of these are the swampy patches along the edge of crops where artificial irrigation ensures a high groundwater table. These dry out only slowly, and the earth remains moist and swampy until well into May and occasionally even later. This is the home of stilts and lapwings. The former had not yet got down to breeding. Ever since their arrival in the Camargue in mid-April—we actually saw the first of them during the last few days of March—they had been keeping close to their breeding places of last year. But they still did not seem to feel like building a nest or laying eggs. The lapwings, on the other hand, had been breeding for nearly three weeks and the first young birds were due almost any day. As soon as we approached their nests the old birds hurled themselves at us, wailing. They certainly had courage. Boldly they dived down on us and streaked close around the horses with loud cries. We had to be careful to see that the horses did not shy. At the Etang du Fournelet we had to enter water for the first time. The horses, not yet used to the wide greyish-blue surface, at first bridled a little and refused to jump down the bank. Firm pressure with one's legs and an encouraging word rallied them. Breathing heavily, they splashed into the water.

Hard by the bank was a flock of flamingos. Most of the rose-coloured birds had heads hidden in their dorsal feathers, sleeping. Only a few of them stretched their long necks, but hardly any glanced across at us. They displayed no fear of the horses and did not seem to regard a mounted human as a threat either. It was easy therefore to approach them to within forty metres or so. Only then did we attract their attention, and calmly, without showing any sign of fear, they moved away towards the middle of the lake. Soon the water got deeper. The horses had long since ceased their first nervous dancing and were now breasting the water with slow, heavy steps. Behind us long wakes showed on the mirror-smooth surface of the *étang*.

On the far side our track for a short distance lay across a high broken edge of bank. The waves here had undercut the bank, biting deep into the soil, and dried cracks showed in the vertical cliff. A narrow track ran along the very edge, where new lumps of soil could break off under every tread. But the horses moved over these dangerous spots with the assurance of a sleep-walker. We had long given them their heads: their sharp senses seemed to us more reliable than our own often belated commands.

From up on the bank we had a magnificent view of the lake and the adjacent *sansouïre*. It stretched ahead for miles—green, uniform, and as flat as a pancake. There were only two points for the eye to seize on in this infinite vastness—to the south the slim white needle of the lighthouse at Gacholle, and in the west the dark green silhouette of the Bois des Rièges on the far horizon. Out on the water was a pair of shelducks. These black, white, and rust-coloured birds with their blackish-green iridescent heads and brilliant red bills are by no means as common as they used to be. Ever since myxomatosis decimated the rabbits there have been fewer warrens about. And it is in these rabbit warrens that the shelduck like to build their nests. Perhaps their number will increase again when the rabbits, now gradually recovering from their plague, once more provide suitable nesting places for these birds, thus enabling them to abandon their enforced breeding in the open and revert to their old breeding habits.

Across Le Cassieu, the elongated flat peninsula between the Etang du Fournelet and the Etang du Lion, we gave our horses free rein. At an easy canter we were making for the distant line of dunes. Dully the hooves drummed against the bare salt ground; the saddlery creaked in the rhythm of the horses' movements; the animals snorted. The head wind was pleasantly cooling on our faces. No matter how often one has done it, to ride through the steppe on one of these splendid horses is a grand experience. Willingly and with evident enjoyment the horses themselves keep up their brisk canter for mile after mile. Rarely do they get tired. The *gardians* are no doubt right when they say that these half-breeds like nothing better than to be given free rein and be allowed to run and run. The true Camargue horses are agile animals, powerful in spite of their somewhat squat build. As mounts they have a number of excellent qualities and perform sterling service to the cowherds in their daily work. True, they do not achieve the turn of speed of the pure-bred Arab or Berber races, or the long-legged Andalusians. On the other hand, their sturdiness and, above all, their endurance far surpass those of the faster breeds. And that is what matters on the difficult and often treacherous ground of the Rhône delta. "Without horses no bulls" the Camarguais say. And that is the truth. How else could the herds of cattle be tended in the pathless steppe or in the treacherous marsh, how else could the often obstreperous beasts be sorted out and corralled together? The Camargue horse, born free and bred in the vastness of this landscape, can stand up to all hardships. It reacts swiftly and surely to the countless obstacles on the ground and it is able to spot dangers long before the man in the saddle. The stallions—and only the stallions —are rounded up according to custom at the age of three to five years, gelded, and broken in. In the past, custom demanded that training should not be started until the horse was seven years old. But it is a great deal more difficult to tame a wild seven-year-old, which was fully mature at the age of five, than to train an animal of three or four years. In either case the capture of the young stallion means a merciless struggle between man and beast. With teeth and hooves and in a hundred different ways the animals separated from the herd and corralled in a pen will defend their freedom against anyone approaching them. Attempts at taming frequently lead to serious injury. The *gardians* invariably try to wait for a favourable moment in order to slip the *seden*—a long rope twisted from horsehair—over the head and neck of a wild young stallion running about the corral. If they succeed the noose is tightened until the captured animal cannot breathe and crashes to the ground, half dazed. Instantly several men pounce upon him to tie him up with further cords. But frequently the strength of the *gardians* is not enough to control the young stallion. Cunning and ruses have to be resorted to, since the animals' instinct for freedom is usually so powerful that they succeed in shaking off the humans and breaking loose. Whenever that happens, woe betide anyone who cannot quickly get out of reach of the raving and furiously kicking animal.

Our cavalcade came to a halt in front of a narrow, deep ford. We let our horses get their breath back before moving into the water. The banks though not high were steep and slippery. Snorting, the animals flung themselves into the water. A flight of greenshanks streaked up from the far bank. Two little egrets rose from a dip in the ground and made off, croaking. We had to take our feet out of the stirrups, otherwise the water would have got into the tops of our boots. Fortunately the ground was firm and the animals, in water up to the girths, did not break in. Once more on dry land we soon crossed from smooth, salt-saturated steppe floor to undulating sandy ground. The first dune thicket, ahead on our right, was rising higher and higher from the *sansouïre*. Already the contours of individual treetops were discernible. Over along the southern end of the Vaccarès lake a herd of *taureaux* was moving in a long file; tiny black spots in the shimmering haze. It had become warm. The sun was near its zenith. Midges whined. Grasshoppers creaked in the dry dune grass. From the bushy forest came a spicy fragrance. A short-toed eagle was circling in the azure sky. Its almost pure white underparts gleamed bright.

Abruptly a wild boar shot out from a concealed waterhole, straight in front of the horses' feet. Two of the animals shied and reared up on their hind legs. The boar for its part bolted in the direction of the *bois*. How about a little boar hunt? We flung ourselves on the horses' necks and gave them the spurs. The boar ran as fast as it could. But the horses were faster and were gaining on it. Over sandhills and across swampy troughs the wild hunt went. The horses were frothing at the mouth, their silky skin sticky with sweat. Their nostrils were dilated. Yes, they understood the game all right. To them the bristly quarry was much the same as a young bull that had to be driven to the branding place. The first rider had nearly caught up with the boar. Suddenly, with a grunt, it turned sharp right. But its second pursuer was nearly on top of it. A moment later it was flanked on both sides, enclosed in a semicircle. Its only line of escape was straight ahead. And all the time the animal kept up a pace that one would not have credited it with. Just then one of the horses stumbled and threw its rider far into the salicornia. At once everybody reined in their animals. The hunt was over. The boar got away. Luckily neither man nor beast was seriously injured. Just a few bruises on face and hands—no more. But the horseman had quite a shock all the same. From now on everybody was more careful. The soil here was riddled with rabbit warrens and these were veritable horse traps which could easily cause broken legs.

A quarter of an hour later we had reached the first *bois*. We had come to the heart of the Camargue, to its wildest and most primordial spot. Dense and thorny the dark green barrier of the shrub forest rose before us. A heavy, sweetly astringent fragrance hung on the air—the perfume of thyme and rosemary, of lavender and rock-roses. This was blossom-time. Everywhere the dark mass of juniper, mock privet, and mastic shrubs was dotted with patches of white, yellow, red, and blue. Here were the heavily perfumed yellow-white flowers of the rock-roses, the bright red or violet flowers of wild gladioli, and the tall, slim stems of asphodels, the flower of the dead which so often adorns the graves in south European cemeteries and which the ancient Greeks believed covered the slopes of the underworld. A delicate pale-blue haze against the rich green marked a patch of wild rosemary blossom. Brightly coloured butterflies tumbled through the air. On glittering wings bees and bumblebees flew from blossom to blossom. Capricorn beetles in gleaming metallic armour were visiting the blossoms as uninvited guests, getting drunk on their sweet nectar. There was ceaseless hectic activity, a continuous coming and going—and so it would continue throughout the warm hours of the day.

To penetrate the interior of the dense thicket is laborious and no longer possible everywhere. The vegetation is too much of a barrier and the few gaps are closed by a much too dense tangle of undergrowth. In particular the thorny shoots of smilax again and again catch in one's clothes and prevent all progress. It is to this tough shrub with its numerous tendrils that, according to the locals, the thicket owes its name. But the plant which imprints its character on this evergreen jungle is a type of juniper, *Juniperus phoenicea,* which thrives only here and among the dunes of the Little Camargue. Magnificent patches of this rare plant cover all eight parts of the chain of dunes. At times they are clumped together, at others they grow in loose groups, sometimes in pure bush formation, at others as trees five to six metres (fifteen to twenty feet) tall, or both forms intermingling. But invariably, whether as a bush or a tree, the Phoenician juniper with its striking silhouette lends the Bois des Rièges its unique appearance.

From the dunes there is a far view both inland and out towards the seashore, whose outline can just about be guessed at in the blue haze of the late morning. In the distance lie the hilly ranges of the Alpilles. In front of them, from horizon to horizon, a changing pattern of water, salicornia, and brightly glistening expanses of dry mud. To the right and left runs the gently curving line of the bush forest. Like a thick separating wall it cuts across the monotonous *sansouïre*—broad and deep green from close to, increasingly pale and narrow in the distance where the dark band is gradually lost between sky and earth. A light breeze stirs the grasses. This, roughly, must have been the sight that offered itself to Noah after the flood—a silent, empty vastness under the shimmering air in which the smell of the earth mingles with the scent of blossoms and resin.

In the Reed Jungle

Along the lakeshore the reeds were thick and lignified. The tall, slender stems were gently waving in the wind with a barely perceptible rustle of their leaves. In the opening which a fisherman had cut for his boat clouds of tiny midges were soundlessly floating up and down in the air. Small fish, as transparent as glass, flitted about just under the surface, their delicate shadows trembling on the flat lake bottom. An olive-green viperine water snake was sunning itself on a clump of weeds which had floated up against the reeds. Swallows flew low down the lane cut throught the reeds, snapping up the midges without apparently reducing their number. Near the bank the ground was covered with a thick layer of dead algae, like cotton-wool. If one stirred it up, black, ink-like clouds would make the water turbid over a wide radius. A smell of decay and rot hung on the air. But out there, beyond the reed thicket, where the sun was reflected in the grey-green sheet of the *étang,* where coots were squabbling and great crested grebes proudly sailing along like Roman galleys, was no smell of decay. There the white lake bottom could be seen shimmering through the clear water. The silvery bodies of fish flashed over it like pale ghosts.

In the northern part of the belt of reeds, which was about a kilometre (two-thirds of a mile) long and almost as wide at its widest point, were the nests of the purple herons. We had frequently seen the large dark birds dive into the sea of reeds in the distance or rise up from it. When the wind was favourable their cries could be heard from the bank. Our attempts to approach the heron colony from the landward side were unsuccessful. Lignified reeds, snapped by the wind and interlocked in thick tangles, formed an unyielding barrier which could only be penetrated with a bush knife. On the lakeward side, however, the tangle was not quite so thick. The first ten or twelve metres in knee-deep water were easy enough. But then, suddenly, our legs gave way alarmingly and we were slithering in viscous mud. It was no fun pulling our feet clear again, pushing on through the thick reeds and plunging again into the morass until at last sole and heel struck firm ground. After a few minutes we were covered in sweat. Our soaked bush shirts were sticking to our skins. The mosquitoes had a feast. Splintered reed stems bruised our arms and hands till they bled, suddenly recoiling shoots whipped our faces.

It is easy to lose one's sense of direction in the twilight of the reeds which grow to nearly twice the height of a man. Wherever one looks, there is nothing but stems and leaves. To the front and to the back, to the right and to the left—light and shade, nothing but light and shade. Even overhead, in distorted perspective, steeply towering green giant canes. And above a narrow blue band—a piece of sky. By that time one almost wonders whether it is in the right place. Hardly a sound penetrates this maze from outside. There is nothing but the breathing and whispering and clicking of the reed forest. Now and then a sound—close one moment and distant the next. The exasperating whine of the midges, the creaking of the reed warblers, the barking of the coots. The whistle of a marsh harrier, the squeak of water rails, the ringing of the bearded tits. And at a still uncertain distance the hoarse croaking of the purple herons. Utterly exhausted after an hour's struggle through water, mud, and tangled reeds, we were delighted to find our own track again, merely to establish that we had walked in a circle.

By May 16th the colony of herons was about three-quarters complete. The nests, which differed a good deal in size, were on broken reed-stems, some of them up to 1·2 metres (four feet) above water-level. Many were still empty, others were still being built. In the majority of them were two to five, and in three instances six, bluish-green eggs. Within an hour we had counted thirty-two nests, completed or under construction. But we were sure we had found no more than half of them.

Two weeks later we had a tent standing on the edge of the heron colony, camouflaged with green netting and thick reed mats, all ready for our photography.

A dozen herons rose from their nests clattering as in the early hours of the morning we made our way to our hide along the narrow partially cleared path through the reed thicket. With loud warning cries the birds circled above us before turning landwards and, vigorously beating their wings, disappearing from view. A week had passed. In nearly all the nests the young birds were hatching—small, ill-proportioned creatures which had little in common with the general picture one has of herons. Rather ugly pot-bellied things with thin necks and with heads much too large for them, dangling haphazardly, first one way and then another. When they open their beaks their red throats seem to take up the whole head.

We swiftly moved under cover. A few minutes later my escorts were able to withdraw again. The sound of their footsteps in the reeds died away. Everything was once more calm and silent. I sat and waited. It was once more one of those timeless moments at the beginning of a long vigil, moments when one is alone with oneself and one's thoughts and memories.

Soon the parent herons returned to the near-by nests: gliding down to the green sea of reeds, dropping their long legs, and touching down with a swish of beating wings. Sometimes their toes only gripped the tips of the reeds. Then the stem would bend under the weight and the birds would stand still for several seconds, wings raised and necks thrust out. The chicks in the nest, only eight metres away, kept quiet. Crowded together into a ball of feathers, they kept motionless. In spite of the shallowness of the nests they were difficult to make out from my hide. The smallest must have hatched last night or during the night. Since the one before it burst through its eggshell as long as four days ago we had assumed that the fifth and last egg was unfertilized.

In the second nest, behind my hide and visible to me through a slit in the canvas, nothing much was happening for the moment. The young herons were sleeping or dozing. Now and then one would lift its head with tired movement, nod, yawn broadly, and sink back into the bowl of the nest. There was no sign of the parent birds. Even so I was not bored. I was kept busy enough by the quite respectable number of midges and gadflies which had found their way into my tent to seek shelter from the cool night. As the temperature gradually rose, the accursed insects awakened from their stupor and soon regained their appetite for biting. Not until the very last insect had been picked off the canvas silently and squashed between thumb and forefinger could I relax. Quite close a great reed warbler was sitting on the top of a reed stem, warbling noisily. He was doing so with such intensity that his throat feathers were bristling under his bill like a shaggy beard. Suddenly he broke off and made for my hideout. A few seconds later I could hear him climbing about the reed mats close above my head. And once more the grating notes rang out: "Karra-karra-keet-karra-keet-keet..."—louder and more obtrusive at this close range.

One of the parent herons from the nest behind me had returned through the reeds unnoticed and was now about to lie down on its young. I had not heard it come. The ability of these large birds to move through the mass of reeds without any sound at all and with scarcely a movement of the canes is quite astonishing. They are helped in this by their long toes which are developed into real prehensile extremities. Awkwardly the bird settled down. Since my last visit it had piled up a wall of dry leaves and stalks on the near edge of the nest, so that only its narrow head with its long dagger-like beak could be seen. During the first few days the heron had clearly not felt too happy about my hide. But in the meantime it had become used to the motionless structure and was no longer taking any notice of it. During the past two days of watching I had noticed the frequent horse-like neighing trill of a little grebe. Judging by the sound, the bird must have invariably been very close to my hide. Once or twice I managed to spot it between the green-and-yellow reed stems. But every single time, just as I got it in my viewfinder, it would dive out of sight and for the next half-hour would remain invisible. I suspected that the bird must have its nest somewhere in the immediate vicinity and made a search with my friends. In vain. I was the more astonished to see the grebe suddenly emerging next to the heron's nest and again vanishing under it. A later inspection showed that it had built its floating nest immediately below the platform of the heron's nest and that there were six eggs in it. What could have induced the bird to hatch its eggs in such an odd spot? Did it feel particularly safe in the deep shadow of the large canopy provided by the heron's nest? Was it just a coincidence? Whichever was the case, the grebe's nest was superbly camouflaged. Unless one knew it was there the bird simply could not be spotted. The reed canes which, higher up, supported the heron's nest formed a curtain around the grebe, with only two small gaps, and in the pattern of light and shade produced by that reed curtain the outlines of the bird's body were completely broken up. This did not, however, stop it from panicking at the slightest unfamiliar sound. As if propelled by a spring it would hurl itself headlong into the water and surface again only at a safe distance. But a minute later it was back again, hurriedly climbing up the blunt cone that formed its nest and acting as if nothing had happened. The same game was repeated many times during the next hour. Having seen the panic the slightest noise produced in the grebe, I got so nervous I hardly dared to breathe.

A cold sulphur-yellow eye was steadily regarding my film tent. It completely filled the small observation spy-hole and its piercing gaze seemed to penetrate the walls of the hide. This was the old purple heron. It was still standing among the reeds, about two metres from its nest—watchful, motionless, as if turned to stone. Slowly I moved towards the viewfinder. The bird's head with its splendid bluish-grey crest feathers almost filled the ground-glass rectangle. And that vigilant eye seemed alarmingly close. Could it be suspicious? I did not think so. The hide now was nothing new to it. It had long become part of the familiar surroundings of the heron's nest. Even so those few seconds under the watchful gaze of the bird seemed like hours. Two minutes passed, perhaps three. Nothing happened. I dared not take my eye off the viewfinder, even though I knew that not even the sharpest eye could possibly notice my movements. The tall reed mats completely screened our camouflage tent. And our peepholes, barely a few centimetres square each, were, moreover, covered with strips of green gauze which allowed a good view out but made it impossible from outside to see into the dark interior. At last the yellow eye slowly swivelled down between the reed stems. The heron's head and neck moved forward, and with two or three long strides the bird climbed up to the rim of its nest. Its plumage was really magnificent. The dark crest contrasted strikingly with the rust colour of the bird's temples and neck. From its dark grey-violet back the long purple mantle feathers fell down over the bird's flanks. Here, in the muted sunlight of the reed thicket, the name purple heron seemed fully justified. The delicately graduated colour scale of its plumage was seen to full effect. Outside, when the birds were standing in the lakes or flying up from the tangle of the ditches and streaking overhead, they just looked dark and almost without colour, with little suggestion of purple.

The young birds in the nest were craning their necks and softly whispering. Cautiously the old heron stepped over them, to the frontal rim of the nest. There, with slow, measured movements it fitted a projecting reed cane more neatly into the base of the nest and then embarked on its protracted toilet. Feather after feather was carefully drawn through the beak. First came breast and belly, then the back and tail. Even the long, thin neck had its turn, although the combing action here at times involved grotesque distortions of the neck. Finally the wings were subjected to thorough treatment. The operation was concluded by a vigorous shaking and a yawn. Slowly, infinitely slowly and cautiously, the bird lay down over its young. Now and again it would carefully probe with one foot to make sure they were properly settled and that none of them was crushed.

It was past ten o'clock and the sun was rising higher and higher above the reeds. A heavy heat was settling down. The old purple heron was still dozing in its nest, its head lying on the rim. Earlier it had stood on the nest, wings opened, to provide shade for the squabbling chicks. But now it had become sleepy. It was shutting first its right eye and then its left. But even so the bird's senses were taut and no movement escaped it. It saw the water rail noiselessly scurrying through the reeds even before it emerged from the thicket to move down the narrow passage leading to its nest. The fat carp which had got stuck between the tangled reed canes and was now noisily thrashing about in an attempt to free itself attracted the heron's attention just as much as did the small Cetti's warbler which had just plunged into the twilight of the reed thicket, its beak full of nest-building material. And it was wide awake the moment a marsh harrier appeared from somewhere and passed close to the nest—so close that its gleaming eyes were clearly visible. The harrier, too, had some chicks of its own in a nest near by; their healthy appetite similarly forced the parent birds into conducting a continuous hunt for food. At such times, therefore, the powerful bird cannot afford to be choosy. Anything it can grab is a welcome prey—the grass snake or the young mallard, the great crested grebe and the green edible frog, the water rat and the coot. For all of them the harrier would remain a threatening spectre, an ever-present danger, for the next few weeks. So long as one of the parent birds keeps watch, the young purple herons have nothing to fear. But woe betide eggs and chicks in an unguarded nest when the death-bringing shadow flits over the reed thicket. A short pulling up, a sudden wheeling—and some young life ends in the grasp of needle-sharp talons. Cruel? Nature is cruel. It kills for the sake of life, and nothing is more alien to it than sentimentality. By its death each individual discharges its contribution to the whole, obeying the inexorable law of survival. Only man disregards this law and believes he may interfere in the balance of forces—but in the end he finds that he cannot do so with impunity.

A swish of dark wings and a hoarse grating broke the mid-morning stillness. I started. A second parent heron had touched down a few yards from the nest and was now striding over the stems, beating its wings. Roused from its sleepy indifference, the bird in the nest got up. It ruffled its magnificent mantle feathers in excitement, it stretched its neck further and further, rocking it in a gentle rhythm. Its head was bent back, its beak pointed almost straight at the sky. There were hoarse sounds of greeting. Nodding its head, the returning heron entered the nest. Both partners bowed until their breasts very nearly touched the edge of the nest. There was deep-throated croaking and a soft clicking of beaks. Both birds straightened up simultaneously. Their necks, twisted round one another, jerked up, parted, and came together again in a playful movement a moment later. The couple circled each other with measured steps, their open wings brushed each other with a rustle. The two bodies seemed to grow together into an over-dimensioned blossom from which the rust-coloured necks rose up like flickering flames. It was a fascinating dance of dreamlike savage beauty.

This ceremony of 'changing the guard' at the nest took less than a minute. Then the birds' movements slowed down and died away. The relieved bird moved to the far edge of the nest, grew longer and longer, and with a vigorous beating of wings took off. For a short while the bird in the nest watched it fly away. Then it turned to the young. Hurriedly I got the camera ready for the imminent feeding of the chicks. But I was unlucky—feeding time was not until an hour later, when the heron which had just flown off once more took over sentry duty at the nest.

On the Beach

May 24th was gone—the day when the wandering gipsies of Europe make for the wide open wilderness of the Camargue each year. The Masses in the fortified church of Les Saintes-Maries-de-la-Mer, the ceremony of the candles, the ecstatic cries of the gipsies as the reliquary with the remains of the two Marys is lowered from the tower chapel to the high altar, through a nave heavy with incense—all these were now a thing of the past. Over, too, was the blare of loudspeakers and the exciting roar of the bullfights in the whitewashed arena. The stirring songs, the fiery dancing in the streets and squares—all these were over. The restless nomadic pilgrims had scattered again in all directions. The first of them had left Les Saintes-Maries in the late afternoon of May 25th. But the great general departure came on the following morning,

38 With the onset of spring begins the gradual drying out of the marshy lowlands

The salicornia steppe *(Salicornietum fruticosae)* of the middle and upper Camargue through the seasons (Pl. 39–42)

39 Its appearance in spring (May) ▷

40 Typical dense growth of *Salicornia fruticosa* during the dry summer period (July) ▷

41 In particularly severe winters precipitation in the Camargue can be in the form of snow (January)

42 The copious rainfall of the late autumn floods large tracts of the steppe (end of November)

43 By the Etang du Fournelet

when caravan after caravan moved out of the village down the road to the north, until they had all vanished in the distant haze. "*A l'an que vèn*"— "till next year!" Then they would all come again, *les gitans,* as punctual as the migratory birds. Between May 20th and 24th their overloaded caravans would move down the hot roads of the Midi, to the estuary of the Little Rhône, to the fortress of their patron saint, of Black Sarah and the Holy Marys.

Left behind on the beach was the motley crowd of sun-hungry tourists who populate this little fishing village in steadily growing numbers from about mid-May. Come to think of it, is this sanctuary of the two Marys still a 'fishing village'? Does it not rather present the familiar picture of a flourishing seaside resort—without the smell of seaweed or of nets drying in the sun, without those picturesque fishing-boats which inspired Van Gogh? Yes and no. The long summer, admittedly, belongs to the visitors who come here from all parts of France and from neighbouring countries in order to enjoy the sea and the sun, or to relive on the backs of the white Camargue horses the romantic Western dreams of their long-vanished boyhood. The natives, from *M. le Maire* down to the simplest pistachio or mussel vendor in the street, do their utmost to profit from this development and rake in what money they can. And who can blame them? At the same time it cannot be denied that in consequence of the tourist explosion in Provence, Languedoc, and the Camargue in recent years a great deal of ancient custom is beginning to turn into tawdry folklore for the visitors, and that rites originally derived from religious needs are being progressively debased to a fairground spectacle. In the late autumn and in winter, at long last, when the stream of tourists has dried up, when hotels and bars have closed their doors, when a dreamy rustic peace has once more settled on the streets and nooks of the little township, Les Saintes-Maries-de-la-Mer reverts to being a simple fishing village whose inhabitants, after a noisy and turbulent summer, begin to rediscover their proper way of life.

There is a world of difference between the overcrowded bathing beach and the quiet strip of coast here in the eastern part of the delta. Over there a hectic rush, a noisy bustle among countless brightly coloured tents and camping caravans—here heavenly peace, the shimmering expanse of sand, the spume of the surf, and the white shapes of fishing gulls and terns above it. The sea, rather choppy during the past few days, has settled down again. Quietly and regularly the waves roll up to the shore, gently lap the moist sand, and fall back again with a lazy semicircular motion. Through these almost glass-like curtains of the waves comes the flash of slender fish bodies out by the sandbank. Like silver arrows they are hurled forward from the toppling waves, clearing several wave crests on their flight.

A long way out to sea, several hundred metres beyond the breaking waves, large white and dark speckled birds are gliding above the turquoise surface. They are hardly identifiable by the naked eye; only the telescope tells us that they are immature gannets. They are regular, though not very numerous, visitors to the Camargue coast. As a rule only a few individuals are present, performing their graceful flying manœuvres in their hunt for fish. Only in the autumn do they occasionally arrive in their hundreds from their breeding places on the island rocks of the North Atlantic—young ones and old ones, the latter with brilliant white plumage and strongly contrasting black wingtips. Their weight is about the same as that of a goose, yet they are a picture of power and elegance as they speed over the wave-tops with a regular quick beat. An even more unforgettable experience is to see them circling high up, looking for fish, and suddenly diving forward, one after another, wings folded back, hurtling headlong into the water like racing torpedoes from a height of twenty or thirty metres (seventy or a hundred feet). It may be assumed that their momentum carries them some five to ten metres (fifteen to thirty feet) below the surface. Almost invariably they have swallowed the fish they have caught by the time they surface again. *"Fou de Bassan"* is what the French call the agile bird. 'Mad' because—as a fisherman assured us—they not only dive into the sea but occasionally also on to the decks of seagoing ships, breaking their necks. I would not care to venture an opinion on this interpretation; personally I never witnessed such 'madness'. But why should not a gannet circling over a ship be tricked by reflecting surfaces and lured into a fatal dive?

It was past midday and the sun was beating down on the vast beach. The sand burnt the soles of our feet. Wherever it is firm and its surface covered by a fine crust of salt, long-legged tiger beetles scurry about, hunting for small insects. They never keep still for more than a fraction of a second. These small, slender creatures zigzag over the bare ground, this way and that, over drift sand and through sun cracks, often difficult to discern against the blinding white background. If disturbed they fly up with astonishing speed—but a few feet away they land in the sand again, heads invariably turned towards the place and cause of the disturbance. To catch these Cicindela beetles—and nearly every bather must have tried this at some time or other—is a difficult and exciting game.

Above the waterline the sand is covered with all kinds of jetsam. When the sea is rough it carries its rejects a long way up the flat beach, leaving them there on its retreat. This is a veritable mine of gnarled roots, the prickly shells of sea urchins, cuttlebone, and the shells of snails and other molluscs. No one had been along yet to pick out the finest pieces. Only the fishermen of Beauduc had driven along the high waterline to the lighthouse in their rickety old pre-war vehicle. Perhaps one should look for some souvenirs to take home as a reminder of an enjoyable day on a sunny Midi beach. To search for Greek amphorae or ancient Roman coins would be almost pointless—they are not disgorged by the sea quite so frequently and generously as the internal chalk shells of the cuttlefish or the fourpointed black egg pouches of the rays. After our highly successful shots of the purple heron we felt our quota of luck was exhausted. But a deep violet starfish or a fine large murex snail with its bizarre spikelike excrescences would make a very acceptable souvenir.

The Rhizostoma jelly-fish deposited along the high-water mark are less suitable as souvenirs. Once removed from their natural habitat these delicate creatures are soon desiccated by sun and wind. In the end, a paper-thin skin is all that is left of their bodies. These helpless lumps of jelly on the beach have little in common with the creatures moving about in the clear water. They have a strange jerky way of swimming, their transparent membranes throbbing in a rhythmical opening and closing motion. They turn about gracefully, they rise up and sink down again in a gentle floating motion.

An astonishing wealth of species can be found among the snails and shells washed up on the beach. There are the small clams which are scraped from the sand with tools like rakes by the locals and provide a tasty dish, then there are the blue-black mussels, likewise a much-valued food, and various other kinds like the thick-walled auger shells, the pelican's-foot shells and the smooth, white-shelled clams *Scrobicularia piperata*. Like folded cut-throat razors the long, narrow razor shells lie scattered about among hun-

dreds of pale yellow cross-striped cockles, and thin-shelled, fine-ribbed scallops. Among the scallops, in particular, there are some very attractive specimens. This species has long been one of the best known shells of the Mediterranean—in the Middle Ages because the pilgrims brought these fan-shaped shells back with them to central and northern Europe as drinking vessels testifying to their pilgrimage to the Mediterranean, and in our own century because they have become the emblem of an international oil concern and are, moreover, used for the serving of *ragoût fin*.

Among the dunes the heat of the early summer day is far more noticeable than out there on the beach. The light breeze which always produces a pleasant sense of freshness on the beach does not reach the dunes. The air shimmers above the hot sand. The slim stalks of the marram grass and the short bristly shoots of the sea-bent stick out stiffly from the glaring white sand. There is not a breath of air to stir them. Sea-rocket and stock, everlasting flowers and spurge, sea holly and common chamomile—all the flowers which during the past few weeks brought a touch of colour to the dips in the dunes, now seem to have become wax copies of themselves, artificial lifeless shapes with faded leaves. All is quiet. No voices of birds, no rustle of wind in the tops of the pines. Only now and then the faint hum of insects. And from afar the muted swish of the surf.

Fat orb-web spiders, relations of our garden spider and yet a totally different shape, are hanging lazily on their webs. Normally such eager hunters of insects, they are now not roused even by the struggling of their trapped quarries. Only if one brushes against their webs by mistake, causing them to swing, do the spiders drop down to the ground as quick as lightning and hide among the stems of the bulrushes. No other creatures are seen today. The dunes appear to be empty and dead. Even the swift Spanish sand racers, those small, warmth-loving lizards, have been driven out of sight by the heat.

Only in the shallow ford which east of the dunes links the *étang* with the sea, and in those waterholes which are already cut off from the outside world, is there life. Here there are swarms of small crabs, barely the size of a man's palm. Wherever one puts one's foot on this slippery ground, covered with brown-black algae, the armoured creatures scuttle away with jerky sideways movements or—a rather amusing sight—adopt a threatening posture with the front of their bodies erect and their pincers opened. But these offensive tactics are of short duration. If the adversary—in this case the human foot—does not instantly retreat at the first threat, the crabs themselves get alarmed at their own courage. As fast as the ground permits they dig into the slimy surface backwards. Their two short pairs of antennae and stalk-eyes are all that remains visible of them.

These creatures in the cut-off waterholes face an unenviable fate. In a few weeks' time the troughs will have dried out and the crabs will have died of heat—unless the lighthouse keeper, some fisherman, or some herring-gull has spotted them first and pulled them out of the water.

On our way back to the beach two Kentish plovers were suddenly trying to attract our attention. One could hardly miss the two graceful birds—they were acting so conspicuously. Wings spread out and frequently trembling, they lay in the sand close to the beaten track, clearly anxious to attract our notice. This meant that their young had hatched. Because if we were now to try to catch these two parent birds, which were reeling in front of us, apparently so helpless, they would run off with dragging wings the moment we got too close to them. They would then lie down again and repeat the act. And we would follow them again, once, twice, perhaps a third time... And with each attempt to catch the parents our distance from the young birds, which must be hidden somewhere close by, would increase. We had found the plovers' nest ten days previously, when we were trying to drive the car from Faraman to the few huts of Sablon. Our rear wheels then spun on a patch of deep sand, and seconds later we were stuck. Before we managed to free the vehicle we discovered, only a few metres away, a plover bravely remaining sitting on its eggs. This was the second Kentish plovers' nest we spotted that day, and the one in the quieter situation. The other pair of birds had laid their eggs on the centre strip of a busy dam track among the salt-pans. Whenever a vehicle approached the broody bird would get up, run to the edge of the dike, and there wait until the vehicle had passed over its nest or, if it was a motorcycle, until it had rattled past. Then it would once more resume its sitting. In spite of this somewhat unusual and certainly dangerous nesting place, the young birds hatched safely a week later and, as soon as their down had dried out, were led away by the parent birds to a safer spot in a clump of salicornia.

Firebirds

The flamingos were increasingly becoming our main headache. Since, along with the Rhône beavers, they are the rarest and no doubt also the most valuable representatives of the Camargue fauna, a particularly extensive sequence had been earmarked for them in our film. We had plans for shooting their courtship and pairing in March and April, and then there were to be shots of life in the 'flamingo city', the breeding colony numbering many thousands. Other sequences were to record their search for food in the salt lakes, their arrival among the salt-pans in the early morning, and their departure for their resting places at nightfall. The flamingos, in short, were to provide the climax of our ninety-minute film.

That, at any rate, was how we had planned it and how it was set out in detail in our scenario. But things had not worked out. We were now halfway through our third summer and we still lacked our flamingo shots. A few brief and disjointed sequences of the birds in flight, and two or three long shots of the hosts of flamingos moving through the water were all we had to show for our trouble. We were beginning to ask ourselves seriously whether we were not perhaps chasing a chimera, an unrealizable utopian dream. Our troubles began right at the beginning of our first season in the Camargue, and they just never stopped. Whatever plans we had made invariably went awry. Either the birds did not found a colony at all, or their nests were destroyed during breeding time by climatic or other external factors. The former point, of course, was one which we knew we had to expect. Nevertheless we had hoped that in the course of several seasons in the Camargue we would be lucky enough to observe at least one instance of breeding and successful rearing of flamingo chicks. But our hopes were not to be fulfilled.

Our own troubles merely illustrated the more general questions associated for a number of years with the propagation of these rare long-legged birds in the Camargue. Apart from a much smaller and less important colonie in southern Spain, the Rhône delta is the only place in Europe where the flamingos breed. In years with good weather the number of mating pairs averages 4000 to 5000. The highest figure reliably recorded is 8000. But these tall rose-coloured birds do not by any means breed every year. Over the past fifty years young flamingos have been successfully reared on only twenty-four occasions. Often their nests have been totally or partially destroyed, or else mortality among the young was very high. Together with many other aspects of the life of flamingos, their irregular breeding habits continue to be an unsolved mystery. The assumption that this is largely due to the hydrographic conditions of the lagoons and salt lakes is probably only partially correct. In the past the birds would build their nests in various *étangs* of the delta, and also outside the 'Rhône island' in the Little Camargue. More recently the salt-pan area in the south-eastern part of the delta has become the proper habitat of the flamingos and their exclusive breeding ground. But there the influx of seawater to the evaporation pans is regulated by flood-gates, so that the lagoons favoured by the flamingos receive a very regular supply of water. There are therefore no, or only very slight, variations of water-level. With an almost constant salt content in this water the composition of plankton, the main constituent of the flamingos' diet, also remains constant most of the time. What is more, it is adequate both in quantity and quality. In this respect, therefore, living conditions for the flamingos in the salt-pans are now better than in any other part of the delta. But in spite of it all their attempts at breeding are irregular, with sometimes a long gap between them. There must therefore be some other reason. But what is it? One must hope that researchers will soon find the answer to this riddle so that ways and means may be found to help the flamingos keep up their numbers.

There are several factors which can have a detrimental effect on the normal breeding pattern—exceptional cold weather spells at the time of mating or hatching, heavy precipitation, wind, egg snatching by herring-gulls, and —increasingly over the past few years—overflights by aircraft, especially supersonic ones. Flamingos are exceedingly sensitive to noise, and low-flying aircraft can produce a quite unimaginable panic among the birds. Two further disturbing factors can be, and in fact have been, checked—the loss of breeding islands as a result of continuous erosion, and human disturbance of the bird colony itself. The latter includes both egg collectors and overzealous ornithologists, and, regrettably, also irresponsible photographers and film men.

But let us return to our failure to get a film of this fabulous bird of the Camargue. Two years ago persistent cold weather interfered with pairing until late into April. The fascinating dreamlike parading, the delicate courting games, began only slowly. They never became that splendid natural spectacle which is presented by the courtship of these birds when fully developed. Towards the end of the month the flamingos crowded on to the breeding island, presently took possession of it, and began laying their eggs. But that, too, did not seem to go smoothly. The number of birds sitting on eggs was far below the normal average, and some of them gradually drifted away from their nests again. Only a few chicks hatched towards the end of May. None of them survived. There can be little doubt that the strikingly frequent disturbances by aircraft and helicopters must have played some part in the colony's failure to breed. Last year the birds did not install themselves on their usual island. This had been flattened even further during the winter by high winds and heavy waves; the banks were deeply undercut by erosion and many of the old nest cones had been washed away. Even parts of the island itself were lost. Although at first it seemed that the flamingos would get down to breeding in a near-by salt lake they nevertheless returned to their former lagoon in the course of April. But this time they founded their colony a few hundred metres away from the breeding island proper, at the foot of a dike. That was a bad choice of nesting place. The nest cones, shaped from earth and salt mud, were here only a few inches above the surface of the water, a circumstance which was bound to prove unfavourable under local wind conditions. In fact, no sooner was breeding time over and the first few young had hatched than a violent mistral churned up the *étang*. Frothy waves beat against the nests and salty foam swamped eggs and chicks. Within a short time the flamingo city was deserted—only some 500 birds clung to their nests for another week and a half. Then they, too, capitulated and the host of about 10,000 flamingos scattered to the winds. That then was our second failure. On both occasions we had been determined not to take any risks and not to start shooting until after the hatching of the young. We felt the flamingos owed us some reward for this show of consideration.

In March this year, as we were getting increasingly desperate, matters took a promising turn. Early in the morning, and occasionally though less frequently also in the late afternoon, the flamingos performed their breath-taking quadrilles in the fine haze of the lagoon. Necks thrust up high, wings beating, and a spray of water—that was the picture in the telescope. Courting was in full swing. It was an unforgettable experience to watch a few heads suddenly jerking up from among a crowd at rest, others being swept along, until the bird army had worked itself into a wild frenzy, into a tumultuous scene of a love dance. These courtship rituals continued throughout nearly two weeks. They were nearing their climax. Then came the mistral. In the middle of the night of March 26th it struck. When dawn broke, a hurricane-strength gale was sweeping over the Camargue. Gust after gust lashed the lagoons. The waves smacked against the flanks of dikes. Columns of spume were snatched up by the wind and carried along. They came down again as a salty drizzle on the tracks along the crests of the dams. It was almost impossible to stand up against the force of the gale.

The courtship of the flamingos had been brought to a sudden end. Indifferent and sullen, the birds were standing in the *étang*. The wind brutally ruffled their plumage and made their brilliant coats look bedraggled.

After four days the violence of the gale abated a little. But it took the best part of three weeks before the mistral had blown itself out and ponds and lakes were smooth once more. But the courting mood of the flamingos had gone. Even after many days of calm there was no sign of any resumption of their abruptly discontinued behaviour. The gale evidently disturbed the birds' courtship at a crucial moment. True, one or two half-hearted preening performances were observed by us later, but these were more like the lazy motions of a few individual birds than a serious resurgence of the mating rites. Certainly such individual skirmishes were no longer able to affect the behaviour of the flamingo army as a whole. And it seems that with these birds, whose entire lives are dominated by collective instinct, much more powerful impulses are needed to trigger off an elemental pattern of behaviour.

A month passed. A second month passed. Nothing changed about the flamingos—or not very much. During the day they would stand in the lagoons or salt-pans; at or just after sunset they would fly across to their sleeping quarters in the Impériaux. When it was quite certain that no further attempt at breeding would be made that season, we decided to close in on the fabulous birds. Our scenario had been cut down accordingly weeks ago. It certainly hurt having to write off these wonderful sequences of courtship and the rearing of the young—but there was nothing for it.

We had now spent three years here—and every conceivable kind of living creature had run, crawled, or flown past our cameras during that time. Only the most interesting creature of the region, the typical bird of the Camargue, the flamingo, had to be different. We just were not in luck.

How, in a wide open lagoon with no cover whatever, does one get close enough to 7000 flamingos without the birds running away or even taking wing? That was our main problem throughout those weeks. Put in this simple form it would not have been too difficult to answer. But in practical terms the question was: How does one get close enough with film cameras, tripod, exchangeable lenses, spare reels of film and all kinds of other clutter? And it was not just a matter of getting close. A length of film had to be shot without the birds getting suspicious.

Our first attempt was with a floating hide. On top of a double timber frame we had erected a tall camouflaged tent, securely tied to its floating base. The film equipment was held in special consoles and sockets fitted to light metal struts. The thing floated beautifully. Once one had paddled it beyond the shallow water along the edge of the lagoon, the man hidden inside was able without difficulty to move up to the birds yard by yard. There was no doubt in our minds that, provided we acted cautiously, the birds would tolerate our approach. But disillusionment came soon. At that time the flamingos were mostly in the southwestern part of a large lagoon. To take pictures in the morning, in favourable light, the hide would have had to be pushed right across the whole *étang* from its eastern shore. But this would not only have taken a great deal of time but was also dangerous because of a number of bottomless mud holes in the middle of the lake.

That left the afternoon. But here we ran into trouble of a different kind. Whereas there was hardly any wind at all in the mornings, violent gusts usually sprang up shortly after noon. The waves they triggered off soon caused the float to drift the moment one let go. What was worse, if the wind struck at the side of the hide cover there was a risk of the whole camouflage outfit being forced below the water. It was as much as a man could do to prevent this happening. And that, of course, left him no time for filming. I remember the disastrous day when, the water being relatively calm, I had succeeded in pushing the hide quite close to the huge white and pink wall of birds. Not one of the many thousands of flamingos had shown any sign of alarm until then. Most of them were asleep. Never before had I seen these magnificent birds at such close range. I was just wondering whether to start shooting or to advance a further ten to fifteen metres (thirty to fifty feet) when a sudden gust struck the tent. Only with a supreme effort did I succeed in forcing the floating frame downwards and preventing the whole structure from turning turtle. Almost at once a second and a third gust struck. Within minutes the mistral was blowing full force. There I was, within a hundred feet of the firebirds, desperately wrestling with wind and waves. Not for a second was I able to let go of the tent frame. The force of the mistral would have blown it down complete with heavy frame and mounted equipment. The retreat which I began an hour later, without having taken a single shot, was not just disappointing but heartbreaking.

Further attempts convinced us that in the circumstances then prevailing this kind of approach was unsuitable. We would have to think of something different. And suddenly we hit on the idea of the flamingo. An over-lifesize flamingo which would hide a man complete with tripod and camera. Two days later the bird was ready—a splendid specimen with brilliant 'plumage' and genuine glass eyes. It was even able to move its neck and nod its head. At a distance it really looked just like a genuine flamingo—except, of course, for its gigantic size. It was a little less than twice as big as its brothers and sisters out there in the lagoon. Its skeleton was a structure of wire and bamboo canes. Canvas reinforced with paint, and with a good coating of paint on top, turned the skeleton into a birdlike mask which, we hoped, would stand up at least in the sight of the flamingos. The rather too broad chest of our 'secret weapon' was fitted with a shuttered opening through which film and stills could be taken by means of a special tripod arrangement. Everything seemed well thought out. The wearer of this rather tight bird costume slipped the whole thing on over his head and chest and, somewhat like a rucksack, strapped it to his back, shoulders, and upper arms. Only his legs were not covered. But these were concealed in the water anyway as he advanced through the lagoon. A small but unavoidable snag was that the cameraman needed a helper for dressing and undressing. Without a helper it was exceedingly difficult to get into the bird or out of it. But that did not seem a serious drawback. We were certainly looking forward confidently to its first operational use. But once again it turned out that we had been over-optim-

istic. That trifling snag of being more or less a captive inside the giant flamingo very nearly meant the end of one of our colleagues a few days later. He had been chosen for the job because he was the smallest of us. In the early afternoon, therefore, he set out, equipped with a film camera and two small tele-lenses. Provided our 'première' went according to plan he should have got close to the flamingos towards four o'clock to shoot the first general sequences. To begin with all went well. Acting like a real flamingo, our friend reached the birds sooner than expected. They seemed to take no notice of the arrival of their giant brother. He was within some fifty to sixty metres (150 to 180 feet) of the nearest flamingos when his camouflage structure suddenly started to sway violently, toppled, and a second later disappeared under the water. Only the head of the miracle bird and part of its long neck were showing above the ruffled surface, like the periscope of a submarine. We rushed off to his aid. The deep mud holes, into which one would break without warning, could be exceedingly dangerous. Our friend, however, managed to scramble to his feet by his own efforts and to start his retreat. We met halfway across the salt lake. He had come to no harm, apart from the fright and a few mouthfuls of salt water, but the camera and the lenses were out of action for the rest of our expedition. One would hardly credit the extent of damage that highly concentrated brine can cause to metal parts. No amount of subsequent rinsing was any use. The next day another member of our party tried his luck; he also went out again the following day. After that I played the flamingo three times before our short friend had another go. But none of these attempts was successful. Although we had no more serious incidents, we came up against a new enemy to whom we had not given a single thought even in our most pessimistic dreams—the herring gulls. About two dozen of these suspicious birds had their habitat on the islands in the salt lagoon. During the next two weeks they drove us to the brink of desperation. The flamingos, who were our real concern, showed no interest whatever in their over-lifesize cousin who arrived from the far shore of the *étang* every day to try to mingle with them. For the most part they just dozed on, their heads hidden in their back feathers. Only rarely did one or another stretch its long neck, take a few steps, shake its wings, and again relapse into its siesta. The gulls, on the other hand, had tumbled to our trick at once. They could tell the difference between a real and a sham flamingo and they realized that some mischief was afoot. And they took great care to broadcast it to all and sundry. By the time one of us had covered half the distance, and often before then, they would be circling over him with loud warning cries. No matter whether he stopped or whether he waded on through the salt lake, they would come lower and lower, screeching and cackling, until the flamingos, alarmed by the noise, would raise their heads and look out for the cause of the excitement.

If only the gulls had stopped screeching then, all might still have been well. The flamingos were still unsuspecting—even their 'look-outs', those specially large birds whose behaviour seemed to give the cue to the rest of the flock. If they remained the whole host of flamingos remained; if they moved away then one bird after another would follow until the whole pink mass was in motion. Indeed, it seemed as if these 'look-out' birds controlled the movement of the rest. But these look-outs at first took no notice of our approach whatever. They were clearly at a loss to discover the cause of the herring gulls' alarm. This invariably enabled us to get a little closer to the birds before the ceaseless screeching of the gulls eventually made them move off after all. I am convinced that the flamingos had no idea what they were escaping from. Their flight was probably an entirely automatic action. This is confirmed by the fact that they never once took wing. They simply moved off mechanically, out into the glistening blue and silver vastness of the lagoon, soundlessly like an army of ghosts. With our much greater bulks and impeded by the bird on our shoulders we just could not keep pace with them. To finish reminiscing about past failures and to return to the present: A month had passed since our unsuccessful efforts, and other work in the meantime had kept us away from the flamingos. But now we had another chance—a fortunate coincidence offered us what would probably be our last opportunity to film them.

For a number of days the birds, after returning to their lagoon in the morning, had been standing around a small island. On the island itself, we had likewise been able to make out a few individuals. There would not be room for many of them there anyway, as it was really no more than a minute, salicornia-grown patch of sand rising from the water. During the past two nights therefore we had managed, in many hours of hard work, to dig a three-foot deep hole on that little island and to fit a camouflaged parapet all round and a roof on top

of it. All work had to be done as noiselessly as possible and in total darkness, so that the 700 or so flamingos who remained in the lagoon even at night were not frightened off. All had gone well. The birds had been alarmed neither by the hole and bare scaffolding on the first day nor by the completed enclosed hide on the next. It seemed a good portent.

I was shivering with cold. The small of my back had gone totally numb and my behind hurt as if I had been sitting for days on my uncomfortable, hard folding stool. Yet I had only been in my hide for about two hours, since two-thirty in the morning. But two hours can be surprisingly long when one's clothes are soaked. And that was quite unavoidable in our mud and brine-filled trench on the flamingo island. It had come as a nasty surprise when, in pitch darkness, I squeezed into my trap. Of course, a little thought should have told us that any trench would very soon fill with ground water. It was now a little after four o'clock. A faint red line along the eastern horizon heralded the approach of the sun. Once more I was enjoying the superb spectacle of daybreak alone in this vast wild landscape. The first faint glow had appeared over the horizon towards three-thirty. The stars began to pale. Very slowly the first grey light reached out into the dark sky; not until much later did the first reflected light lift the lagoon as a slate-coloured, dully luminous sheet out of the black landscape. The beacons at Beauduc and Faraman went out. Now and again the faint sound of flamingo chatter came over the water. An early stilt was complaining on the dike. Then the grey over the *étang* grew lighter, pearly. A pale yellow glow rose up in the east. The flamingos which spent the night in the lagoon began to stand out against the dark background. There were only a few of them and they were a long distance away from the island. A cool breeze was blowing over the salt lake. Two herring gulls glided past without a sound.

That was a quarter of an hour ago. Now the sun was rising over the horizon, pouring liquid fire over the sheet of water which was gently ruffled by the dawn wind. The dikes and salt dumps over at Salin-de-Giraud flashed reddish-gold. Steeped in gold also was the tall, slim shape of the lighthouse at the southern end of the lagoon. And here they came, the firebirds of the ancient Greeks—coming from the north-west over the big dams. In triangular or wedge formation their rose-red squadrons moved under the morning sky. The air was filled with trumpet-like shrieks. With a roar the first birds passed low over my hide. I could see the black on their outspread vermilion wings, the delicate red of their breasts, the outstretched necks, the narrow heads with their peculiarly shaped bills, and the long light-coloured legs. Now a huge flock was losing height, making a wide turn round the lagoon, and approaching the island at low level. Slowly they were touching down—wings spread out, long legs starting their running movements as if trying to cross some invisible bridge. Then they were in the lake. Like a flame being doused, the fiery turbulence of raised wings was extinguished. Ear-splitting shrieks accompanied the touchdown. More and more squadrons appeared over the lagoon. Some were only small groups, others numbered hundreds or thousands of birds. Their fabulous plumage shone magnificently in the light of the low sun. They glided closer, and with necks grotesquely turned and legs stretched far back, angled at the heels, they settled on the water—lightly and gracefully like snowflakes. Exactly like this, huge rose-red clouds of flamingos would now be settling on the lagoons of the Nile delta or the salt lakes of East Africa and Central Asia. There these birds live in even greater numbers than here in the Camargue. Hundredthousands of them populate the shallow bays, forming scintillating bands of colour against the bluish-green sheets of water.

The flock of flamingos was moving along with measured tread. There must have been some five or six thousand of them, but new flights were still appearing, wheeling over the lagoon and joining them. Two groups had now formed —one close to the island, the other, more numerous, towards the spit of land on the western shore.

The sky meanwhile, after changing from orange and pale yellow to turquoise, had now become its customary brilliant forget-me-not-blue. Life in the surrounding lagoon was awakening. Common terns and black-headed gulls were flying over the island. Avocets were squabbling. On the near-by dike a pair of shelducks were sunning themselves. The fluting of the redshanks was continuous. But all these splendid birds paled before the grandeur of the flamingos, those fabulous birds of the Camargue. Words are weak and meaningless to describe the magic beauty of these creatures. Only he who has encountered them himself, out there in the boundless solitude of the salt lakes, will understand that enthusiasm for these birds is more than mere romantic sentimentality. They were now standing quite close to the island, in the shallow water—a wall

of white with a faint cast of pink. Seen from close to, they appeared large and oddly proportioned. A long, thin neck bears a strikingly small head terminating in a stubby bill which, from about halfway along, is markedly bent down. Its small yellow eyes lend the bird something rigid, inscrutable. The pink legs are enormously long and thin, and the short toes are connected with genuine webs.

Apart from their size and shape the colouring of the flamingos is of particular interest. The delicate colour and texture of the plumage has been responsible over the past few centuries for the birds having to pay a heavy tribute to the caprices of human fashion. The white of the plumage is touched, over large areas, with a delicate pink; this is particularly brilliant on the bird's neck, chest, and back. A deep vermilion, visible only when the wings are opened, extends over the upper surface of the wings. The powerful wing feathers on the underside are deep black.

Not all birds show the same deep colouring. Just as there are considerable differences among them in shape—any flock will contain downright pygmies and giants—there are considerable variations in the colouring of the plumage. All possible graduations exist between bright red individuals and almost pure white ones. This variation in colour bears no connection, as far as is known, with the age or sex of the birds. On the other hand, it is assumed that the smaller ones are always females and the larger ones males. Whether the striking difference in egg size similarly suggests the sex of the chicks is not yet known.

Let us look again at the bill of the flamingo. In conjunction with the bird's tongue and its function it represents an anatomical masterpiece. The upper bill is much weaker than the lower one. Flattened from top to bottom—in much the same way as the duck's—it shows a pronounced bend at the middle. The lower bill is flattened from the sides and with its turned-in edge and the numerous horny cross-strips forms a kind of deep trough. This large, hollow space is filled almost entirely by its thick, fleshy tongue which the bird can move only forwards and backwards. In order to get the flamingo's tongue out of its bill one would have to push it right back until it was all out of its 'channel' and then pull it forward. A strange and unusual construction.

The two large forces of flamingos had moved closer to my island; soon it would be entirely surrounded by them. Nothing in their behaviour betrayed any definite intention.

45 Wild boar *(Sus scrofa)* enjoying a mud bath

46 Young rabbit *(Oryctolagus cuniculus)*

47 A herd of white horses moving to new pastures ▷

48 Pratincole *(Glareola pratincola)* and its superbly camouflaged eggs

49 Stone curlew *(Burhinus oedicnemus)* about a month old

50 Nesting cliff of bee-eaters ▷

51 Bee-eater *(Merops apiaster)* displaying tropical splendour of colours ▷▷

51

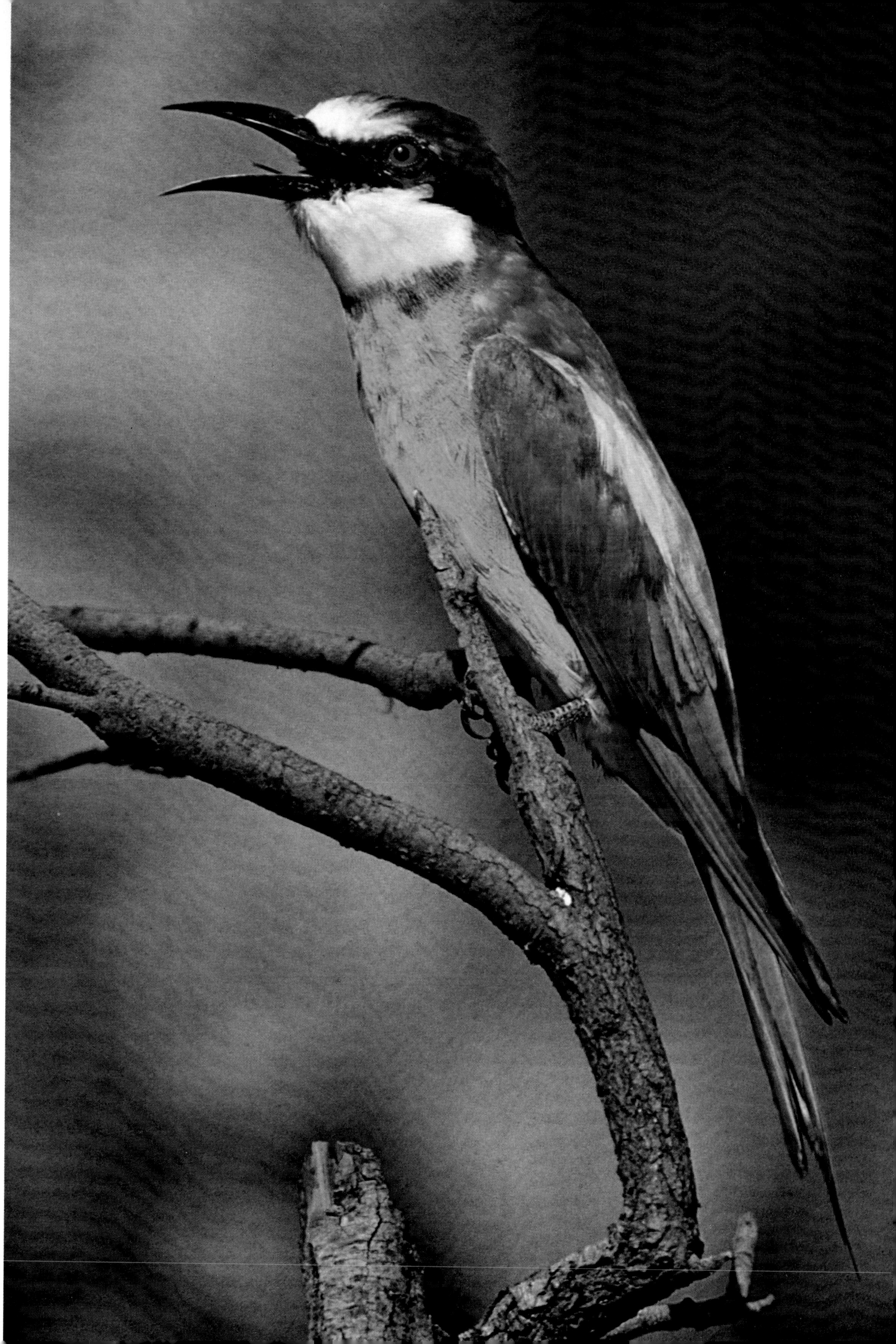

52 European praying mantis *(Mantis religiosa)* in somewhat menacing or impressive posture

53 Close-up of the grotesquely helmeted male of *Empusa pennata*

54 *Acrida mediterranea,* a grasshopper

55 Stick insect *(Clonopsis gallica)* ▷

56 The false mantid *(Mantispa styriaca).*
    The leg sheath of its left prehensorial instrument is opened ▷▷

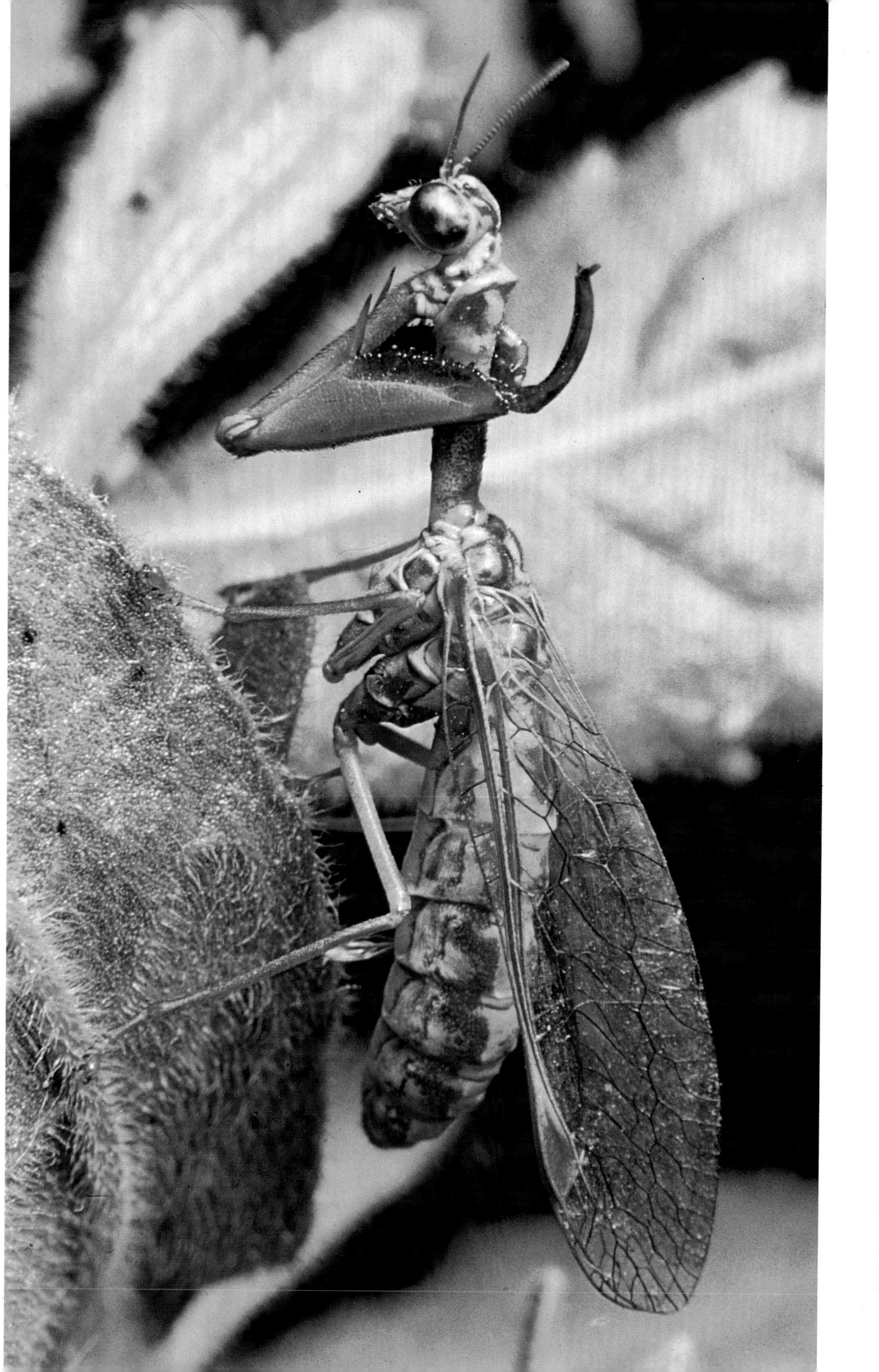

57 Grass-type vegetation cover of the higher-lying, drier and less saline regions of the delta. In the background tamarisks *(Tamarix gallica)*

58 Shield bug *(Graphosoma semipunctatum)*

59 Female workers of *Polistes gallicus*, a wild wasp.
   Eggs and larvae can be seen in some of the open cells

All movements of this pink mass appeared to be dictated by chance alone. And who could tell—perhaps a happy chance would cause some firebird or other to step on land, across the narrow bank of shells, to stop in front of me, preen itself, or just sleep. This would be the fulfilment of two and a half years of ardent hopes, and also the culmination of our encounters with these giant birds. To have made their acquaintance has been the happiest of the experiences which the Camargue has to offer. Nothing in this remote world set between sea and land, between water and sky, is more impressive than a flock of flamingos rising white, red, and black out of a blue lagoon towards a blue sky. It is a picture which embodies the whole poetry of untouched nature.

Under the Mediterranean Stars

Dusk had wrapped the land in deep peace and silence. Like a huge ball of fire the sun plunged into the lagoon at the far end of a blinding trail. The waves were like liquid gold as the glowing sphere sank into the haze on the horizon and its blinding halo was extinguished. Now the afterglow was gradually fading away over the water. The waves were darker, more shadowy; they were barely audible as they broke against the steep bank. The silhouettes of the tamarisks, bent by the gales, still stood out clear against the purple twilight of the lake surface. The glow in the sky had disappeared and the last flickering purple rays swept over the edges of the clouds. Deep shadows were lying between the trees; darkness was spreading. Softly the night rose from ditches and marshes. The true grandeur of this wilderness is revealed not in the early morning or under the scorching noonday sun, but in the evening, at dusk. The mysterious span between day and night, when trees and shrubs lose their dimensions, when the shapes of the birds in the ponds and lagoons dissolve, and the bulls out on the steppe melt into the darkness. Only a thin, pale yellow line of light was left low down on the western horizon. Soon it would disappear too. The plaintive flute-like call of the stone curlew rang out across the *sansouïre*.

An hour had passed. By now a starry sky, such as is seen only on a clear Mediterranean night, was stretched out above the seemingly sleeping land. In the east the orange disc of the moon was rising over the dark barrier of the Rhône forest. To the south the lighthouse of Beauduc was winking in its regular rhythm—one, two, three—pause—one, two, three—pause. A light wind was fanning the tree-tops; through the reed thickets wafted the warm breath of the early night. Our eyes had long accommodated to the darkness and were again perceiving details. A thousand different sounds struck our ears. The night was not sleeping, as a casual glance might suggest. From bushes and trees, from ditches and rice paddies, came the powerful chorus of the tree frogs. Their real numbers are difficult to estimate. There are certainly tens of thousands of them, and probably hundreds of thousands.

Among the hedges all round our tent the nightingales were singing. Ever since nightfall their song had come ceaselessly from the thick undergrowth. By no means every bird is a master singer—many never get beyond half a dozen different phrases. But there are some whose song far surpasses in harmoniousness and variety that of their mates. In perfect harmony, softly fluting phrases alternate with brash metallic ones, plaintive tunes with gay ones, strongly accentuated ones with lyrically soft ones. While one tune may start softly, gradually gaining in strength and eventually dying away in a drawn-out sob, another may open with notes of emphatic harshness, supplanted presently by melancholy fluting or exuberant trills. Night after night we are sung to sleep in this manner—but sleep is possible only provided the very last whining mosquito in the tent has first been killed.

The petrol lamp under our canopy attracts a multitude of moths and flies. The number of insects pressing towards the flame is quite astonishing. There are the minute silvery and golden pearls, the thin-horns with their enormously long, thin antennae, the snow-white plume-moths with their deeply fringed wings, the reddish-brown knot-horns, the insignificantly coloured owlets, the prominents with their striking crests, and the magnificent garden tigers with their black, white, and yellow markings. And, of course, a multitude of restlessly dancing mosquitoes. A surprise awaited us outside the tent entrance. Soaring between the tents, like bats, were large, heavy moths. A few of them had alighted on the lit gauze curtains, others were sitting on the tent pole. They were emperor moths, the largest moths of Europe, and—it could hardly be otherwise—all of them were male insects. Males on their wedding flight, in search of a newly hatched female. More and more of the huge moths came towards us out of the darkness, attracted and deflected from their path by the light burning in the tent. I was reminded of Jean-Henri Fabre, the great French entomologist and brilliant chronicler of the life of insects. Near Sérignan, not very far from here, he studied the nuptial flight of the large emperor moth in all its details and made it the subject of one of his finest accounts.

The moon meanwhile had climbed higher in the sky and plunged the scene in a brilliant silvery light. How about a short walk? The night was mild and full of scent—and besides it was too early to go to bed.

The soft grass muted our footfalls. In front of the bramble hedge rabbits were out grazing—grey shadows which scattered at our approach and made for the cover of the sparse shrubs. "Tongg, tongg" came the warning signal drummed on the ground by their hindlegs. *"C'est le tam-tam de la sansouïre"*, the *gardians* say whenever the tom-tom-like beating is heard from the steppe.

In the dark of the poplar grove, where the moonlight penetrated to the ground at only a few points, the lanterns of the fireflies were winking. Like emerald-green sparks the flying males zig-zagged among the foliage while the females, incapable of flight, the aptly named glow-worms, were emitting their light while sitting in the grass. To this day man, otherwise so inventive, has been unable to solve the mystery of this cold light. To manufacture the luminous substance of the glow-worm in the laboratory is the dream of many a scientist and would probably turn our present-day methods of illumination topsy-turvy.

Along the irrigation ditches the rats were squeaking and scurrying. We would rather meet these long-tailed rodents out here than on their impertinent visits to our camp. From the trees came the hollow hoot of a tawny owl. The young birds in the rotten elm had by now learnt to fly, but they were still being fed and led by the parent birds. Their begging call could be heard first in one place and then in another. Bats flitted down the footpath like spectres; a barn owl swept over our heads without a sound.

Our route led past the open sheep-pen into the cultivated fields. The warm, pungent smell of the sleeping animals was wafted over to us. Now and then a faint tinkling of bells came from the dark opening in the wall. Over there, in the shepherd's hut, the light was still burning. Should we

drop in for a few minutes? Some other night perhaps—but not on a night like this, on a night which was irresistibly alluring with moonlight and the sparkle of stars, with the rustling of leaves and the whispering of the reeds. Who could resist this magic, who could remain unmoved by the ocarina-like call of the Scops owl or the hoarse croaking of night herons moving overhead unseen? We must go on, out into the steppe, to the marshes and ponds.

The deciduous forest was getting sparser, the trees now stood less close and gradually yielded to low shrubs. From among the dark foliage we stepped into the silvery light of meadows and fields. One could see a long way—each clump of tamarisks, each patch of reeds, and each sandy hummock was clearly discernible in the pale light of the moon. Outlines seemed preternaturally clear, bushes and trees enlarged to twice or three times their natural size. The air was filled with the shrill chirping of the crickets. Behind us, from the tall willows, came the intermittent call of the Scops owl. There was a soft rustling to our right. A hedgehog was hunting for snails and insects along the edge of the path. If it was lucky it might find a nest of young mice or a pheasant's nest. The latter was by no means impossible since the hens were fond of laying their eggs on the edge of the path, under the overhang of tufts of grass.

We soon left pasture and vineyards behind us. Through salicornia and dry bulrushes our path led into a marshy hollow. The croaking of the marsh frogs was growing louder and more urgent; moorhens shrieked, alarmed mallards rose from the ditches and, chattering excitedly, made off. As during the past few nights, the dull boom of the bittern again came from the depth of the reed thicket: "Ee-whumb, ee-whumb." The loud call, more like the roar of a bull than the courting call of a bird, could be heard for miles: "Whumb, whumb, whumb." Only the soft opening syllable was lost at that range.

Zoologists for a long time have discussed the manner in which this strange far-carrying boom is produced. It used to be assumed that this heron-like bird produced this exceptionally powerful sound by putting its bill in the water. Brehm in his *Tierleben,* for instance, records the following observation which he regards as trustworthy: "The artist (he is referring to the bittern) was standing on both feet, body held horizontal, bill in the water, and at that moment a growl rang out which made me start. I realized that these sounds, which are so loud only at the beginning, are produced when the bird has filled its throat deep with water and hurls it out with much greater force than usual." This is what Brehm thought. Today we know that this information is incorrect and that the assumption that the bird places its bill in the water when producing its call is mistaken. The fact is that the male bittern is able to inflate his oesophagus—his gullet—which in any case is enlarged during the mating season, to such an extent that it becomes an ideal sounding-board which amplifies his call and makes it audible over long distances.

The ground underfoot was getting softer and damper. Almost imperceptibly the track was lost among beds of sedge. Our boots were sinking deep into the marshy ground; water softly gurgled under our soles. The ponds gleamed dully among the black reed thickets; somewhere a fish splashed; from somewhere among the reeds came the trill of a little grebe. A fresh wind was blowing from the steppe, gently ruffling the water and making the mirrored disc of the moon tremble. "Cra-eek, cra-eek" came the harsh call of a heron.

Suddenly, directly ahead, the sound of violent threshing and breaking. Reed stems snapped, water splashed. Grunting and snorting. And like the devil himself with his infernal cohorts a pack of wild boars burst from a hidden lair, straight past us. For a few seconds the black sow, the last to burst from the bulrushes, hesitated over which way to go. It was a nasty moment. Not until the beast had disappeared over the high dike on the far side and we were sure that there were no more of them hidden in the reeds did we continue our journey.

So deep is the silence over the *sansouïre* that at times one believes one can hear a soft, high note as of a violin vibrating on the air. Nothing moves. The round clumps of salicornia stand crowded together like sleeping sheep, back arched next to back, only rarely broken by bare patches of ground shimmering with salt or by the matt, silvery, snaking line of the sandy track. The pungent smell of the salt steppe hangs over everything. From the ground the stored warmth of the past day is wafted up. Here and there a solitary tamarisk rises from the vast light-drenched landscape. It was time to turn back. Our watches told us that it was nearly midnight and we had a good distance to cover yet to our camp. Salicornia twigs scraped against our boots, dried-out shells crunched under our feet. A hare rose from a

dip in the ground. A little owl hooted from the leaning doorpost of a tumbledown enclosure and inquisitively turned its head towards us.

On the edge of the low-lying marsh a herd of *taureaux* was settled down for the night. Large and massive, the dark bodies of the animals towered against the pale back-drop of the tall tamarisks. Above the drooping heads the long sickle-shaped horns gleamed white. Most of the animals had settled down in the thick bulrushes and were dozing; black mountains in a sea of molten silver. Only the twitching of ears, the flicking of tail-tassels, and an occasional muted snort suggested the presence of life in the resting bodies. We had become genuinely fond of these noble creatures during our life and work here in the Rhône delta. Noble creatures? Certainly they were noble, having preserved the characteristics of their free, wild race through thousands of years, in spite of being bred by man. Neither in life nor in death did they submit to man—not even in the fight for the *cocarde* in the sun-scorched arena. Of course the *razzeteurs,* who vastly outnumber the bull, will succeed now and then, by cunning or by skill, in snatching the 'trophy' from the animals' horns—but this can be seen as a defeat of the bull only in a purely symbolical sense. The fighting spirit of the *taureaux* is unbroken even after a fifteen-minute bout, and many a *razzeteur* has come to feel the dangerous, dagger-like horns of a bull at the very last moment of an encounter. If the Marquis Folco de Baroncelli, the disciple of Frédéric Mistral, who more than anyone else championed the preservation of ancient Provençal and Camargue customs, described the bull as the soul of the Camargue, then this was the highest tribute he could have paid not only to the animal but also to the land and its people. The stranger does not at first find it easy to appreciate the Camarguais' interest in and the strong feelings which they display for these cattle. Only gradually does he understand. But then he too becomes convinced that the black bulls, just as the horses and flamingos, are an indispensable part of this primordial landscape. And suddenly he will understand that far-sighted and responsible breeders are anxious to preserve the Camargue cattle for reasons far more weighty than the momentary advantages of the tourist industry.

Half an hour later the sun-faded roofs of our tents could be seen in the distance. Our nocturnal walk was coming to an end. Bushes and shrubs along the path were getting thicker, the outlines of the poplar avenue were already discernible. The chorus of tree frogs was getting steadily louder, the first trills of the nightingale came from the near-by thicket. From directly overhead came the loud and protracted fluting of a stone curlew. Instinctively one's eyes went up to the night sky with its myriads of stars—each one a world of its own, suspended in an infinite universe.

Island of the Birds

It was day again. A high pale-blue sky was arching over the dreamy early-morning landscape. From the eastern horizon came the first flashes of the sun, promising heat and a shimmering haze for the hours to come. The inhabitants of the small island out in the lagoon had come to life. Flocks of narrow-winged terns and gulls floated like black silhouettes in front of the orange disc of the sun as it rose from the water; the gentle morning breeze carried their shrill cries over the vastness of the *étang*. Island of birds—this is not just a label, a handy name for an island where hundreds or thousands of birds are breeding and bringing up their young. It is a whole small world of its own, a world with its own customs, its own rhythm of life, even its own laws. No matter whether we are at a Sandwich tern colony on a sandbank in the North Sea or on a guillemot rock in the Atlantic, or among Peruvian guano gannets, or in the flamingo city in the Rhône delta—everywhere this self-sufficiency will be the strongest and the most lasting impression. It is the same in the gull and tern colonies of the brackish lagoons of the Camargue. The first fascination perhaps may come from the sheer mass of the birds—after all, there are several thousands of them nesting in an extremely confined space. But the longer one is concerned with the population of such a breeding island, the more one is captivated simply by the bird colony's self-sufficiency and seeming remoteness from the rest of the world.

The long approach in the first light of dawn had been rather tiring. True, the water at its deepest had come up only to our hips. But the large fields of water plants and the slippery pads of algae on the lake floor had slowed us down a good deal. The deep mud holes, moreover, had made the transport of our heavy equipment a very tricky operation. What was particularly unpleasant was the coldness of the water in the early morning, in spite of the advanced season. After three-quarters of an hour of wading through the truly boundless sheet of water one just could not shake off this sense of chill. I felt greatly relieved, therefore, when the small island eventually rose from the glistening surface as a thin line and when the first avocets flew up to meet us with loud warning cries.

We were now barely 200 metres from the edge of the island. Alarmed by the ceaseless cries of the avocets, the terns and gulls had now also noticed the approaching invasion and were rising from their nests, shrieking and cackling. The beating of wings and the deafening screams of a thousand birds were all round us—we could barely hear our own voices. Some 5000 birds were now in the air—black-headed gulls and avocets, common terns, little terns, and gull-billed terns, oystercatchers and redshanks. While a few avocets came down on the water in front of us, pitifully beating their wings and pretending to be injured and incapable of flight, other particularly daring terns and gulls made their mock attacks on us. Abruptly they dived from among the noisy swarm and zoomed close over our heads, so that a collision seemed unavoidable, but at the last moment they would wheel sharply, climb up again, or come down in the water. While swimming they would keep their wings half raised so as to be able to take off for a new attack at once. Excrement was smacking into the water all round, with well-aimed shots very close to the target. The unnerving screech of the birds increased further in intensity as we were stepping across a long, gently rising bank of shells on to the south-eastern part of the island. This then was the breeding colony proper. By now not even the most persevering birds had stayed in their nests. White bodies of birds were swirling around us, in front and behind, to both sides and overhead. But we had to turn our eyes away from the screaming parent birds and concentrate on where we were going. Particular care was necessary because thousands of eggs and young chicks were lying on the shell banks, in the salt mud, and under the salicornia plants—some easy to spot, others just as easy to miss. Eggs and young birds had such excellent camouflage colouring that they were apt to escape even a careful scrutiny. Especially the young chicks, which by pressing themselves motionless into the ground frequently seemed to have lost all substantiality.

Ten minutes after our arrival I moved into the hide we had previously constructed, and not much later my colleague was on his way back again, wading out into the grey gleaming vastness of the *étang*. I did not envy him; he had a long, exhausting journey back through the lagoon, and for a whole hour he would see nothing around him but water, water, and more water. He would have the depressing feeling of merely marking time, of not making any headway in spite of continuous motion. Only when at last the outline of the shore rose from the distant mists would he be reassured that this walking was really getting him nearer his destination. In the late afternoon he would come out again to get me out of my hide and help me get our delicate equipment safely back on land. This was just another of the many tasks associated with film-making.

Slowly the island was settling down again. The excitement was dying down, the wild screeches had ceased. The birds were returning to their nests. Once more there was a crescendo of squeaking and screeching as the common terns on my right all landed almost simultaneously on the shell bank. There was a certain amount of vicious squawking before each parent bird had pushed its way through to its own nest, turned its eggs over and sat down again on them. The real sufferers in these disturbances, however, are not the old gulls and terns but those young birds which leave their nests while their parents are away. Suddenly they find themselves in the middle of a lot of excited and aggressive strange old birds. Woe betide those which do not at once find their way back to their own nests or to their waiting parents. They risk being hacked at by beaks, and being pushed around from bird to bird like a helpless ball. There is a real danger that young birds which have escaped from their nests may be badly mauled or even tortured to death. And while each female tern or gull shows quite touching solicitude for its own young, it will not normally tolerate any strange chick near it. An additional danger for the larger chicks is escape into the water. Although they are able to swim from their very first day, strong waves or a steep bank frequently prevent them from clambering back on land. This means that they are doomed to drowning. It is quite obvious, therefore, that all disturbance—and man's appearance among the birds invariably is such a disturbance—must be confined to the bare minimum if one must penetrate into a breeding colony at all.

Each species has its own nesting areas on the breeding island and their boundaries only rarely overlap with those of neighbouring species. Strange species are rarely tolerated in the breeding zone. With loud shrieks and furious determination, terns and gulls pounce on any unfortunate creature which strays into their colony. They will not leave it alone until it has been finally driven away.

A truly unfortunate pair, as far as relations with their neighbours were concerned, was a pair of avocets which had their nest away from the large avocet colony at a spot surrounded on all sides by common terns. Whenever one of the birds wanted to get to its nest it had to run a terrifying gauntlet. No matter how much it tried to sneak through, unobserved, among the broody terns, they would not leave it alone. From all sides bills and wings hammered away at it. Whichever way it turned, nothing but hostility. It was pitiful to watch the two avocets being forced, time and again, to beat a retreat when, after much anxious ducking and dodging, they had very nearly fought their way through to their nest. At the last moment they would lose heart. Plaintively they would back away, full of despair and incomprehension—if one may attribute to them these human emotions—to settle down in the shallow water outside.

There was no such hostility between black-headed gulls and gull-billed terns. Indeed, the nesting places of the latter were pretty well mixed up with those of the gulls in the south-western part of the bird colony. A model of peaceful coexistence. The reason most probably is that the two species are about equal in strength and size, and display much the same kind of fighting spirit. In consequence, it is invariably the black-headed gulls and the gull-billed terns which most vigorously oppose and even chase away all intruders to the island, such as herons or marsh harriers. It is no coincidence, therefore, that redshanks and plovers, little terns and avocets, are fond of nesting all round the gulls and terns. Why should the weaker not profit from the superiority of more powerful neighbours?

Life among the little terns on the large sheet of dry mud in the south of the island is also very quiet and well ordered. They are peaceful creatures, these graceful birds. They breed quietly and inconspicuously, and they are very easily missed in the large mass of birds. As yet they had no chicks. Their first preserve had been swept away by high waves and they had thus been forced to start breeding all over again. Fortunately, the young little terns grow very quickly from minute chicks to fully-fledged birds. They take only sixteen days. But then these delicate birds go in for all kinds of records—every egg of theirs, laid by the females who weigh about forty grams (one and a quarter ounces), weighs no less than one quarter as much as the hen bird itself.

A male returning from a search for food often brings a little fish along for his mate who is sitting on her eggs. With wings raised and trembling the male will touch down alongside the nest—a simple hollow in the ground, occasionally adorned with shells—place himself next to the hen, and hold out his gift in his bill. If the fish does not arouse the expected degree of interest the snubbed donor will trip away again excitedly, but will soon return and offer his present a second time. Almost invariably this is now accepted by the female, whereupon the male stretches his head upwards in a truly triumphant pose and extends his wings away from his body. If, however, the adored female continues to be cold and persists in refusing the offered fish—a pattern of behaviour more frequently observed during courting time—then the gift usually disappears down the donor's own throat.

Three and half hours had passed since I became a voluntary prisoner in my small tent on the island. Three and a half hours of bustling life and noisy activity, each minute filled with new pictures and new impressions. At first I was unable to do any productive work—I just sat and gazed, enjoying the noisy and colourful activity like a child. I was swept along by the turbulent happenings, forgetting my task and becoming a mere spectator. It is hard to see how anyone could resist succumbing to the magic of a bird island. The birds very soon convinced themselves that my film tent was no threat to them and tolerated it in their midst unafraid. Even the capricious avocets, which elsewhere had forced us to spend whole days advancing our hide inch by inch, did not seem too shy on this island. Very soon, incredible as it seems even to me, I was within a metre and a half of a pair of avocets sitting on their eggs. The fact that I could move my tent from inside, unseen, was a great advantage. It was a most satisfying achievement to be able to work amidst this lively bird community without being regarded as a disturbing factor. Sequence after sequence was recorded on my film—avocets in their bath and at their toilet, avocets returning to their nest, turning their eggs over and settling down on them, the 'changing of the guard' at the nest, when the returning partner stands by the side of the nest, lays its long, upward-curved bill flat on the ground, and makes backward jerking movements with its head. Close-

ups of the eggs and of hatching chicks, a portrait of the hen bird cleaning her young, and a shot of the cheerful little heads peeping out from under their mother's wings. Then there were overall shots of the shell bank and the island's edge, with sections from the territories of the avocets, the terns, and the gulls. A great many fragmentary sequences which later, ordered and put in logical sequence, would convey a living picture of a day at this colony of sea birds.

At regular intervals of about twelve to fifteen minutes the entire company of gulls and terns would rise up into the air with a terrifying noise. Screeching, the birds would fly a few circles round the island and then settle down again on their eggs. For a period of several seconds an impenetrable white wall of birds' bodies, wings, and tails would then hang in front of my tent, and I never ceased being amazed that in this crowded confusion the birds did not knock each other to the ground. The first time it happened I had quite a fright. I thought there must have been some outside disturbance. But when I found I was wrong, when I discovered that these spectacular round-flights were taking place with almost mechanical precision and regularity, I ceased being alarmed and got used to it. But I never succeeded in discovering any cause for or meaning behind this strange behaviour. It seems as if some inner unrest drives the birds to make these flights as if at a word of command. As the time for the next flight approaches they get more and more excited. Heads and necks jerk up, the general tension builds up rapidly, until suddenly one of the many thousands of birds triggers off the turbulent start.

The sun had passed through its zenith, and what in the morning had been a pleasant warmth had now given way to heavy heat. The island and the lagoon were under a grey cover of haze which stifled all colour. My camera motor had long fallen silent. The equipment was standing in a corner of the tent, all packed up, while I had settled down as comfortably as I could under the hot canvas.

Everything was quiet now in the colony. Gulls and terns were sitting on their eggs or sheltering their young. Only rarely did all the birds now fly up from their nests together to repeat their turbulent flights. The rays of the sun now were too dangerous to eggs and chicks for them to be left unprotected. One of the parent birds was continually on watch by each nest. Only now, during these still, heat-throbbing hours, did one fully realize the isolation of the island. A small patch of bare land, scarcely five hectares (twelve acres), sparsely covered with salicornia and a few thin patches of bulrushes, with a few shell banks and sheets of dry mud. And all round, as far as the distant horizon, the blue-grey, mirror-smooth surface of the salt lake.

One of the two oystercatchers whose surreptitious activity caught our attention on our arrival in the morning is wading in the bay. No doubt these magnificent birds have their three greyish-yellow black-speckled eggs lying somewhere in the shell sand of the western shore. A redshank is having a bath just off the little mud island. He bows gracefully as he wets his breast plumage and in so doing flashes his white rump. We should have loved to devote a whole day, or several days, to these oystercatchers and redshanks, and also to the brightly coloured red-crested pochards, a few pairs of which have their nests on the island, to discover more about their lives. But there are too many tasks and we simply have to confine ourselves to the essentials—even though this is not always easy with such a multitude of magnificent subjects. Nothing very much is happening at the moment. The half-grown black-headed gulls which, like the redshank, had spent a few hours bathing and attending to their plumage, have long withdrawn to the scant shade of the salicornia. Now and then some common terns arrive over the lake with small fish in their beak, or gull-billed terns with frogs and large insects—the former coming from the south, from the sea and the brackish ditches, and the latter from the north, from the grass steppes and the rice paddies, from foraging expeditions which have frequently taken them far beyond the confines of the delta. Then the young will scrabble out from under the protective wings of the parent birds and from under the salicornia, to accept their mouthfuls of food. These mouthfuls do not always slide down their throats easily. Often the morsels are too large and have to be manœuvred a little before they are swallowed. Sometimes the chicks can be seen gasping and choking in a quite alarming manner, but in the end they usually get their food down all right.

As the sun rose in the sky the shadow cast by my hide had been getting narrower and narrower. Now, shortly after noon, the sun was almost vertically over the island. There was hardly any shade to be seen anywhere. Two young common terns soon discovered the pleasant coolness of the rapidly dwindling dark area on the ground and patiently moved back with it. In this way they got nearer and nearer to the front wall of my tent. Then came the moment when their cool dream was at an end—there was no shade left. The only protection now was inside. Before very long they discovered that they could slip through just below the bottom edge of the canvas. Since then—for a little over an hour—they have been lying in a corner of my small abode, lazy and evidently content. They only slip outside when father or mother arrives with a small fish in its bill. After feeding time, however, they immediately come back into the tent.

Hour after hour passed in this way. A glassy, unreal quiet hung over the lagoon. From time to time the startlingly loud shriek of a gull or tern broke the heavy silence. The heat produced a desire to sleep—not only among the thousands of birds, many of which were now dozing with eyelids dropped. I myself, inside the tent, had to struggle hard not to drop off. Breathing had become difficult. I had long opened all the observation flaps, but they were much too small to let any refreshing current of air pass into the sticky interior.

The heat persisted until late afternoon. Only when the sun had got appreciably nearer the horizon and the grey haze over the island and lagoon began to dissolve, did the oppressive, sultry heat abate. Gradually the cries of the birds started again. The number of birds arriving and leaving rapidly increased. Shortly after five I had finished my filming work for the day and was waiting for my assistant to arrive. Just then a flock of herring gulls came swinging up across the lagoon from the south, from the direction of the sea. They were a force of raiders. Almost every day this hungry lot would appear in the sky, singly or in formation, in order to seek their prey among eggs and young chicks. Much larger and more powerfully built than the terns, the black-headed gulls, and the avocets, these herring gulls would invade the colony unimpeded, noisily sucking the eggs, killing newly hatched and half-fledged young birds and getting all spattered with their blood. Why should they worry about the screaming of angry parents? What harm could the boldest attacks by gull-billed terns or avocets do them? In front of the parent birds' eyes they would hack away at the eggs or kill the chicks. These herring gulls are a veritable scourge of the breeding islands, demons in white raiment exacting their toll of blood even among the flamingos, even among those thousands of tall, long-legged birds. Unless man interferes here by way of checking an excessive increase in herring gulls, their brutal assaults may result in the extinction of the sea-bird colonies. Patiently the marauders were circling over the island, swooping lower and closer all the time. Their drawn-out wailing heralded disaster. But they dared not strike at the colony. My film tent right in the middle of the island made them suspicious. It was a new and strange object to them and for the moment was keeping them away. Greedy, importunate, and impertinent as the herring gulls may be, unafraid as they may be of humans in ports or on ships on the high seas, in these breeding grounds here and along the deserted coastal regions their behaviour was different. Suddenly those fearless birds would act shyly and over-cautiously. Their eyes seemed to be everywhere and their reaction to any human approach was immediate flight. That, at least, was our experience in the Rhône delta. Indeed, from the point of view of the cameraman, the herring gull is one of the most difficult birds to get close to in the whole of the Camargue.

Having flown over my hideout several times with loud screeches, the whole flock of large gulls suddenly wheeled away towards the open water. They quickly gained height and before long they were out of sight.

For once caution had been stronger than appetite and greed. And even though the failure of this latest raid could have no possible effect on the future prospects of the sea-bird colony, I could not help feeling pleased that my presence on the island had succeeded in saving its inhabitants from attack by the insatiable egg-robbers for at least a few days.

Among the Nests of the White Herons

This was the third day we had spent in the small pinewood among little egrets and night herons. It was to have been our last, since we had not budgeted any more time for our filming of the herons. But it was clear already that we would have to add a day or two. For two days now the mistral had been shaking the trees almost ceaselessly, and our camera hide high up just below the top of one of the highest trees was swaying about like the crow's nest on some late medieval caravel on a stormy sea. Little wonder that we had so far been able to take only a few shots while most of the time we had been busy just watching the bustle among the treetops. This heron colony—the biggest of the region—this year comprised some 1300 to 1500 breeding couples. Of this total about four-fifths were little egrets and one-fifth night herons. Here and there one of the very shy Squacco herons could be seen among them. This species, which is not very common in the Camargue, with its white wings and delicate light-brown

back and brown plumage, was again represented in this mixed colony by at least a few pairs. Unfortunately, in spite of a strenuous search, we could not find any of their nests. It is by no means easy to make a moderately reliable estimate of the number of nests in use. Frequently the thick branches of the pines bar the view from the ground, or at least obstruct it sufficiently to prevent the counting of nests. One is then reduced to guess-work or to falling back on average figures —unless, of course, one decides to climb every single tree. An average of ten to fifteen nests per nesting tree is probably pretty near the truth. But the size of a heron colony is often subject to considerable fluctuations, and a year later the number of breeding couples here or in any other colony could well be totally different.

If any of the many different birds of the Camargue arouses the interest of every visitor, including the non-ornithologist, then it is surely the little egret. These graceful white stilt birds can be found hunting for frogs, water insects, and small fish throughout all habitats of the alluvial region, from the cultivated zone in the north all the way down to the sea, as well as in the adjacent areas to the east and west. Frequently their hunting grounds are a long way from their breeding place, with the result that the birds, once there are young chicks in the nest, must undertake extensive flights in search of food. The delicate, elf-like appearance of these small herons has frequently been compared to Chinese porcelain figures— and a very apt comparison it is. Especially when standing motionless in the shallow water of rice paddies, pools, or *étangs,* waiting for their prey, do these birds resemble delicate, fragile figurines. Yet this picture is entirely at variance with the lively temperament displayed by the little egrets in their nesting colony.

So long as the majority of the birds were busy sitting on their eggs there was more or less quiet in the pinewood. The only disturbance came from parent birds flying in for the 'changing of the guard' at the nest, and only occasionally did their hoarse squawking come from the tree-tops. But ever since the young hatched in nearly all the nests, with a good many of them now already half-fledged, the peace has gone. Now the wood rings with the bleating and squeaking of several thousand heron chicks from morning until night. Whenever we approach our tree in the early morning our arrival invariably produces both a visual and an acoustic tumult. Hundreds of beautiful birds fly up from the tree-tops with cries and beating of wings. Noisily

61 Black-winged stilt *(Himantopus himantopus)*

62 Rare colouring of the European tree-frog *(Hyla arborea meridionalis)* ▷

63 Winter evening by a freshwater lake in the eastern Camargue ▷▷

63

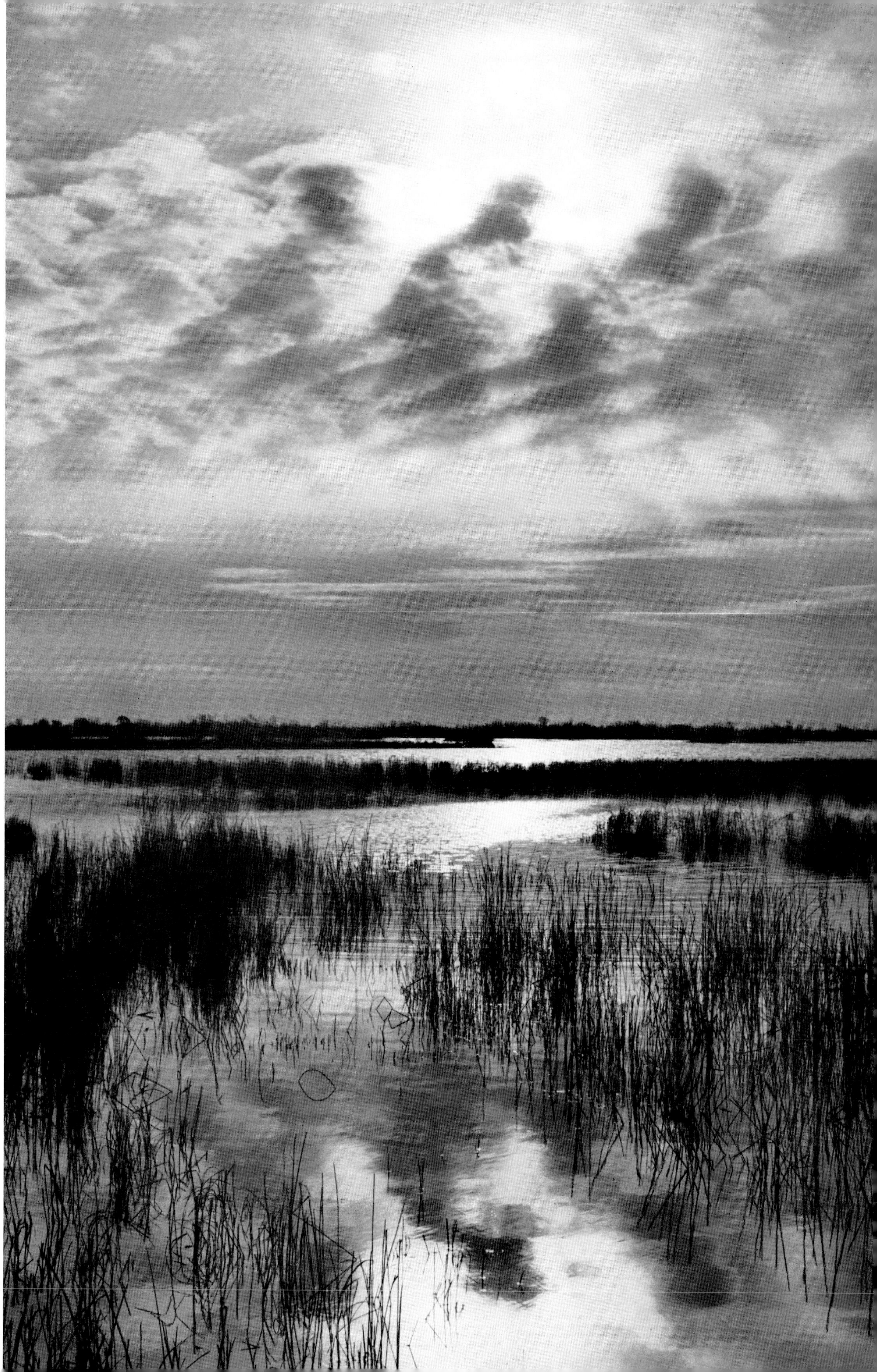

64 Shoveller drake *(Spatula clypeata)*

66 The air over the wintry waters is filled
with the roar of many thousands of wings.
Teal *(Anas crecca)*

67 Skeletons of tamarisks *(Tamarix gallica)* marked by wind and weather

68 Lapwing *(Vanellus vanellus)* climbing up to its nest in a flooded meadow

69 Family of whiskered terns *(Chlidonias hybrida)* on their floating nest

73 Shore of the Etang de Vaccarès, the largest inland lake of the Rhône delta

they flutter around each other, their many-voiced croaking spreading through the colony like an echo. Seconds later a huge cloud of birds is floating over the waving dark-green tree-tops. The wild confusion is almost invariably triggered off by a few night herons sitting on the bottom branches of the pines or stalking about on the ground clearing up the food vomited up by frightened heron chicks, or dropped during feeding. They are up and gone before one even spots them. Instantly all the birds up in the tree-tops are alerted. A screech of protest against the disturbance rises up from three or four hundred, or even more, herons in the air. The noise is enough to make one scramble up to one's hide as fast as possible. There one then sits, for the next four, six or even eight hours, right among the nests with the young birds, without the birds being aware of it. By no stretch of imagination can this prolonged sitting in the tree-tops be described as comfortable. The hide must necessarily be devised as small as possible, which means that the cameraman has very little freedom of movement. This is particularly noticeable when reels have to be changed or when one tried to exercise a leg that has gone to sleep. On the other hand, one has a superb view of the gently waving pine-tops with their many hundreds of white dots among the rich, deep green of the pines—herons sitting on their eggs, sheltering their young, or just resting. There is also a pleasant, fresh scent of pine needles and resin, and—the peak of delight—a mosquito-free air. Matters are very different down on the ground. The forest floor, as well as the few shrubs and bushes below the nesting trees, are whitewashed with bird excrement, and its pungent smell, mingling with the stench of decaying fish, is enough to make any stay in the colony exceedingly unpleasant. Added to which are the millions of blood-sucking mosquitoes which concentrate in the thicket where they are sheltered from the wind. True enough, they can be found anywhere in the Camargue—with the possible exceptions of the beach and the wide-open salt-grass steppe. Things are particularly bad at supper-time in our camp—in spite of the many thousands of yellow, red, and brown dragonflies which have been our allies for the past few days in our bitter nightly battle against the plague of mosquitoes. Shortly before sunset these dragonflies arrive near our tents in huge squadrons to stage a vigorous hunt on the mosquitoes. It looks just like a real raid. They will sweep right into the open anteroom of our large living tent in pursuit of their quarries. After

that they will invariably sit down on the edge of a used plate or of a soup- or salad-bowl. These elegant insects are not in the least shy. If one stands outside the tent and holds up one's forefinger one of the dragonflies will alight on it at once. One of our colleagues soon discovered that these creatures are evidently fond of having their bellies tickled. If one gently strokes their underside from head to tail they will remain perched wherever they are and curve their abdomen obliquely upwards.

Conditions did not look too promising for my shots of the egrets. During the past two hours the mistral had clearly gained in strength. The tops of the pines were bending under the gusts, the shock being transmitted through the tripod to the camera. Nevertheless, I had to hold on until about four in the afternoon. Not till then was I due to be relieved. I was getting a little anxious about the chicks in two nests situated obliquely below my hide. They were the most advanced young of all the twenty-eight nests of my tree and were already finding the small structure of dry sticks too cramped for them. At first they used to spend most of the time between feeds sitting on the edge of the nest; then, gradually, they would climb up to the neighbouring boughs and branches. Now they were spending most of the day outside the nest, returning there only at feeding-time or for an occasional rest. On a windy day, however, sitting out on the branches is a dangerous business for the young egrets who are still unable to fly. True, they are surprisingly good climbers, but the force of the gusts of even a moderately strong mistral should not be underrated. Frequently they bring down eggs and young birds. The birds, as a rule, first drop some way through the branches, but although they are caught lower down in the tree they are unable to work their way back up again and soon crash down, exhausted, to the forest floor, where foxes, large Montpellier snakes or jewelled lacertas soon finish them off.

From my elevated airy hide I had an effortless view of nine nests of little egrets and one nest of night herons. Six of these were in my own tree, and three in the next pine. Between them they provided an almost continuous picture of the various stages of development from the eggs to the nearly fully fledged bird. That, in fact, is one of the most fascinating experiences for the wildlife photographer—that, with a little luck, he can take in one and the same bird colony shots of parent birds sitting on their eggs or feeding the newly hatched chicks, as well as of half-grown and fully fledged birds. The nest on my left, so close that its loosely intertwined twigs were almost touching the camouflage sacking of my hide, still contained a complete set of eggs. This proximity did not seem to worry the parent birds at all. No sooner was our hide built than they started using it as an intermediate landing place on their way to their nest. As a rule they would alight on a branch well above me and then climb down skilfully across various other branches and the roof of my hide, as though it were a ladder leading to their nest. On arrival they would very carefully turn their pale blue eggs before sitting down on them. All that separates their eyes from mine is a thin sheet of material. Less than half a metre lies between me and the broody bird—it seems hardly credible. Yet there the parent egret is sitting, magnificent in its long, soft mantle plumage with its delicately fringed ends. These feathers, loosely dangling one moment and the next erect on head, back, or breast, envelop the bird as in a soft veil and, moreover, betray its mood. The strange, muted white sheen of the plumage, particularly noticeable at this close range, is due to a bluish powder produced by powder glands distributed along the bird's flanks. It takes the place, in these egrets, of the fat produced by the rump oil glands of other birds and used by them for greasing their feathers.

In a nest about two and a half metres away and slightly higher up among the branches the young chicks are just hatching, while a more than usually solid nest over to my right contains three young egrets about eight days old. Immediately below, a pair of night herons are keeping their chicks under their wings. These birds, stockier and plumper than the graceful egrets, are extremely suspicious. In this respect the two species are totally different. Whenever the night herons are in the least apprehensive they will spend an enormous length of time sitting on a branch or behind their nest, motionless, half hidden behind the boughs, watching my hide with anxious eyes. They are beautiful red eyes which look like signals among the green twilight of the pine-tops. Now, at breeding-time, the night herons can be seen making regular flights even during the day. Normally they would come to life only about dusk and then make their foraging expeditions to fresh-water ditches, rice paddies, and ponds. The hoarse cries of the roaming birds can be heard till late in the night.

In the nest of little egrets, upon which our filming efforts are chiefly concentrated, the young birds are barely two weeks old. They are still too small to climb out of the nest. But soon they too will find its confines cramping and start ranging farther afield, exploring the neighbouring branches.

The age of three weeks is represented by the young birds in the two nests immediately below the camera hide. They are beginning to show the yellow toes which are characteristic of the adult birds. At the same time, their legs still have their greenish-grey colouring so that the impression of 'bare-footedness' is not as marked as with fully grown little egrets.

Two nests in the next tree, finally, contain some roughly month-old birds whose plumage is nearly fully developed. In daytime these birds are very rarely seen in their nests now. They spend most of their time climbing among the dense branches, where they are now also fed by their parents. Only at nightfall do they return to the nest, first one and then the other, to spend the night in it or close to it. Their daily activities, apart from feeding and sleeping, include a good deal of exercising of wing muscles. Gaily they hop about the branches, beating their wings like mad, and performing the most grotesque leaps. Frequently their eagerness to exercise proves infectious so that suddenly two, three, or even four young birds can be seen dancing around as if demented. A parent egret has just landed in my pine-tree. Croaking noisily, it is climbing down the swinging branches. The young birds in the nest have stretched out their necks and are whispering excitedly. Four bills are thrusting impatiently at the parent bird, which stops for a moment, watchful, before entering the nest and turning to its young. What follows now is a normal feeding performance but at the same time an exceedingly turbulent scene. No sooner has the parent bird stepped into the nest than its young pounce upon it; a scene of wildest confusion ensues. The young birds snap at the old bird's bill, grip it, pull it and shake it, push it, and tear at it so that the parent bird is forced, time and again, to open its wings to keep its balance. The purpose of these somewhat rough begging gestures is to induce the parent bird to spew up the food it has brought back in its crop either into the chicks' throats or into the nest. The rough manners would come as a surprise to the unsuspecting observer whose mental picture of the feeding of young birds is a scene of gentle parental love. But there is no suggestion here of any solicitous stuffing of little beaks or of considerate mothering—on the contrary. The whole thing is much more like a brutal assault, the young simply forcing their parents to surrender their booty. Even when the parent bird has no more food to disgorge, the cackling, wing-beating, and hopping about of the four young birds continues. So long as the parent bird remains in the nest they will not settle down. In the end the hard-pressed parent has to tear itself away from its importunate offspring and withdraw to a branch behind the nest. But even there it is not safe. From the edge of the nest the young birds continue to beg with necks stretched out, and only when the parent has fled higher up into the tree-top do the young gradually quieten down. For a few more minutes they continue yapping and blindly hitting the air with their beaks. Then, exhausted by the long struggle, one chick after another drops back into the hollow of the nest. There they lie, flat on their bellies, as if dead. Heads and necks are twisted in a seemingly impossible manner. Looking at the young birds at this moment of utter exhaustion, one would not believe that just a few minutes earlier they had created such an uproar or that they would produce a similar tumult at the next parental visit to the nest.

Flying Gems

The heat of the second week of July lies heavily over the land. The song of the birds, their eager calls and cries, have increasingly fallen silent. A pale veil of haze lies over steppes and marshes, stifling the gay colours of the early summer. Even in the morning the thermometer shows 25 °C (77 °F) or more. Lazily the air shimmers over the hot ground.

Above the steep banks of the Etang de Vaccarès brilliantly sparkling bee-eaters float in the air. At times they hang almost motionless in the washed-out blue of the sky, like small dark crosses. They like this oppressive heat. The more mercilessly the sun beats down from its zenith, the happier these tropical creatures are. Watching them sitting on the edge of the loess cliffs or in piles of washed-up algae on the shell banks, dozing, wings held apart from the body, ruffled head bent backwards, and beak half open, one can see how they enjoy the warmth.

In spite of the heat and the painful mosquito bites, the hours which we have been spending in our low hide in the shallow water just off the bank in front of a small colony of bee-eaters have been among the most satisfying of our work in the Rhône delta. From just under two dozen holes in the bank the heads of fully feathered young birds are peeping, noisily demanding food from the adult birds sailing past. It is about four weeks since they hatched from their eggs in the darkness of the nesting holes. Now they are almost ready for their first flight. Curiously and at the same time anxiously they watch everything that is happening outside their loess cliff. They are particularly interested in the flies and beetles which run around the creviced edge. Often their eyes are fixed on them for minutes on end. But we have never once seen one of these young birds trying to capture such an insect, not even when it was running up and down straight in front of the earth hole, literally presenting itself to the young beaks. For these young bee-eaters, as indeed for other birds of that age, the concept of food seemed still to be exclusively linked to the person of the parent bird or to a food-from-the-bill pattern. Or perhaps these birds, which when fully grown will hunt insects in flight, do not recognize them as a prey when they are moving on the ground. Indeed, the young birds are afraid of the larger insects, such as big dragonflies. Whenever one of them rustles past the steep bank the young birds jerk back their heads. The sparrows, on the other hand, who now and again visit the colony and shameless push their heads into the nesting holes of the bee-eaters, do not seem to frighten the young birds in the least. Almost invariably it is the sparrows who make off as soon as the bee-eater chicks get too importunate with their begging gestures.

A few metres off the bank some massive old tamarisk skeletons stand in the shallow water. They serve the lively birds as favourite look-out posts, and as a place where they can rest or from which they can take off in pursuit of insects. One of these skeletons, in particular, a tall, slender one with strongly ramified branches, seems to attract them especially. Frequently ten or more bee-eaters can be seen rocking on it simultaneously. Their turquoise breast feathers flash in the light of the low sun as though the bare branches were studded with huge gems. But the tamarisks seem to attract not only the bee-eaters. Magpies settle on them frequently, and one cuckoo flies in regularly over the steep bank in order to give a prolonged concert among the dead tamarisk branches. Other occasional visitors are kestrels and turtle doves, swallows, great reed warblers, and corn buntings. A hoopoe, performing its morning toilet within a few feet of our hide, provided an unscheduled sequence of shots. But the rarest visitor, hardly ever expected, is a little bittern. One late afternoon one such little bittern, a bird belonging to the heron family and about the size of a pigeon, came paddling across on the water. It was a male, its back black with a faint sheen of green and with light ochre colouring on its throat and underparts.

He settled down, crouching, among the exposed roots of a tamarisk and stared motionless into the shallow water by the bank. But the bee-eaters overhead presumably were too noisy, for very shortly the bittern moved off and disappeared in the near-by reed thicket.

Work in the bee-eater colony proceeded without any problems. The colourful birds proved exceedingly trusting and within a few days most of our shots were taken. Often the birds were basking in the sun so close to our hide that it was impossible to focus on them to get a sharp picture. We usually worked two shifts—from six to ten in the morning and from three to six in the afternoon. As a rule, the morning was used for filming and the afternoon for photography. Intensity and angle of incidence of the light were of considerable importance here in view of the strong reflection provided both by the steep bank and by the shallow water. Only at a few definite times of the day was it possible to photograph the bee-eaters in such a way that the magnificent brilliance of their plumage would be caught on the film. But the birds themselves made things very easy. Not a single cameraman or photographer had any complaints, and we soon had a complete set of pictures 'in the bag', from an overall view of the nesting cliff to a close-up of a calling bird.

We had only one disappointment—we missed an almost perfect piece of drama on one of our last days in the colony, a scene performed jointly by a bee-eater returning with food and a young, newly fledged blue-headed wagtail. At the crucial moment our reel ran out, and by the time the second camera was ready for action it was all over. What happened was that the bee-eater arrived in the tamarisk, with a cicada in its bill, and landed close to the young wagtail. In order to render harmless a possible sting, the bee-eater knocked its booty against a branch several times and kneaded it in its bill. While it was doing this the wagtail moved closer and closer to it. It took some time before the bee-eater noticed it and, somewhat alarmed, moved away.

Instantly the young bird hopped after it and forced it to retreat again. This time the bee-eater put a couple of feet between it and its pursuer, but it had not allowed for the persistence of the young bird. It again followed close on its heels and with beak opened wide tried to snatch the cicada from the other bird. Again the bee-eater withdrew. This entertaining performance went on until both birds had reached the extreme end of the branch and the pursued had no further room for retreat. As the wagtail again lunged at it the bee-eater hurriedly swallowed the cicada and when the young bird continued to harass it it slipped off the branch and flew off. Whenever the bee-eaters hunt their prey over the *étang* or over dry land their outstanding flying skill can be observed in action. Like an arrow from a bow-string they streak off in pursuit of their prey. With lightning speed they react to the slightest change of course of the insects and invariably snap them up in the air. Frequently one can see the hunting birds fluttering or hovering in the same place above the edge of a steep bank, waiting for a dragonfly, a bumblebee, or some other insect to appear. Instantly they pounce, often diving after their quarry, for which there is no escape. If an insect tries to escape by flying straight up, the bee-eaters instantly zoom up in a steep looping manœuvre, gaining height and catching their prey. They glide back to their waiting posts and start 'knocking out' their victim. The short, hard blows can be heard quite well at a distance of nearly thirty metres.

During the last few days before the young birds try out their wings for the first time they are almost invariably fed at the entrance of their nesting holes. Very rarely does a parent bird now enter the nesting tube. Instead, the food is frequently passed on from a hovering flight. As soon as a young bird is sated it disappears backwards in the nesting tunnel to make room for its brothers and sisters.

All day long the shrill but not unpleasant cries of the colourful birds ring out along the nesting bank. Softly the waves lap the shore, with its yellow-brown shells. The hours creep slowly by under the scorching sun.

One morning, when most of the nest entrances were still in the shade, the first young bee-eater left its nesting tube. For a quarter of an hour or more it had been sitting at the nest entrance, calling for its parents. But the old birds, seemingly unconcerned, were perched on the tamarisks, stretching themselves in the early sunshine. Now and again one or the other took off to describe a wide arc. In doing so they passed close to their young each time before returning to their perches. Further and further the young bird would lean out from the hole, until the whole of its upper body was outside. Then, suddenly, it let itself fall. Vigorously it struck its wings, it was gaining height and climbing higher and higher—so high that it missed the approach to the tamarisk. Only at its second attempt, after an arc out over the lake, did it succeed in landing. This meant the beginning of a new phase in the breeding colony. That same morning a second young bird left its nest.

The next day another two followed suit, and before the week was out all the young bee-eaters in the steep bank had started flying. They were now fed in the tamarisks or somewhere along the top of the cliff. More and more often they would now accompany their parents on their flights around the immediate neighbourhood. But at night they would still return to the bank in order to sleep in the holes which had protected them during the first thirty days of their lives. Our job among the bee-eaters had thus come to an end. There were new tasks waiting for us. We felt a touch of nostalgia as we pulled our small hide out of the shallow water on to the beach and for the last time carried our equipment across the shell bank. We were sorry that the chapter of the bee-eaters was now concluded. But perhaps one always felt a little sorry to leave any of one's four-legged or feathered film-stars when one had spent days or weeks in their immediate vicinity. One had taken such an intimate part in their lives and become part of their immediate environment. Unaffected by one's presence, the creatures had acted out the parts that nature had given them.

The Sorrows of a Cameraman

Filming does not always go quite so smoothly. Only a few days later we had one of those experiences which remind one from time to time that animals, after all, are very different from human performers. Humans can be directed how to act in front of the camera and if necessary can be made to repeat their performance. Animals, on the other hand, are altogether unpredictable creatures, and no matter how well one thinks one knows their behaviour one may still find oneself faced with new problems.

After a long search we had at last found a family of rollers. Not just any family, but one which answered the requirements of the scenario on nearly all its major points. These were: a hole in a tree, half-grown chicks, location of the nesting tree in a sparse deciduous forest. The last condition was the most difficult. We knew of several nests in holes in the ground, in steep banks, or in gnarled olive-trees standing in the open. But we still needed some sequence showing the roller. And the shots had to be taken in the bird's proper habitat. Of course, we could have cut in some shots of rollers from a totally different habitat at a later stage, and this would certainly have been simpler and saved a lot of time. But we did not really believe that this kind of deception would come off and the idea did not appeal to us. Consequently, we spent a whole week searching for a roller nest which conformed to our 'script'. Unfortunately, since nothing on earth is perfect, it had one serious drawback—the nest was sixty kilometres (forty miles) from our camp. That meant a round trip of 120 kilometres each day. And even the most optimistic of us did not believe that our first attempt would end in success.

Preparations took two whole days. The hole in the tree was only five metres (sixteen feet) above the ground, which was a good thing, but on the other hand the neighbouring trees had a rather thick foliage and lighting was not too good. We therefore had to cut a narrow clearing through the screening branches, just about big enough to allow a weak ray of sunlight to strike the opening of the hole between eight and nine-fifteen in the morning. Later in the morning the angle of incidence of the light would be too steep, and in the afternoon the sun would be on the far side of the tree.

Even when the purely technical problems of filming or photographing wild animals or birds have been solved, one great unknown factor remains—how will the creatures react to the changes in their environment which have been or are about to be effected, such as hides, lighting equipment, camera or flashlight devices, and suchlike? By no means does each individual animal react in the same way—not even under identical conditions. Some are a great deal shyer than others. Indeed, frequently an individual belonging to a notoriously shy species will behave like a tame animal used to the presence of humans, while individuals belonging to species not normally afraid of man can reduce a cameraman to despair by their timid behaviour. The same species of animal often includes both extremes. One thing is quite certain—the behaviour of animals and birds can never be predicted.

Even while we were still building our hide we discovered that the two parent rollers were extremely nervous. Our first camouflaged tent, placed some ten metres from the nesting tree, proved a complete flop. Although the canvas had been painted in a colour matching the surroundings, and although we used plenty of natural camouflage material, the birds kept away from their nest for an hour and a half. Throughout that time they were flying through the wood, uttering hoarse warning cries, or else they sat up in the tree-tops, suspiciously viewing our hide. There was nothing for it but to move it. The next day we tried our luck at a distance of fifteen metres and with even more camouflage around the tent. But the result was the same as on the first day. By late afternoon we had moved again.

We then decided to take our sequences through one of our most powerful tele-lenses, and this enabled us to move away another five metres. We would have preferred to do without this sixty-centimetre (twenty-four-inch) focal length, because this kind of heavy gun has a lot of snags to it. But in the circumstances it was our only hope.

A thick patch of shrubs enabled us to set up a hide in natural surroundings. We were able to dispense with the tent altogether and merely use one of our dark-olive canvas sheets for overhead cover. On all sides we were adequately hidden by thick shrubs and undergrowth. Now at last the rollers ceased being suspicious. In the course of one hour during which we watched the entrance to their nest from this respectable distance a bird flew in twice to feed the young. It seemed a favourable omen for the following day.

The tree-tops were glowing in the fire of the first sunrays. Playfully the light moved from leaf to leaf, danced from twig to twig, swept trembling and flickering over the branches down to the tree-trunks. Slowly it sank down to the ground, among the shrubs and bushes, into ditches and thickets. The last shadows of the night were yielding. A hedgehog was attracted to a pile of dry twigs, a belated badger was hurrying towards its set; red woodmice rustled through last year's dry leaves. Only when a shadow detached itself from a branch overhead did the scurrying creatures on the ground suddenly fall silent. The tawny owl was making its last hunt for prey before retreating to its daytime hide in the old white poplar. In the rotten oak on the edge of the patch of woodland, high up on a long, bare branch pointing towards the sky like a finger, a roller was sitting and enjoying the warmth of the morning sun. Its turquoise plumage gleamed, or rather sparkled, in the early light, so much so that for a moment I felt that I was not in a sparse forest in the south of France but in a tropical rain-forest in Africa or Asia, that I was surrounded not by ash, poplar, and oak, but by palm-trees, philodendra, and bromeliacea. The young birds in the hole, hacked out originally by a green woodpecker, did not budge. No ray of the sun had yet reached their nest. Too many near-by trees provided a tall green roof of foliage to let the dancing sunlight through into the interior of the forest. A few feet above the

entrance to the hole sat the second parent bird. Slowly it was picking over its plumage, fully absorbed in its morning toilet. It was so large and clear on the ground-glass viewer of my camera that I could almost count its feathers. The violet-blue edges of its wings and the chestnut-brown back contrasted strongly with the bird's pale azure head and breast. Its dark lores lend this bird a particularly vigilant expression. It is a truly splendid creature. Rarely have I been so fascinated by a bird as by the roller. Ever since I first encountered it two years ago its picture has been haunting me—sitting in my warm room on long winter evenings I could see them hunting for locusts in the steppes of South Africa or sunning themselves on palm-trees and oleanders in Moroccan wadis. I could see them perform their magnificent courting flights above the evergreen bushes of Provence and squabbling with jackdaws in the poplar groves of the Camargue. And all the time I had been getting increasingly anxious to catch these flying jewels on my film so that I could make the tropical brilliance of their colourful plumage come to life again. And now, two years later, I was sitting among the still shady bushes, with the bird in my viewfinder for the first time. I could feel my pulse racing and my hunting fever increasing from minute to minute. The temptation to pull the camera trigger was almost irresistible. But what would have been the use? A shot showing the shape of the bird but not the brilliance of its plumage. No, I must wait for the rays of the sun to penetrate to the rollers' nesting hole and hope that one of the parent birds would just then come back to feed its young. If only there were not so many mosquitoes about. They made this long wait a torture. The tightness of my hide and my fear of betraying my presence by moving compelled me to watch idly as the mosquitoes calmly plunged their jaws into every part of my body they could reach. Their abdomens would inflate, revealing through the transparent skin the blood they had just drawn. But all one could do was clench one's fists and swear silently.

Just then the roller above the nest moved off, and passed low over the patch of grassland adjacent to the forest. It disappeared over the tree-tops on the far side. The second bird, up on the oak, followed a few seconds later. They were setting off on their hunt, evidently. This meant one had to be doubly vigilant, because when they return with food these shy birds are particularly furtive in their movements. And once one had missed their approach there would probably be no time left for a good shot. There was certainly plenty to watch in the meantime—so much, in fact, that one had to be careful not to be distracted from one's main purpose. Long-tailed tits were climbing through the branches, a Sardinian warbler was flitting out from among the brambles. In the elms overhead the jackdaws were fighting over a dead blindworm—or was it a small snake? A melodious warbler was very persistently singing its song on the next tree. A jay, that harlequin among forest birds, was hopping along the edge of the grassland. Suddenly there was a rustling between my feet. A mouse? Hard as I tried I could not make out the cause of the noise for some time. Then, suddenly, a dry leaf was raised just in front of my toes, and a caterpillar hunter, gleaming metallically, appeared from the rotting cover of the forest floor. The large, strongly built beetle was hunting for caterpillars. Its armour had a steel-blue sheen, a gleam of golden-purple lay on its basically green but longitudinally striped wing-cases. Among European beetles the caterpillar hunter, also known as the handsome beetle, is one of the most remarkable, and not only because of its size and colouring. To satisfy its craving for the caterpillars and chrysalises of butterflies it will skilfully climb up the trunk of trees and pursue the caterpillars among the foliage. Since it also attacks and kills such harmful ones as the processionary caterpillar, as well as the chrysalises of this and other species on the ground, it is a highly beneficial creature in the forest. This fact has been utilized in North America, where the caterpillar hunter has been imported to fight the butterfly pests (likewise introduced from Europe) which had been ravaging the forests and orchards chiefly of the eastern states. The beetle is now properly established there and appears to perform its task of hunting caterpillars to the satisfaction of its hosts.

I watched the beetle raking over the dry leaves for nearly a quarter of an hour. Then it moved slowly away and I had to concentrate on my job again, since the entrance to the rollers' nest was now fully in the sun. If only the parent birds would arrive now to feed their young!

But they did not arrive. Neither at eight-fifteen nor at eight-thirty. By nine o'clock there was still no sign of them. The young birds could be heard calling softly from inside the hole in the tree. At five past nine a deep shadow appeared just above the hole. Inexorably it was creeping downwards. At twelve minutes past a golden oriole flew past the entrance to the rollers' nest. At a quarter past the shadow had reached the upper edge of the hole. Now was our last chance, now they must come. At twenty past the hole was half in the

shade. In the distance I could hear a roller croaking. Then it was twenty-five past nine, time was up, and our opportunity was gone. Until tomorrow morning the entrance to the nest would remain in the deep shadow of the tamarisk foliage. Thus ended our first morning's vigil—an unforgettable experience but wasted as far as work was concerned. Nothing out of the ordinary had happened. What we did not know that wonderful summer morning—and it was fortunate we did not know it—was that this day would mark the beginning of twenty-one days of downright incredible bad luck.

Here, to illustrate this period, are excerpts from our diary.
July 19th: Reveille at 0400 hours. Followed by one and a quarter hour's drive to the rollers' nest. No parent birds in sight as we take up position. 0730: a roller arrives in the tree and spends the next fifteen minutes sitting on a branch in the shade above the nest. No feeding before 0915.

July 20th: Reveille at 0400. Drive to our hide. A parent bird leaves the nest as we arrive. Feeding at 0740—twenty minutes too soon. Next arrival of a bird at 0950.

July 21st: Reveille at 0400. Taking up position in hide at 0600. At 0825 a parent bird makes for the nest but remains at its entrance for less than three seconds before leaving again. Sequence too short. Fifteen minutes later another roller arrives. Flies off at once.

July 22nd: Reveille at 0400. Vigil from 0615. First bird arrives 0930. By then nest already in shade.

July 23rd: Departure from camp 0415. Puncture halfway. Had to change wheel. Arrived at nest too late.

July 24th: Reveille at 0400. First feeding 0745; no light yet on nest entrance. Both parent birds seem nervous; frequent warning calls. Next arrival with food 0912. First of three envisaged sequences shot.

July 25th: No birds arrived before 1000. Both parent birds somewhere near nesting tree. Young birds calling loudly. Camouflage of our hide in need of renewal.

July 26th: Reveille at 0400. Held up by road check and arrived at rollers' nest too late.

July 27th: Vigil from 0600 to 0830. One roller comes near the tree but does not approach nest. After 0830 disturbance from workers on near-by farm.

July 28th: Reveille at 0400. Sky overcast, but set out nevertheless. Cloud cover beginning to break up after 0700. At 0810 a roller lands on branch below nest. Why couldn't he do so a little later? No feeding. But feeding at 0850. Difficulties with focusing and lose valuable seconds. Sequence too short.

74 *Triops cancriformis,* a Branchiopod, floating on its back

75 Male of the bearded tit *(Panurus biarmicus)* feeding one of its young ▷

76 'Changing of the guard' at the nest of the purple heron *(Ardea purpurea)* ▷▷

July 29th: Reveille at 0400. Arrival at hide 0530. Our tarpaulin has gone and cannot be found. Makeshift repair to roof with hay and green twigs. The former (a pressed bale) 'found' in near-by field. Start vigil 0700. Feeding at 0832. Bird flies off the moment camera motor starts. Perhaps sensitive to noise? Five minutes later arrival of second bird. Same reaction to camera noise.

July 30th: Overslept.

July 31st: Reveille at 0400. This is the fifteenth time we have covered this sixty-kilometre distance between our camp and the rollers. Done 1800 kilometres so far—and what a poor result! Unfortunately we cannot keep a man permanently on watch at the nest. Can hardly cope with the other work as it is. After 0700 rapid build-up of cloud-bank. Discontinue watch at 0830 because of poor light.

August 1st: Young chicks are quite large now and almost fully fledged. They often put their heads out of the hole now and call for their parents. Six arrivals between 0800 and 0915. All of them very short—none longer than four seconds. Too short for either of the two sequences planned.

August 2nd: Take up position at 0615. Both parent birds uttering warning cries and only slowly settling down again Feeding 0730—too early since no light yet on nest entrance. Second arrival not till 0926—too late since light has gone. Exasperating!

August 3rd: Departure from camp 0415. Heavy cloud, but beginning to clear at 0600. After 0800 only sporadic cloud-banks. Feeding at 0820 and 0843. Infuriating, on both occasions the arrival of the parent rollers coincides with a short period of shade. To shoot would be pointless. The bird's colour would not come out.

August 4th: Shot second scene (close-up of bird bringing food). Also try to shoot the third and final sequence, but the necessary change of lenses takes too long. No second feeding within the suitable time span.

August 5th: Watch from 0600. Very warm and close morning. Mosquitoes worse than ever. Both parent birds close by. At 0730 arrival of farm labourers. Grass being cut in adjacent meadow. No feeding before 0945.

August 6th: Reveille at 0400. Our car on strike—engine refuses to fire in spite of every possible effort. Spent until 0630 trying to get car started. In vain. End up with totally exhausted battery.

August 7th: Reveille at 0400. In a borrowed car out on our twenty-second trip to the rollers. When will this impossible episode end? Probably not until all the young have flown. Of the five, there are three left in the nest at the moment—the other two have been fed on near-by branches since the day before yesterday. Arrival of parent bird and feeding at 0805. The scene turns out too short again since the roller does its feeding while hovering. Next feeding not until 0939.

August 8th: Reveille at 0400. Watch from 0610. Isolated cloud until 0740, afterwards clear sky. The third chick left the nest yesterday. First feeding at 0805; the roller just still in the full shadow of a branch. Half an hour later a parent turns up again with food in its bill (huge—*Palpares libelluloides*). For at least a minute it sits on the small branch below the nest. Take two shots and with them conclude the sequence.

After twenty-three days, after 2520 kilometres covered, and after a watching time of sixty hours we had at last made sure of fifteen seconds of film sequences showing rollers.

Midsummer

It is nearly four months since we last had any rain. Day after day the sun beats down from a pale cloudless sky with undiminished strength—scorching, crushing, killing. Not a breath of air, not a thundery shower which would at least give the illusion of refreshment. The marshes have become still and quiet, the steppes are monotonous and disconsolate. The heavy heat lying over the landscape makes breathing a torture. Mirages, shimmering reflections in the air over the parched ground, suggest the proximity of non-existent water. The small and medium-sized ponds have long dried out; ditches and water-holes have been empty for weeks, their banks covered with a yellow-brown fringe of wilted bulrushes and sedges.

Even the large inland lakes are rapidly losing their water. Almost visibly their edges recede inch by inch. The exposed belt of mud dries out rapidly, hardening into an unattractive grey mass. Wherever the water lays bare mud and earth a bizarre lattice-work of fine cracks and fissures opens on the crusted surface. As the humidity in the soil diminishes these cracks open wider and wider to form a huge network of miniature ravines on the brilliantly bright surface. Sand racers and small black spiders scurry

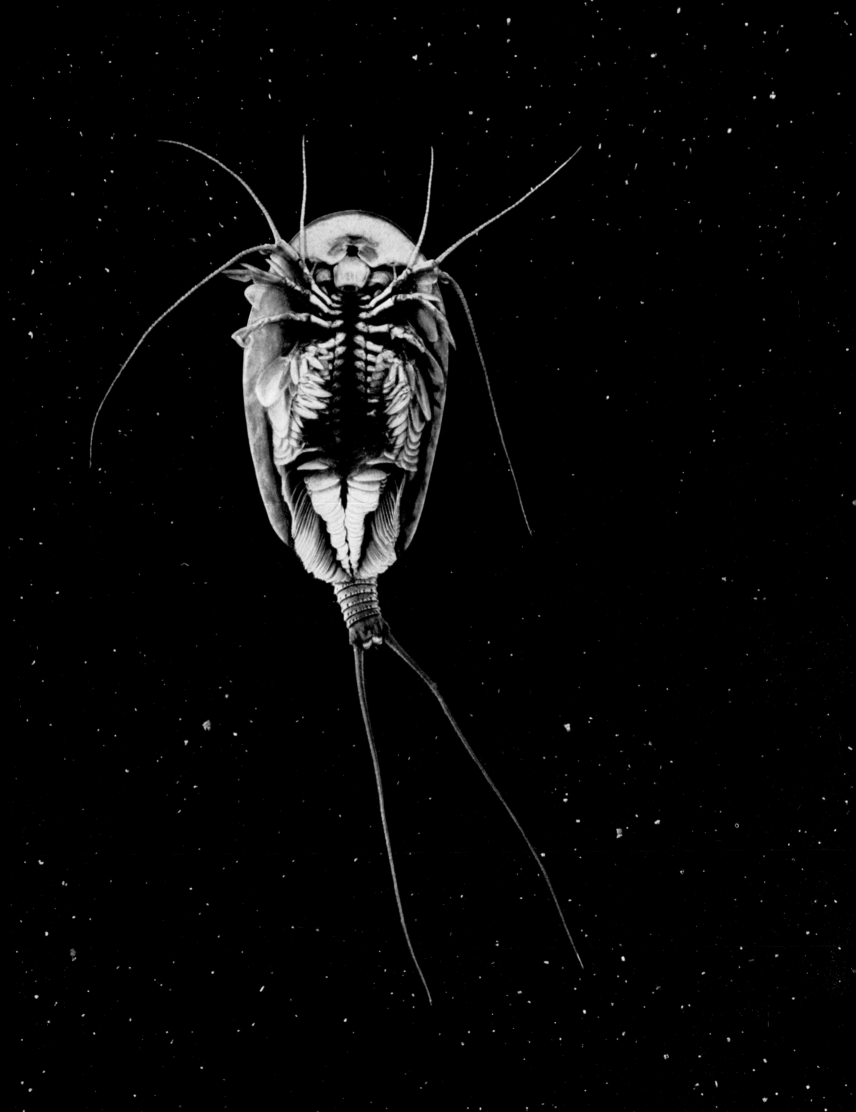

79 Little owl *(Athene noctua)* with nearly fully fledged chick

80 Tarantula *(Lycosa narbonensis)* outside its hole in the ground

81 La Crau, the former estuary area of the Durance

83 Mediterranean Garrigue at the foot of the Alpilles

85 Southern smooth snake *(Coronella girondica)*

86 Viperine water snake *(Natrix maura)*

87 Montpellier snake *(Malpolon monspessulanus)*

88 Ladder snake *(Elaphe scalaris)* with adult skin

89 Caterpillar of the spurge hawk moth *(Celerio euphor-biae)*

90 *Palpares libelluloides,* an ant-lion

busily through this endless maze of cracks, vanishing and reappearing, to be lost again in one of the countless rills. The large brackish lake which we had crossed in mid-May on our journeys to the bird island, and whose water then came very nearly up to our hips, has disappeared. In its place stretches a grey desert plain, extending far into the haze of the distant horizon, its silent infinity varied only by occasional shimmering white efflorescences of salt or the bleached armour of dried-out crabs.

From the steppes, too, all life seems to have disappeared. In vain does the eye seek the lively Kentish plovers, in vain does the ear listen for the trills of the larks or the fluting song of the stone curlew. The flocks of sheep which, a few weeks previously, had wandered through the *sansouïre,* feeding on its sparse greenery, have moved off to the northern hinterland, exchanging their rough diet of hard grasses for more succulent mountain plants. Not till the late autumn will they return to the Rhône delta to winter here.

The low salicornia plants along the paths and tracks are covered with a thick layer of yellowish-grey dust. The dry crust which forms on the ground when the water has evaporated cracks in the scorching heat and gradually crumbles to dust. Wherever one puts one's foot a clear imprint is left in the soft surface. As soon as the wind springs up huge clouds of fine soil are driven across the plain, coating shrubs and plants and even dusting the tall tamarisks with a white layer of powder. Hundreds of *Cepaea* snails have climbed up grasses and shrubs, bushes and fencing poles, in the hope of escaping death. On the parched ground they would now be slowly scorched. They cling together in huge clusters like grapes, or like twisted chains. Many will perish in the long run, but others, those at the centre of the clumps, may escape death by scorching and survive the dry season thanks to the protection of their fellows.

So far, heat and aridity are still holding sway, and there is no sign of a change in the near future. Hardly a bird voice can now be heard. Only the cicadas chirp ceaselessly in their trees right through the day. Their irritating shrill noise is increasingly getting on everybody's strained nerves. We are all beginning to feel the effects of lack of sleep during the past few weeks. The sultry nights bring no refreshment, and the temperature drops only a few degrees below that of the daytime. The heat is trapped in the tents and prevents one from sleeping. Soaked with sweat, one tosses and turns on one's camp-bed. One's throat is parched with thirst and one's tongue clings to one's palate. To reach for the water-bottle has become an automatic reflex action. But the more one drinks the more eagerly do the mucous membranes absorb all humidity and the more one starts sweating. Three times we tried to sleep with our tents open, and on all three occasions the rats gnawed holes into our mosquito curtains to pay us a midnight visit. By now these beasts have got entirely used to us and have become real tame domestic animals, entering and leaving as they please. Returning in the evening, after dark, one is welcomed from afar by delighted squeaks. As soon as one of us sits down by the petrol lamp to make an entry in his diary, at least one of the rodents will come up, stand on its hind legs, or boldly leap up towards the bread basket which hangs from our ridge pole. And later, when the lights have been put out and all has become quiet, there is much whistling and rummaging, scurrying and squeaking, biting and fighting. There is a clatter of empty food tins as two of the lithe little rats grab each other in the refuse box. Or else one of the impudent beasts will climb to the top of the pile of cooking pots and bring the lot down with a crash and clatter. Nothing, positively nothing, is safe from these importunate animals. Neither bread nor cheese, neither soap nor soup powder. Tea and tobacco are eaten with the same pleasure as half-ripe tomatoes, and wax candles seem no less tasty than chocolate. The only things which do not seem to interest them at all are the rat traps which, carefully baited, are scattered all over the place.

The days pass in dull heat, heavy and monotonous. The air trembles over the hot ground, the hard light steeps the landscape in a dull grey-green haze. Now is the worst time for water creatures, especially the fish in marshes and ponds. The steadily dropping water-level increasingly compels them to congregate at the few remaining deep spots. Communications with other sheets of water have long been cut off, and there is no line of escape. The salt content of the water increases, soon the oxygen will no longer be sufficient for the desperate creatures. Here and there the first flashing dorsal fins are seen above the water. In their agony the first fish leap out on land to die there in the sun. A feast has been laid out for herons and kites. The herring gulls, too, those hyenas among the birds of the Camargue, are not long in coming. Circling at great height over the patches of water, gliding slowly before dropping down to begin their meal. But once they have started...!

I had taken up position in our hide on the small island at day-break. Everything was still quiet, only two night herons flew off soundlessly as we approached across the hardened sheet of mud. The water began to seethe as I took the few steps across it to the edge of the island. Masses of fat-bellied carp scattered to right and left, got into the shallow water at the extreme edge of the hollow, and there stuck in the viscous mud. Some of them no longer had the strength to fight their way back into the deeper water, no matter how they twisted and turned—mouths wide open, they remained stuck in the glutinous mass. A few times they flung themselves into the air, came down on their sides with a smack, furiously whip-ped the mud with their tail fins, and suffocated. More food for the herring gulls which had been circling over the island for the past two minutes. I could see them as small white dots high up in the blue morning sky. There must have been about a hundred or more.

Less than fifteen minutes later they came down with a hoarse caterwauling to have their feast. Abandoning all caution, the big heavy birds pounced on the dead fish. Ruthlessly beaks hacked at the swollen bodies, tearing the guts out of the fish bellies. Greedy swallowing, violent choking, and spiteful screeching. Bodies floating on the water were seized by the tail and dragged on land. Hard blows with the bills caused the rotten flesh to burst with a sharp hiss. Mouthful after mouth-ful disappeared down the wide throats of the gulls. The man-ner in which they attacked even fish which were still alive and hacked out their eyes was revolting. One or two well-aimed blows, a pull to the left, a turn to the right, a good jerk—and all that was left was the yawning, empty eye sockets. A macabre scene acted out before a backdrop of hundreds of creatures in an agony of dying.

Scattered all around were stripped skeletons, some of them still covered with tatters of skin and scales. Ripped-off heads were bleaching in the sun. And amidst it all the blood and mud-spattered crowd of executioner birds were fighting over the tastiest pieces. Their noise did not stop for a single moment. Their drawn-out mewing and groaning, and the caterwauling ending in a kind of diabolical laughter, still rings in my ears.

Suddenly my attention was caught by a large black-and-white shape drawing its majestic circles high up in the air. It was an Egyptian vulture, drawing its wide spirals without any wing beat whatever, carried only by the thermal currents.

Superbly elegant, remote from all earthly gravity. These black-and-white soaring birds with their peculiar wedge-shaped tails do not nest in the Camargue. Their nests are among the inaccessible rock faces of the Alpilles, high above the evergreen Garrigue, and from there they make their far-ranging flights which occasionally take them down into the Rhône delta. As a rule they come at the time of the mass dying of the fish, when the number of stinking cadavers grows from day to day.

But the vulture did not come down to feed. For a while it continued circling over the island, higher and higher. Then I lost sight of it. Could it have been suspicious of my hide—itself less greedy and therefore more cautious and vigilant than the herring gulls? Or did it just not feel like joining that noisy squabbling crowd on the ground?

The greed of the gulls really knew no bounds. It totally over-rode their usual caution and pronounced mistrust. My small camouflaged tent was surrounded by herring gulls gorging themselves on dead fish; all round me were piles of inflated evil-smelling fish bodies. The sickly smell of decay which hung over the whole scene was beginning to affect me. My still empty stomach began to rebel. I had been here since early morning and I was now praying for my relief to arrive soon.

Thunderstorm

One day is like another in its scorching grey monotony. July ended in parching heat, and August followed, burning and parching. The murderous heat continues to claim its victims. Every morning one hopes for a thunderstorm or a rain shower. In vain. Not even a cloud-bank to hide the sun for a while. The proverbial perpetually blue sky of the Midi disap-points our last hopes of a break in the weather. The heat pro-duces a general irritation. Any enterprise suddenly seems too much, even the smallest task seems too much trouble. Only with reluctance does one do any work at all.

During the night of August 8th to 9th, at long last, in the early hours of the morning, a change seems imminent. The day starts leaden grey. The sky is overcast and lowering over the landscape. For the fist time in many weeks the sun is not moving along its glaring trail. An unusual stillness has fallen over steppes and marshes, a stillness that is different from that of the preceding, heat-pulsating days. There is something frightening, something menacing about it. The air is oppressive, and mosquitoes and gadflies seem to have gone mad. Tens of thousands of them are swarming around the clumps of bushes and among the trees. They will pursue a man far out into the *sansouïre* with their painful bites. The morning does not seem to be getting properly light. Perhaps the longed-for rain will come today after all.

Towards eleven o'clock it gets darker still. From the sea a black bank of thunderclouds is approaching. A strong wind has sprung up, rapidly driving the clouds landward. Dust swirls up and is swept in long trails across the steppe. A rustling runs through the tree-tops. Alarmed birds flee into the undergrowth.

The first flashes of lightning! The dark wall of elms and poplars behind our camp is steeped in sulphur-yellow light for several seconds. An elemental roar of thunder, crashing and echoing among the trees. The earth trembles under the weight of the pressure wave. Hurriedly we set our storm guys. It is now as dark as at night. A violent gust strikes—leaves and dry grass swirl through the air. The fly-sheets of our tents are billowing furiously. Once more a flash of lightning plunges the landscape into brilliant light. A crash of thunder follows. Heavy raindrops smack against the bone-hard ground, sporadic at first, then thicker and following each other more quickly. Within a second the rhythm of their striking has speeded up to a racing staccato, to a wild drum-roll.

The heavens open. Like a great flood the rain beats down on the parched earth. Lightning flash after lightning flash streaks from the black sky; ceaselessly comes the roll of thunder. The flood-gates are opened as though to compensate the land for the drought it has had to suffer.

Soon there are large puddles on the grassy steppe, in ditches and in dips of the ground. Only slowly is the water absorbed by the hard-baked soil; minute after minute the sheets of water on the ground are growing. Where a moment ago there was dusty leached-out steppe there is now a slippery, swampy morass.

Along the banks, in hollows of the ground, and along sloping tracks the water masses are in motion. Dirty yellow waves roll down between the salicornia, carrying with them the loose layer of dust and washing deep runnels into the ground. For the moment they are halted in the ditches which are filling rapidly. But the thunderstorm rages on,

lightning flashes, thunder cracks. And the rain still comes beating down. Ditches overflow and the loamy water spills over the *sansouïre*.

All round our camp the puddles have grown to alarming size. Our drainage ditches are full to the edge and are unable to cope with further rain. Under the canopy of our main tent everything is under water. Whether we like it or not we have to go out into the inferno to build emergency dikes. The whole area of our camp is now soaked soft. Whenever a spade is brought down vigorously into the ground fountains of mud spurt up. Soon we are soaked to the skin and spattered with earth and mud from head to toe.

Until late in the afternoon the thunderstorm continues over the Camargue. It seems unable to get beyond the arms of the Rhône in the north; it is flung back time and again and now moves to and fro between the sea and the two estuaries. Large tracts of the salicornia steppe and the saladella grassland are flooded. They lie under nearly half a foot of water. In the woodlands the gusts of wind shake thick veils of drops from the trees; small silvery torrents rush down the tree-trunks. One of our storage tents has half collapsed, a mighty gust having carried away the fly-sheet and ripped open a side wall. To attempt a repair while the storm is raging is quite out of the question. So, in the pouring rain, we evacuate all our food stores and finally release the guys. We cannot risk any further damage to the tent.

Just as suddenly and unexpectedly as the storm hit the landscape it also ends, towards the evening, after hours of savage raging. Abruptly the rain stops, the darkness lightens, and the last flashes die away in the distance. On the low horizon the cloud cover is rent open and, for the first time this day, the rays of the sun break through to strike the earth which has assuaged its thirst.

Autumn

Now the land is wearing the colourful garb of autumn. With more than generous palette the great painter has passed through steppes, marshes, and reed thickets, lavishly applying his brilliant colours. Red and yellow to the salicornia, dark green to mock privet and bulrushes, deep blue to ponds and lakes and to countless small sheets of water in the flooded *sansouïre*. Reed stems are garnished with gold, and the smooth trunks of poplars and the small, rounded leaves of the *buisson blanc,* the saltbush, with silver.

But among these brilliant colours there is also a multitude of delicate pastel hues. The sedge beds of the freshwater marshes are tinted pale yellow, and above the wilted brown of the lake shores tower the dry fruits of the bulrushes. The bare deciduous forests along the banks of the Rhône are thin bluish-violet lines in a hazy grey distance. In their undergrowth the deep vermilion of the brambles glows from among the wet rotting leaves. Olive-green and chestnut-brown, ruby-red and smoke-grey are the favourite colours with which autumn, that incomparable artist, enriches his brilliant canvas.

But although this autumnal symphony of colours clearly marks the turn of the seasons, it is by no means the most important of the changes in the rhythm of life in the delta. Autumn above all means a turning away from the exuberant joy of summer, from a deep-blue sky, from the heavy scent of plants, from bird song and the hum of insects. Autumn for the Camarguais also means an end of the exciting feasts in honour of the black bulls and the white horses, an end to the cheers of an enthusiastic crowd. It marks the beginning of a time of reflection, of preparation for the coming winter, the time of peaceful rest for man and beast.

Only the change from summer to autumn marks such a dramatic caesura in the natural life of the Camargue. Spring comes gradually. Summer betrays itself by an increasingly unbearable heat, by a growing insect plague, and by the drying out of the marshes. Winter is heralded by the arrival of northerly ducks and divers among the lagoons and brackish lakes, by horses and bulls alike growing thick woolly coats, and by a thin crust of ice forming along the edges of ponds in the morning. But autumn—autumn arrives abruptly, unmistakably. After the long weeks of rain in October and early November, one day, after a stormy night when gales have raged over the wide open spaces of the delta and turned steppes and marshes into a vast watery desert, the sun will rise in the east and welcome the first autumn morning. Suddenly the pale sky seems higher, the plain wider, the lakes deeper than usual. The sea seems immense. A great tranquillity and silence has arrived. Not a single lizard now scurries over the rotten tree-trunks, not a single snake suns itself on the carpet of algae

in the quiet ditches. There is no whirring of cicadas and no rustling of dragonflies, no humming of beetles and no chirping of crickets.

Many, indeed most, of the striking species of birds of the Camargue summer have left the delta and moved to their winter quarters—the brilliant bee-eaters and rollers, purple and night herons, the graceful pratincoles, the charming stilts and avocets, turtle doves, hoopoes, and nightingales, swift warblers and the quicksilver penduline tits, the golden orioles and the cuckoos, the wheatears and the short-toed larks, the whiskered and the little terns. Inconspicuously they have all vanished from the scene and left a noticeable void.

In the early morning and the late evening white veils of haze lie over the seemingly dead steppe. The wind blows down the last colourful leaves from the trees. The large flocks of sheep again wander through the land. Well-nourished, the animals have returned from their summer grazing in the mountains. Now they are facing the meagre winter of the Camargue. As long as the weather permits the shepherd drive them out every morning to those stretches of grassland which are not yet flooded. His calls and the tinkling of the dogs' bells ring out over the wasteland. Restlessly the long-haired black sheepdogs run around the large flock, understanding and executing each order of the master. They are not beautiful or well-groomed dogs, no thoroughbreds with a long pedigree. Their origin is rarely known and even cynologists might find it difficult to determine their exact breed. But the shepherd cares little about that. To him obedience matters more than pure blood, reliability and affection more than appearance. The dogs form part of his life, and throughout many weeks and months they may be the only creatures with whom he maintains silent communication.

The nights have become damp and cool. The gnarled, bare branches of the tamarisks grope out from milky wisps of fog like spectres. Remote and cold, the stars stand in the sky; the magic of warm summer nights is nothing but a memory. The pale sickle of the moon steeps marshes and steppes in a mysterious twilight. Like phantoms the massive silhouettes of wandering bulls emerge from the mists. Soundlessly, as if floating, the dark shapes move past and are swallowed up in nothingness.

There is a great deal of activity during the autumn nights on the islands in the river and under the overgrown banks of the arms of the Rhône. The beavers, those most secret animals of the Camargue, are at work. Now more than at any other time of the year they are busy laying up adequate supplies of food near their lodges before the onset of the winter. Frequently they will leave the lodges, which are built in the river-banks with entrances beneath the water, while it is still twilight. Bubbles of air and rings in the water mark the spot where an animal will appear the next moment. Almost at once its head breaks surface. Two small button eyes glint out of shaggy fur; short, round ears are turned towards the bank, listening. For a while the beaver will let itself be carried downstream. Only the upper half of its head and a small strip of back can be seen. Presently it will turn and make for the bank. Cautiously it will climb on land. Having clambered up the short but steep bank, the animal crouches on its hind legs, once more makes sure there is no danger from any side, and then vanishes among the dark undergrowth.

Tree bark, leaves, and the soft shoots of willows and poplars make up the favourite diet of the beavers. To gain possession of these they will not shrink from covering even extensive distances on foot—though they prefer to cover them by water. Favourite 'transport routes' are the many canals and irrigation ditches leading from the Rhône into the adjacent farmland. On a bright night, with a little luck, one can see the animals paddling about or, especially in the autumn, floating suitably cut boughs and pieces of branches downstream. The felling of a tree and the cutting up of its branches are usually done during the same night. Trunks of bigger diameter are sometimes felled in two consecutive nights or at greater intervals. If the animals do not succeed in cutting the boughs and branches down to their proper size and moving them away in one single shift, then, provided the spot is quiet and undisturbed, they will come back again and again until all transportable material has been taken away safely. The nearer the trees stand to canals or irrigation ditches, and the less the beavers are forced to leave their native aquatic element, the better. The direction in which the felled tree will fall can sometimes be so arranged that the branches come to lie straight in the water. In this way the animals are saved the long overland haul and transportation is greatly speeded up. Not infrequently one of the canals used by the beavers for the transport of their house-building material carries too little water so that the load gets stuck somewhere. On those occasions the Rhône beavers, which otherwise hardly ever build

dams, remember their skill and with simply incredible speed pile up branches, driftwood, and sticks into dams at suitable points. Soon the water-level will rise in the canal, and within a few hours it will be deep enough to ensure a smooth 'shipment of goods'. By now the water has been dammed up high enough to make the canal overspill its banks and flood the fields. The next morning a farm worker will come to make his daily inspection of the irrigation ditches and will discover what has happened. And he will not be pleased—either over the dammed-up water or, even less, about the additional work this makes for him. Grumbling, he will start pulling sticks and branches out of the ditch and removing the obstacle, cursing the beavers all the time under his breath.

"Tous calus ces p...s de castors. On a jamais vu ça! Ah non, ça ne peut plus continuer comme ça; ils rongent les peupliers et bouchent toutes les roubines avec leurs foutus barrages. – Bon Dieu! – Et nos poissons? – Ils les mangent tous.

Et le patron qui dit: 'Il y en a plus beaucoup, il faut les protéger.' – Les protéger! – Ah, quelle bêtise! Je vais les détruire – oui – les détruire!"

But an hour later, over a belated breakfast, with the obstacle removed and the water-level in the canal back to normal, the man will be laughing again. With a shake of his head he will recount the beavers' nocturnal misdeeds, adding:

"Vous savez, ce sont des bêtes très intelligentes, ...parfois plus intelligentes que les gens! Remarquez, elles font des barrages pour mieux transporter leur nourriture dans les roubines! Ah, ça on peut le dire que ces castors en abattent du travail en une nuit. – Et puis bien sûr, ...ils mangent tous nos poissons... Mais enfin 'peuchère' on est habitué à les voir, et puis... Ah! on les aime bien quand même."

When it is pointed out to him that the beavers are not interested in fish but confine themselves to a purely vegetarian diet, reconciliation is complete. How long it will last will depend solely on the beavers and how much consideration they will show for the harassed farmworker. Thus autumn passes. The days are getting shorter and the still nights longer and colder. Gradually the brilliant display gives way to more sombre and muted colours. The sky is an overcast bluish-grey, a pale sun shines through the tears in the clouds. Above the harvested rice-fields the wind plays with the lapwings, tossing them through the air like white rags. The jackdaws perch in the tall poplars, with ruffled feathers and apathetic expressions. From the tamarisk groves come flights of thrushes. Flocks of finches arrive; buntings flit through the bare branches singly or in small groups. The first formations of northern duck have settled on the open ponds. Grey is also the colour of the vast beach and, beyond it, the sea. With crests of spume the surf crashes against the shore fortifications. The waves pile up high and burst in the wind. Foam tears off and mountains of white bubbles cover the path on the dike. Herring gulls sit on the massive stone blocks of the breakwaters. Others float over the water on grey-and-white wings—up and down, this way and that, departing and returning ceaselessly. Their cries are swallowed up by the rough sea whose thunder can be heard a long way off in the dunes and in the hinterland.

Lonely the *sansouïre* lies spread out behind the dike. A dismal sight of depressing vastness. Water and salicornia, bright patches ruffled by the wind, dotted with dark brown skeletal shrubs as far as the eye can see—full of variety and yet always the same in the monotony of its severe pattern. Only rarely does one now encounter another human being—just possibly a *gardian* roving through the area looking for lost cattle, or the lighthouse keeper, or a fisherman on the beach. Of the visitors, a colourful flood of whom had swamped the near-by villages during the summer months, not one has remained, and even those natives who are not actually compelled to cross this treacherous solitude with its bottomless mud holes full of rotting morass prefer to sit at home and warm themselves by the open fire. The crackle of dry vines on the fire is a far pleasanter sound than the howling of the gale across the open plain. Marshes and lagoons, steppes and reed thickets, are now the unchallenged possession of birds and beasts. Soon the winter will invade the plain of En-Fore. The frost will hang out delicate gossamer threads between the twigs, and the water among the salicornia will freeze. Never-ending flocks of duck will wing their way under the evening sky, and an icy wind will carry the barking of the foxes through the long December nights.

Symphony of a Winter Day

The date is December 27th. An icy wind is lashing the plain with short, violent gusts. It is eight in the morning and bitterly cold. Only a few days ago there had been almost summer temperatures about midday, and the natives were beginning to ask themselves whether winter for once would stay away altogether. The careful observer, however, would not miss the rather anxious expressions on their faces. For the longer the cold weather failed to arrive, the worse it would be when it came.

But then, abruptly overnight, frost invaded the land. The thermometer took a mighty plunge—the mercury dropped and dropped and dropped. Only when it had reached —9°C (16° F) did it come to a halt.

That was at the beginning of the week. Since then the thermometer had never climbed by more than one or two points. Soon the water in the steppe, between the dry salicornia, was frozen solid. Along the edges of ponds glittering ice collars began to grow, reaching farther out into the open water each day. The fine spray whipped up by the wind from the *étangs* against the dikes and far into the land crystallized instantly into cold, glassy jewels.

Only slowly and hesitantly is the twilight receding from the land. The sky is overcast. A pale, yellow-red glow on the distant, indistinct horizon merely serves to make the monotony and infinite vastness of the wintry Camargue seem more boundless than ever. In the reed thickets the stiff northerly wind is playing with the dry stems. Ice cracks under the soles of our boots. Our breath turns into white puffs in front of our faces. From overhead comes the ring of invisible flights of duck.

Unless a man loves solitude he had better not visit the Rhône delta in winter. The flooded steppes and the swampy marshes are now more forbidding and remote than at any other time of the year. Paths and tracks are sodden after long rainfall and impassable; deep ditches and mud holes can often be spotted at only the very last moment. Where only yesterday the salt-sodden ground showed the tracks of bulls and horses, a foot of water may lie today—merely because a sudden veering of the wind has swept vast masses of water from the lagoons into the *sansouïres*. Once more nature has set clear bounds to human comfort. If, in spite of all this, a man is still attracted by this quiet and gloomy wilderness, then he must make his way on foot or on horseback. For hours on end he may well ride across the waste land without meeting another human being. Only a handful of people now have any business out there in the wilderness between the dike and the woodlands of the Rièges. Towards ten o'clock a bright spot appeared among the low cloud and unexpectedly the sun broke through. It steeped the land in brilliant light, but it gave no warmth. The gusty wind continued to sweep across the plain, stinging our faces in spite of a turned-down hat and a turned-up collar, jerking the tears from our eyes. It was difficult to make any headway; time and again one's boots broke through the new ice and stuck in the rotting mud hidden underneath.

On those parts of the freshwater ponds which were free of ice thousands of duck and coots were crowded together. They showed as dark bands on the greyish-blue waves. From time to time the birds rose into the air with a thunderous roar. Sometimes a hunting marsh harrier will make them fly up, at other times they take wing for no obvious reason. Squadron after squadron of birds takes off from the water, gaining height with a hasty beating of wings, and uniting over the marshes into a huge cloud of birds darkening the sun. Eight, nine, ten, or twelve thousand birds will fly up, climb, and dip in well-drilled formation, soaring up skywards one moment and diving steeply right down to the water the next. The air is filled with a vast roar as, after repeated passes over the lake, the birds bank sharply and touch down. Just then a small force of shovellers was approaching across the narrow tongue of land. The drakes' bright plumage glowed magnificently in the sun. Already the birds were gliding down with outspread wings when suddenly they spotted a red fox unashamedly trotting across the open ice with a moorhen in its jaws. Quacking, the small flock climbed again and wheeled away landwards. At the same moment a slim grey shape detached itself from the topmost crossbar of the steel high-voltage pylon—a peregrine. With swift wing-beats it appeared above the duck, which were scattering in alarm, and with a sudden thrust, so sudden that its swish was audible, it pounced and slammed its talons into the back of the last drake. There was a dull thud and a flurry of feathers. In a steep arc the bird came down with its prey and with it dropped into the salicornia. The short drama on the edge of the marsh had caused one more alarm among the many thousands of duck there—the whole pond was in turmoil. Even the cormorants, which had been sitting in the lee of the

big island with wings open to let their wet plumage dry, had flown up with the rest. Like black crosses they were now describing wide circles in the sky while below them over ten thousand teals and several hundred shovellers and gadwalls were performing twists and turns. But the alarm would not be of long duration. Soon the birds would calm down again and settle on the water off the ice.

The sunshine was equally shortlived. An hour later another thick cloudbank moved over the milky disc of the sun, and steppes and marshes were once more plunged in a dull grey. The force of the wind continued to increase; its howling had long drowned any other sound. The biting cold was increasingly cutting through one's clothes and getting a hold on one's body. A drop of hot coffee now would be exceedingly welcome. Along the dry and ice-free edges of the path large numbers of earth-coloured skylarks and crested larks were scurrying about. The number of these birds rose dramatically at the onset of the cold weather—a sure sign that there had been a big influx from northerly areas. Robins, yellowhammers, chaffinches, linnets, and a few other species of songbird were also far more numerous than two or three weeks previously. Continuous heavy frost had driven them from their customary winter quarters down the Rhône valley to the Mediterranean coast. Here they would stay for a while, until warmer weather allowed them to return or colder weather still compelled them to seek out even more southerly regions. Immediately after the abrupt drop in temperature an exodus of various species of birds began also from the Camargue. Thus, among others, many of the flamingos which stayed here in the late autumn had now disappeared from the salt lakes, and several thousand duck had moved on to marshlands in Italy or southern Spain. If the frost continued a much more marked exodus of native and foreign birds must be expected. On the other hand, new visitors, some of them rare, would arrive from the far north to take their place. Soon also winter would claim its first victims. A few more days of cold and ice, and the numbers of birds would begin to thin out rapidly. The first victims would be the weak, the sick, and the old. Later, if the frost was particularly severe, many birds at present still healthy and strong would follow suit. This was what happened two years ago when three severe cold spells caused the death of vast numbers of flamingos and of hundreds and thousands of coots, water rails, and many small birds, and when other animals died after being weakened by hunger and cold. It was shocking to watch the rose-coloured firebirds standing in the lagoons half-frozen, incapable of flight because of their iced-up feathers, so apathetic that they let themselves be seized by humans. Would this winter see a similar tragedy?

In the early afternoon the temperature rose. The wind dropped a little but it still had sufficient force to raise high waves on the *étangs,* drive them against the border ice, and force reeds and dry bulrushes down on to the matt green ice cover. Dark clouds obscured the sky and produced an atmosphere of gloomy dusk. Across the wide plain the gale roared and howled. There was no other sound. Only occasionally did the high-pitched neighing of horses or the lowing of cattle come across the ice-covered ponds as sounds tattered by the wind. A spotted eagle had been sitting on the broken trunk of a white poplar, snapped by the mistral, for the past two hours, its head drawn in. Throughout that time it had hardly moved, shaken its plumage, or shifted its weight from one leg to the other—a motionless grey shape against a grey background in a monotonous grey hazy landscape.

Towards nightfall it began to snow. The swirling flakes were not entirely unexpected because the feel of snow had been in the air throughout the day. One could almost smell it. Nevertheless, a sudden snowfall is a strange experience. Heat and drought, thunderstorms and howling mistral, weeks of rain, and even occasional ice during a rainy winter—all these are part of the familiar picture of the seasons in the Camargue. But snow is a rare occurrence and experienced by no means every winter.

Thicker and ever more impenetrable the white veil comes down over the land; already visibility is down to a mere twenty metres. Furiously the wind lashes the falling snow. It drives it along almost horizontally, it blows it under the bare black salicornia and mock privet, it sweeps it into ditches and furrows. Against even the slightest unevenness in the ground the stiff north-westerly whips the wildly swirling snowflakes. Soon most of the hollows have been evened out by a smooth snow cover, and knee-deep drifts have been piled up wherever major obstacles obstructed the driving snow. The *sansouïre* with its patches of glasswort has become a vast relief in black and white, with wild sows crossing the open steppe from their reed thickets, like long lines of massive earth dumpers.

For the next few hours the blizzard continues with undiminished violence. Night has long since fallen—a long, lonely winter night. In a few days the year will end. No-one knows yet what the remaining one hundred hours will bring. More snow? More ice? Or a rise in temperature and a thaw with more rain?

Now, just before midnight, the snow is still falling. But the gale has abated and only an occasional weak gust now disturbs the flakes as noiselessly and evenly they settle on the ground. Marshes and steppes, ponds and lakes, shore and dunes, have all become one. They are all sleeping. And perhaps, under their white blanket, they are dreaming of those distant spring days, flooded with light and warmth, when new life will pulsate all around—provided man sees to it that this life can continue.

92 *Saturnia pyri,* a large nocturnal moth very similar to the Emperor moth. Pairing: the male in the foreground, the more heavily built female behind

93 Enlarged picture of the eye spot on the forewing of *Saturnia pyri*

94 Bee orchid *(Ophris apifera)* ▷

95 Cicada *(Cicadetta montana)* ▷▷

96 The Lesser Rhône a few miles above its estuary ▷▷▷

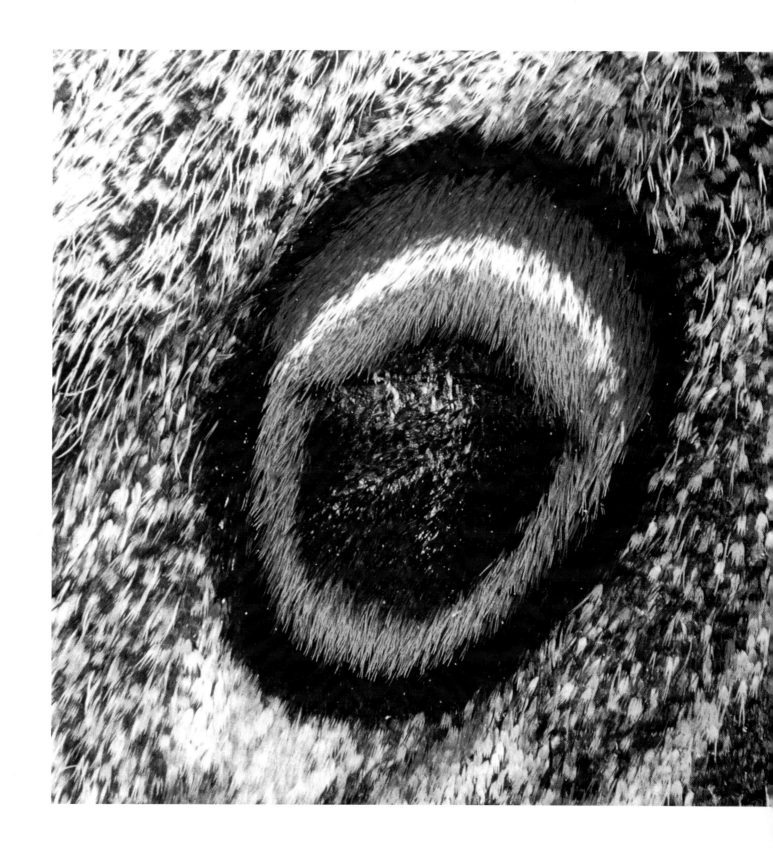

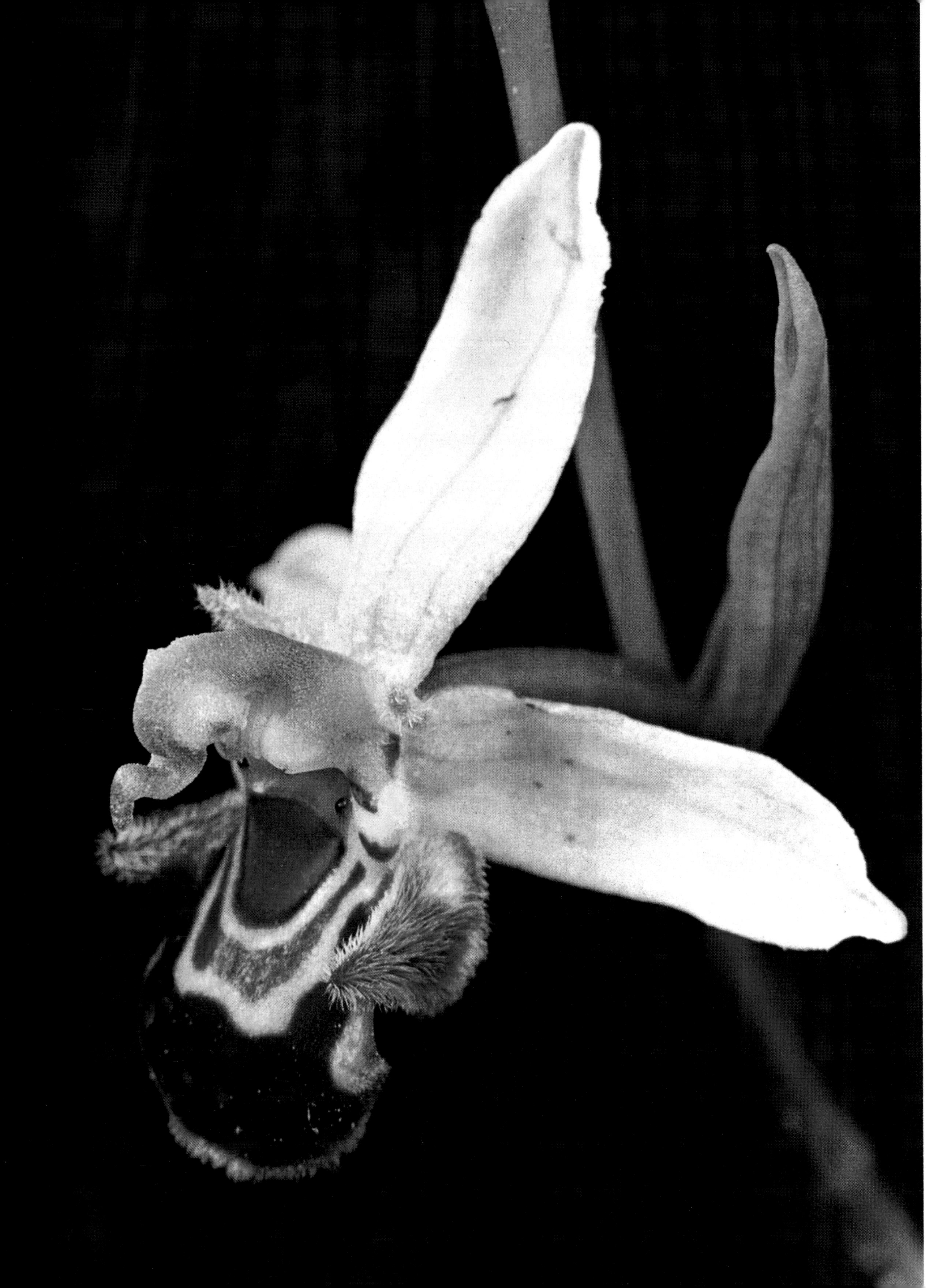

94 9

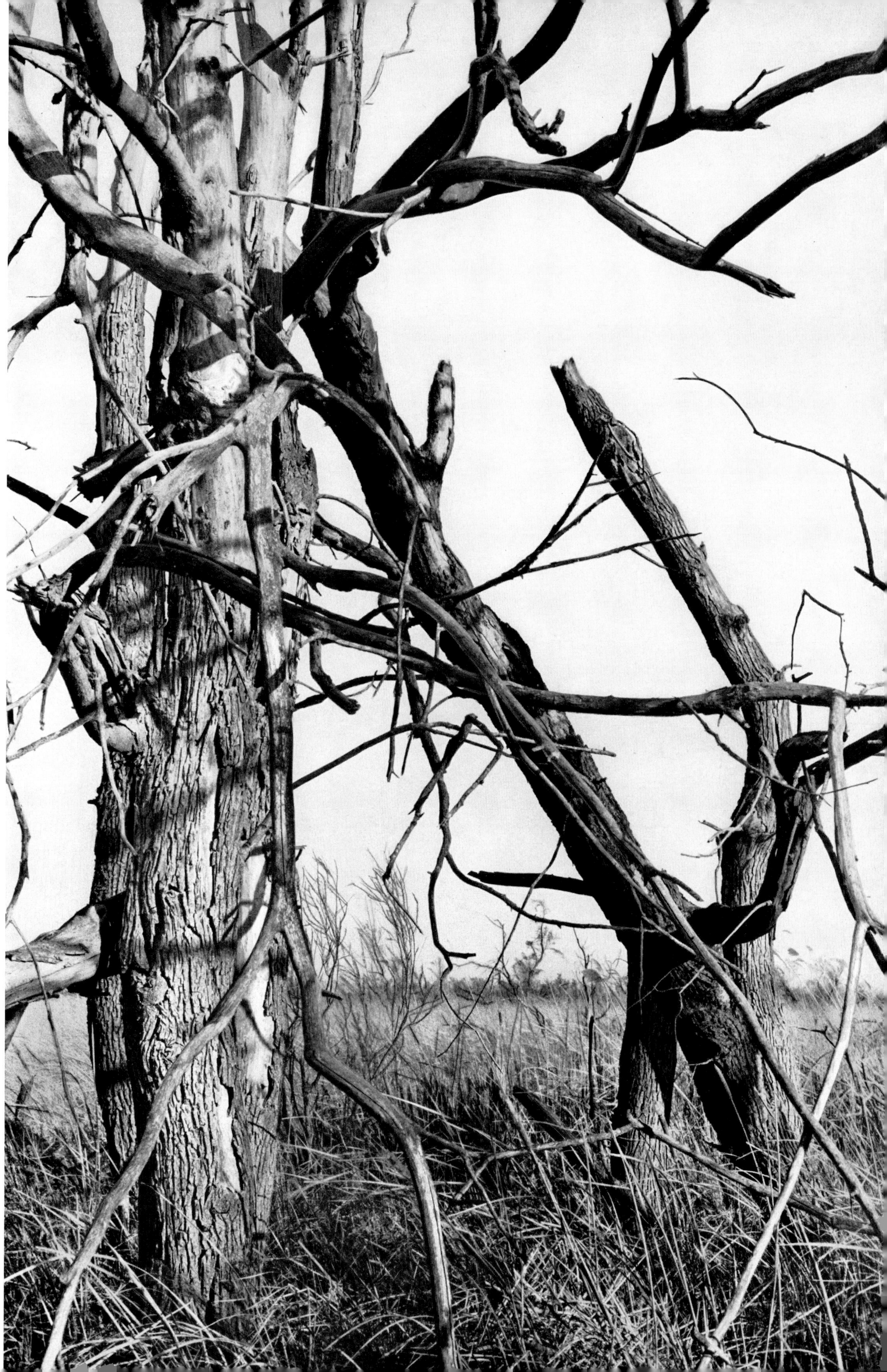

101 Beaver *(Castor fiber)*, the secret inhabitant of the overgrown banks of the Rhône

102 Hoopoe *(Upupa epops)* ▷

103 Scops owl *(Otus scops)* ▷▷

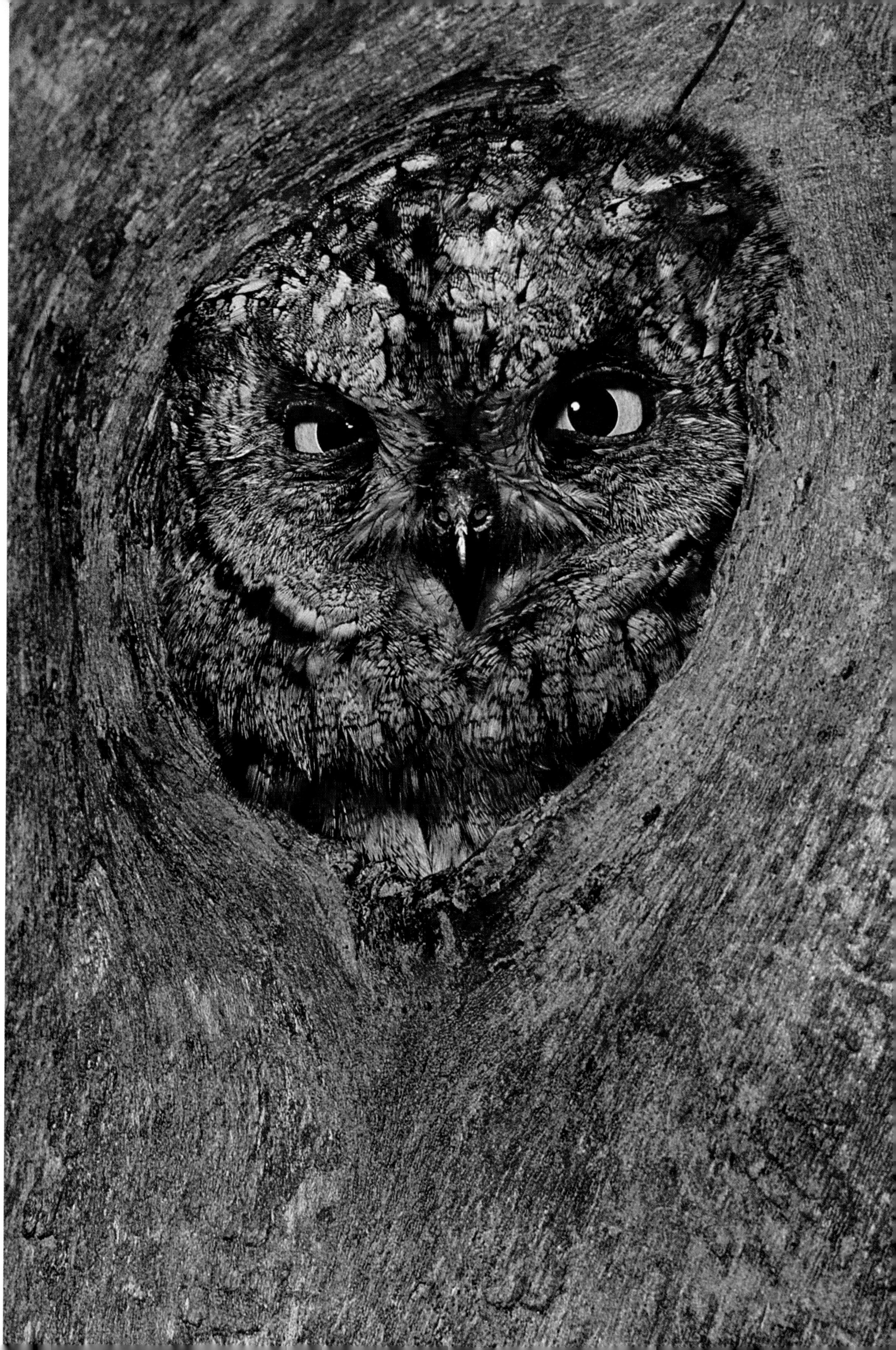

Notes on the Plates

1 The Mediterranean forms the geographical boundary of the Rhône delta in the south. But this boundary is not rigid. For thousands of years its course has been determined and changed by the ceaseless struggle between river and sea. Each year the Rhône deposits tens of millions of cubic feet of clay, sand, and detritus off the estuaries of its two arms, and there pushes the coastline further to the south. But at other points the waters of the sea eat deeper into the accretions of the river and compel man to fortify the shore. Thus the two primeval rival forces continue their struggle for the 'island' of the Camargue to this day.

2 Strong winds cause drifting of sand on the beach. The dry sand is swept across the level ground in white waves or long wisps and only settles down in front of or behind small obstacles. Clumps of grass or jetsam will arrest it and will gradually produce small sandhills. The bigger the obstacle in the way of the drifting sand, the more material is deposited and the higher the dune grows as more sand is delivered. But anything the wind has built up the wind can carry away to set up in another place. Only if vegetation succeeds in establishing itself in good time, in fixing the dune and growing with it, can a shifting dune be arrested and progressively anchored by the plants' roots.
The dunes between Fos-sur-Mer and Grau-du-Roi reach a height of 7 to 9 metres (25 to 35 feet). This makes them the most important dune formations in the western Mediterranean zone.

3 The dung beetles, mostly medium-sized black beetles, like hot, sunny patches of loose soil. Their food consists exclusively of dung of animal or human origin. For that reason they are often encountered on the beach, on sandy pastures, or along caravan routes. Fresh dung is spotted by the beetles at considerable distance and approached with a buzzing flight. They can consume astonishing quantities of food within a short time. As the 'dinner-party' increases in numbers with the arrival of other beetles, one or another soon starts to separate a piece of dung from the mass. This is done with the aid of the beetle's serrated, rake-like head-plate and its equally serrated forelegs. By means of kneading, pressing, and rolling with its long hind legs

the beetle shapes the severed piece of dung into a ball or pellet of sometimes considerable size. This pellet, which may be several times the size of its owner, is then rolled by the beetle with its hind legs, in a kind of 'hand-stand', to a suitable spot where the ground is soft. If the beetle succeeds in getting its pellets there without being challenged by other beetles, it digs a chamber for itself and the dung pellet, where it can continue its meal safely and undisturbed. Occasionally the buried pellet represents a store, protected from desiccation by the sun.
For the production of a 'breeding pellet', produced by the female without aid from the male and generally also buried by the female, the standards required of the material are somewhat higher. For this purpose only entirely fresh and juicy dung is used. The chamber dug is deeper than a storage chamber, and at its end contains an enlarged breeding chamber. There the pellet is finally deposited and worked into a regular pear-shape. At the upper end of this shape, at the narrow end of the 'pear', the female then makes a small hollow and into this places a fertilized egg; she then covers the chamber with loose dung. The chamber is linked to the outside by a tunnel loosely filled with material, but allowing for the passage of air to the breeding pellet. After hatching, the larva, which resembles a small caterpillar, feeds on the dung of the breeding pellet and develops within it. After repeated moulting it pupates and makes its way to the surface as a fully developed beetle.

4 The Sandwich tern *(Sterna sandvicensis)* is one of those large terns which are only rarely found over dry land. Its realms are the coast and the open sea. A bird of outstanding flying skill, it is distinguished by long, narrow wings, a short, forked tail, and a slender black bill with a yellow tip. Its elongated feathers at the back of its crown, black both in the summer and winter plumage, are erected when excited and lend the bird a shaggy appearance. Its voice is noisier than that of most terns.
The Sandwich tern is relatively not very numerous in the Camargue, but an increase in the numbers of breeding pairs has been observed over the past few years. On their winter journey the Sandwich terns cover considerable distances. Some of them fly as far as the southern tip of Africa.

5 Along the whole region of the Little and Great Camargue, from Grau-du-Roi west of the Lesser Rhône to Fos-sur-Mer, a long, flat, sandy beach extends over some 100 kilometres (60 miles). It is broken only by the two estuaries of the river, the small town of Les Saintes-Maries-de-la-Mer, and by a few lagoons linked to the sea—former estuary arms of the Rhône. Its width varies considerably and in some places amounts to several hundred metres before the belt of dunes behind is reached. When the sea is calm one can distinguish between a moist zone with only slight deposits of light flotsam and a zone of dry sand littered with branches, roots, and heavy tree-trunks deposited there by stormy seas.

6 The strong, firm stems of *Erianthus ravennae,* a reed-like grass, reach a height of some two metres, together with their white silky panicles which are 30 to 50 centimetres (12 to 20 inches) long. The very long leaves of this hardy plant, from 0·6 to 1·5 centimetres (0·2 to 0·6 inches) wide, stand in thick clusters around a creeping rootstock. It grows on sandy river-banks and along the coasts of the entire Mediterranean region. It flowers from August until October.

7 *Pancratium maritimum,* in appearance much like a lily and a narcissus, flowers on the dunes from July to September. The plant grows from a bulb and is native to the whole Mediterranean area. Its numerous grey-green leaves, broadening upwards, grow from ground-level. The strong stem, up to 40 centimetres (16 inches) tall, carries an umbel of three to twelve brilliant white trumpet-shaped flowers, each 10 to 15 centimetres (4 to 6 inches) long. The narrow outer petals form a twelve-pointed funnel-shaped secondary whorl at their base. In spite of the dearth of nutritive substances in the insoluble quartz sands, these dune plants thrive exceedingly well since the sand contains not only the fragments of the chalk shells of marine animals but also a great many minerals.

8 Picturesque jetsam. How did it get to the hot coastal sands of the Midi? Where was the seed planted from which it sprang, where did its fruits ripen? And who tore it from the ground? The wind? The water? Or Man himself? And how long was it tossed by the waves before the sea spewed it out on this deserted beach? And will the waves snatch it up again soon to carry it to even more distant shores?

9 The species of elecampane in the picture *(Inula crithmoides)* is common throughout the coastal regions of the Mediterranean and Western Europe, where it thrives particularly on saline soil. Its small flowers stand singly on the short branches of a stocky, leaf-bearing stem. The leaves are succulent, smooth, glossy, and club-shaped. It flowers from August until October.

10 Towards the end of the last century the peasants began to reclaim the formerly fertile land of the Camargue which had meanwhile been lost through water, wind, and salination. That was when the enclosing sea dike was built from the estuary of the Lesser to the Greater Rhône. Only a few controllable sluice-gates now allow the sea-water to pass into the lagoons.
In terms of landscape geography, the dike cuts across the brackish lagoons and low-lying steppe areas of the lower Camargue in their southernmost part and separates them from the coastal strip. In some places this boundary runs immediately behind the flat beach or the dunes, while elsewhere it may run several hundred metres away from the coastline across the *sansouïre.*

11 The low-lying *sansouïre* covers all parts of the lower Camargue as well as the areas east of the Greater and west of the Lesser Rhône. In the north it extends beyond the shores of the Etang de Vaccarès. Between Grau-du-Roi and Fos-sur-Mer it covers an area of about 500 square kilometres (200 square miles). The average altitude of this zone is only a few centimetres above sea-level and, especially in its southern part, where it forms the immediate hinterland of beach and dunes, it is broken up by a large number of seasonal and permanent brackish lakes. The soil is rich in salt and supports only a specific saline flora.

12 Among the great variety of webs built by spiders the orb-webs constructed with frame, spokes, and central hub are the most highly developed. The best-known representatives of orb-web spiders in Central Europe are the garden

spider *(Aranea diademata)* and the yellow, black, and white banded *Argiope bruennichii.* A further species found in the Mediterranean area is *Argiope lobata.* This is related to the garden spider but differs from it considerably in shape and colouring of body. Its large, broad abdomen, as the Latin name suggests, is lobed— *i.e.,* it bears massive lateral bosses. The black, grey, and white upperside is deeply grooved. The basic colour of the underside is a light greyish-brown overlaid with a dark mosaic pattern.

This spider, so long as it is undisturbed, always sits at the hub at the centre of its web. Unlike the garden spider it does not build a hiding-place outside the web with a signalling thread leading to its centre. Since it lives on large insects, such as beetles, locusts, dragonflies, mantises, etc., the web is built very robustly but with a not particularly fine mesh. Its suspension is stretched over a big distance and frequently uses a horizontal main cable of over a metre in length. The plane of the web is always inclined to the ground at about seventy degrees. The spider hangs and runs exclusively along the downward-facing side of the web. In this way its own weight pulls it away from the net and, moreover, enables it, in the event of danger, to let itself drop rapidly from the web.

Argiope lobata, just like *Argiope bruennichii,* reacts to vibration. When its prey has been caught in the web the spider establishes its exact position by repeated tugging of several of the spokes with its legs. Invariably the prey is first enveloped in threads before the paralysing or killing bite is applied at a soft spot on its body. The prey is then covered with the spider's digestive saliva and the resultant pulp is consumed *in situ* unless the prey is to be stored away. Strongly chitinous parts, such as the wings of beetles and dragonflies, are not digested but are detached from the prey.

13 Once the sheets of water produced by heavy precipitation in autumn and winter have disappeared through evaporation, the muddy soil is soon dried out by sun and wind. As a result of capillary action the salt rises from the shallow water table to the surface and there crystallizes. Fine hair cracks form on the surface, widen as the soil dries out more, and eventually produce a bizarre pattern of deep fissures.

14 The Kentish plover *(Charadrius alexandrinus),* which is native on many coasts of Europe, is found also on the sandy beach of the Rhône delta. Together with the black, white, and red oystercatcher *(Haematopus ostralegus),* which, however, is much bigger, it is the only bird whose nest can be found in the sand in the immediate vicinity of the sea. On the other hand, the bird is also found far into the centre of the delta, wherever there are dry, sandy tracks or sparsely grown salicornia steppe with bare patches of ground. The Kentish plover sometimes chooses rather strange spots for its nest—which is nothing more than a hollow made in the sand or the loose gravel—such as the dried cowpats of the Camargue cattle or the central strip of dike roads and tracks. The fact that, in the latter case, motor-cars repeatedly run over the nest during the daytime does not seem to worry the bird.

The Kentish plover differs from the other two small plovers—the little ringed plover *(Charadrius dubius)* and the ringed plover *(Charadrius hiaticula)*—by the absence of the complete black band on the breast, the blackish legs, and the black bill. All plovers are essentially birds which use their eyes in hunting for insects. The birds can be seen running around hurriedly, suddenly pulling up, staring fixedly at a certain point, and pouncing at the next moment to snatch their prey.

15, 16 Typical of the low-lying *sansouïre* is its mosaic pattern of glasswort *(Arthrocnemum glaucum = Salicornia macrostachya).* This forms low, irregular, sometimes circular, cushions of vegetation with extensive bare patches of ground between the individual clumps. From late autumn until spring the major part of the salicornia steppe is flooded. In the very low-lying parts the water covers the plants completely, whereas in the slightly higher marginal zones they can be seen showing above the surface. The fauna of the low-lying *sansouïre* is poor in species and mainly confined to a number of invertebrates.

17 The shape and movement of the avocet *(Recurvirostra avosetta)* reflect a degree of harmony rare among animals. This is equally true of its movement on land, in the water, and in the air. Its contrasting black-and-white plumage, its long lead-blue legs, and its slender,

upcurved bill are in themselves fascinating features. But its graceful gait over a shellbank or its run in front of an approaching wave reveal the full elegance of this bird. Its pointed, upcurved beak prevents the bird from grubbing for food in the mud or on hard ground. It catches its prey in the shallow water. For this purpose it runs to and fro with its head down and picks up small shrimps off the surface of the water by a rapid 'side-sweep' of its bill. The avocet also feeds in deeper water, and occasionally even while swimming. On such occasions several birds sometimes form a kind of semicircle and chase their prey in front of them.

The avocets nest in colonies on sandbanks, flat islands, or exposed sheets of mud. Their loam-yellow eggs with black-brown or grey speckling—four as a rule—are laid on a bed of little twigs or in a flat hollow in the ground. The chicks show a markedly upcurved bill as soon as they hatch.

Over the past ten years the avocet population of the Rhône delta has been declining steadily. The number of breeding pairs dropped from 700 or 800 in 1956 to roughly 200 in 1966. This reduction is chiefly due to man-made changes in the birds' habitat and also to the strong increase in the herring gull population.

18 The herring gull *(Larus argentatus michahellis)*. Greed for food and a wish to deny food to other birds would appear to be the most marked characteristics of this large gull—apart, of course, from its great flying skill. The herring gull will eat anything—eggs, young birds, fish alive or dead, crustaceans, insects, carrion, and garbage of all kinds. It tries to seize the prey of other sea birds; frequently it attacks exhausted migrating birds and kills them by striking their heads with its bill. It cracks the armour of sea animals by dropping them from a great height. Anyone who has watched the brutality with which these birds of prey ravage a breeding colony of terns, avocets, smaller gulls, and flamingos, smashing nests, killing, and devouring newly hatched and half-grown chicks, will find it difficult to forget this macabre experience even when watching the magnificent display of the birds sailing through the air.

Equally varied as its food is the voice of the herring gull. Apart from a repeated strident "kyow" and its warning note of "gah-gah-gah", the bird also produces barking, mewing, groaning, and laughing notes.

Juvenile herring gulls are uniform brown with darker primaries and a darker tail. Second-year birds have a whitish rump but their tail is still black. Not until their third or fourth year do they adopt the colour of their parents and become sexually mature.

19 The black-headed gull *(Larus ridibundus)* at breeding time has a chocolate-brown head and a slender crimson bill and legs. In winter it lacks its dark cap, of which only two faint patches remain near the ears.

Its breeding ground covers the whole of Central Europe up to the Arctic circle, including the British Isles and parts of Iceland. Breeding colonies can be found both along the coast and inland. On the breeding islands in the Camargue the black-headed gull plays a dominant part. Colonies of 800 to 1300 pairs are nothing unusual. As a rule, the black-headed gulls are the first to occupy an island in spring and to start building their nests and laying their eggs. These nests, almost always hidden among the salicornia bushes at the highest point of the island, are close to one another and form solid nesting areas. Other bird species, such as terns, avocets, and redshanks, join them later and settle all round them. It seems that they benefit from the black-headed gulls' superior strength and aggressiveness in dealing with birds of prey or predatory animals. Rice paddies, flooded meadows, and freshly ploughed fields are the main hunting grounds of the black-headed gull. Its diet consists chiefly of insects and their larvae. Everybody must have seen a horse-drawn plough followed by a dense flock of screeching gulls.

20 The little tern *(Sterna albifrons)*. Less than 24 centimetres (10 inches) long and with a wing span of about 35 centimetres (14 inches), this is the most graceful of all terns. It is easily distinguished from other terns by its diminutive size, its black-tipped yellow bill, and its white forehead. On the breeding islands they like to occupy isolated spots some distance away from other noisier species. The average weight of the egg of a little tern is 10 grams (0·3 ounces), about one-quarter of the body weight of the hen bird (40 grams). The female, who spends most of her time sitting on her eggs, is fed

regularly with small fish by her mate. The little tern hunts by hovering and diving, chiefly over the sea, the lagoons, and pools of brackish water. The chicks, barely the size of a man's thumb, hatch after three weeks but grow very rapidly and are capable of flight at about sixteen days old. The bird's call is a rasping, rapidly repeated "kirri-kirri-kirri". With the exception of Scandinavia and Sicily, it inhabits all European coastal areas and frequently penetrates far inland.

21 Among the many inhabitants of the breeding islands one bird in particular attracts attention. Its call, unmistakable and difficult to imitate, can be heard long before the bird itself is seen. This is the gull-billed tern *(Gelochelidon nilotica)* whose rasping two- or three-syllable 'laugh' is quite distinct from any other bird call. In flight the powerful bird with its strong black bill and black cap looks like a small gull, but it can be distinguished by its slightly forked tail. When standing, the bird is distinguished by its tall, solid, black legs.

The gull-billed tern breeds in compact colonies in proximity to black-headed gulls, common terns, little terns, and sometimes avocets. Their courage and readiness to defend themselves are remarkable. If necessary they will attack even marsh harriers and enemies the size of herons. They lay an average of three eggs, mostly on a thin layer of dry salicornia twigs and blades of grass. Hatching takes twenty-two or twenty-three days.

The gull-billed tern's range of operations is astonishingly large. Its hunting grounds are usually scattered all over the delta, a long way from their nesting place, and sometimes extend beyond the two river arms. More commonly than by the sea or in the coastal areas, the bird is found in the freshwater zone of the upper Camargue, over rice paddies and dry steppe. Its diet differs markedly from that of all other terns. The gull-billed tern rarely dives for fish, but instead, while in flight, snatches its prey from the surface of the water or from the ground, or else catches it in the air. Its most common prey are beetles, locusts, and insects of all kinds, as well as crustaceans (Branchiopods) and frogs.

22 The slender-billed gull *(Larus genei)* is a rare bird in Western Europe although it breeds regularly (even if not every year) in the Camargue. Its proper home is the Black Sea coast, the swampy lowlands at the confluence of Tigris and Euphrates, and the regions around the Persian Gulf. It is also native to the Caspian Sea and the Aral Sea. Other western breeding grounds are the estuary of the Guadalquivir, Mauretania, and the southeastern coast of Tunisia.

The name slender-billed gull should not lead us to believe that the bird has a particularly slender or delicate bill. Compared with the black-headed gull *(Larus ridibundus),* for instance, in whose neighbourhood the bird usually nests in the Camargue and which it resembles greatly in its transitional and winter plumage, the slender-billed gull certainly has a somewhat narrower bill, but on the other hand a clearly longer and stronger one. What is typical is its narrow head and its long, slender nape.

Its breeding association with the black-headed gull does not, on the whole, seem to be to the advantage of the slender-billed gull. The former tend to regard the greatly outnumbered slender-billed gulls as intruders and attack them whenever possible. These violent attacks are directed both against the adult birds and against unprotected eggs and later the chicks. At any rate, this pattern of behaviour was observed in the Camargue on repeated occasions. It may be assumed that a considerable number of young birds of this rare species perish as a result.

23, 24 Black, white, and vermilion flames seem to shoot up whenever a flock of flamingos *(Phoenicopterus ruber)* flies up from the salt lakes into the deep-blue sky. It is for the sake of these grotesquely proportioned long-legged birds with their long, thin necks, their small heads, and their strangely shaped bills that countless ornithologists, bird enthusiasts, and naturalists visit the Rhône delta year after year. They are the great attraction, the sensation of the Camargue —its fabulous birds.

Just as the shape of the flamingos is strange, so their way of life and manner of propagation is precariously balanced. Only in the salt-pans and salt marshes, where only few animal species can thrive, do the flamingo find their specific plankton food. On the flat islands in this environment they build their potter's-wheel nests from earth, salt mud, and trampled-down salicornia shoots. A single egg is laid on each such mud column and hatching time is over a month. But the birds do not breed every year—far from it. They form their breeding colonies at entirely irregular intervals. During the past fifty years the flamingos in the Camargue have bred successfully only twenty-four times. On several occasions their eggs were totally or partially destroyed and heavy losses were suffered also among the young birds. If fifty survive out of a hundred this is regarded as a good breeding year. It takes the young birds six years to reach sexual maturity. The number of breeding pairs in climatically favourable years averages 4000 to 5000. The highest recorded figure is about 8000 pairs in 1960. About one-third of the total flamingo population winters in the Camargue. In very severe winters with prolonged cold periods this may result in considerable losses among the birds.

Nobody knows for certain why the flamingos—whose distribution extends from India to the Cape Verde Islands but which have lost no fewer than 120 or 130 of their traditional breeding grounds over the past 100 years—propagate so irregularly in the Rhône delta. Various factors which might have an effect, either on breeding itself or on the subsequent phase, can be identified—exceptional cold during the courting period and the normal start of breeding (March to May), rain, wind, herring gulls, and, increasingly in recent years, overflights of the delta by aircraft, in particular jets. Their noise is apt to throw the whole colony into a wild panic from which it takes a long time to settle down again. But which of these factors is decisive? Is it one definite factor—or are there several of them operating jointly? Or is the cause to be sought elsewhere? It must be hoped that those who are concerned with the study of this problem will succeed in preserving for these birds their two European breeding grounds, the one in the Rhône delta and the other in southern Spain, so that many more generations of humans may be thrilled by the magnificent spectacle of a formation of flamingos crossing the sky.

25, 26 In the south-east of the delta and in the Little Camargue the commercial recovery of sea salt is practised on a steadily increasing scale. The sea-water is admitted through a system of flood-gates into large dammed-in lagoons and from there pumped through various inter-mediary stages to the evaporation pans which are arranged on a strict geometrical pattern. From each stage to the next the salt concentration increases until total evaporation is achieved by sun and wind in the final stage. The entire process takes about a year. The intake lagoons and the first intermediary stages provide excellent feeding conditions for the flamingos *(Phoenicopterus ruber)*. The birds also establish their breeding colonies on the salicornia islands situated in the intake lagoons.

27 The landscape of the lower Camargue is broken up by a large number of communicating saltwater and brackish lagoons. Their shores are populated, during the spring and autumn migration periods, by large numbers of wading birds. In the summer thousands of breeding terns, gulls, and avocets inhabit the enclosed islands, while numerous and often very large flocks of duck winter in the lagoon area. The seeds and tender shoots of a pond weed widespread in these waters, *Ruppia maritima,* are a favourite food of the duck. In very hot and dry summers the enclosed lagoons dry out partially or totally owing to the intensive evaporation produced by high temperatures and strong winds.

28, 29 South of the Etang de Vaccarès, at the centre of the low-lying *sansouïre,* rises the Bois des Rièges, a bushy forest chain consisting of eight parts. About 5 kilometres (3 miles) from the present beach, it represents the remains of an ancient dune formation. The patches of wood, in some places almost impenetrable thicket, are cut off from the mainland by lagoons and their communication ditches for most of the year. This has led to the evolution of a unique flora of great interest to the botanist. The rare juniper species *Juniperus phoenicea* here reaches a height of 6 metres (20 feet). Tall shrubs like the evergreen buckthorn *(Rhamnus alaternus),* the mock privet *(Phillyrea angustifolia),* and the mastic shrub *(Pistacia lentiscus)* form a closely knit barrage up which *Smilax aspera* climbs. Among magnificent flowering plants mention must be made of the asphodel *(Asphodelus cerasifer),* the rock-roses *(Cistus spp.),* the narcissus *(Narcissus tazetta),* and the narcissus-like lily *Pancratium maritimum.* The eight patches of woodland on the ancient dunes extend over a distance of some 7 kilometres (4 miles).

30 The rock-rose *(Cistus albidus)*. This bushy plant, anything from 40 to 100 centimetres (16 to 40 inches) tall, is found throughout the western Mediterranean region from Spain to Italy and from Morocco to Tunisia. Its short, elliptical, stemless leaves are thickly covered with hair on both surfaces. The crumpled pink flowers grow in small clusters at the upper ends of the branches. They have a diameter of 4 to 6 centimetres (1·6 to 2·4 inches). The fragrant plant blooms from April to June.

31 One of the most striking flowering plants of the Camargue is the milk thistle *(Silybum marianum)*. It stands 60 to 150 centimetres (24 to 60 inches) high and grows, often in large clumps, along paths or the banks of freshwater canals. It blooms from mid-May to early July, producing large purple flowers which undoubtedly belong to the most beautiful among the numerous kinds of thistles. The brilliant green leaves, variegated with white, carry strong yellow thorns. The plant has probably spread to southern Europe from the Middle East.

32 The asphodel *(Asphodelus cerasifer)*, a flower typical of the Mediterranean region and commonly used to adorn graves in southern Europe, grows on sandy soil. The white star shaped flowers with their rust-red veins give off a strong perfume. The asphodel, which reaches a height of about 150 centimetres (60 inches), flowers from March to May.
As soon as the seeds in their spherical berry-like capsules have matured the long stalks quickly wilt and collapse. The luscious green clusters of leaves, on the other hand, which grow from ground level, survive a good deal longer.

33 Large patches of yellow flag *(Iris pseudacorus)* are frequently found in marshes and along freshwater canals during May and June. From a thick creeping rootstock grow short flowerless stems and long flowering ones. The bluish-green sword-shaped leaves are alternate in one plane and end in long leaf sheaths which partially or totally envelop the stem.
From the upper leaf-axils on the long stems spring multiple-flowered stalks. The odourless flowers consist of three outer curved petals with a dark marking and three inner erect narrow ones, three stamens, three

petal-like stigmas, and an inferior ovary. The seeds in the three-segment capsule contain an air space under their envelope. This enables them to float on the water and to be carried by waves and current to new germinating locations.

34 The wild gladiolus *(Gladiolus communis)* is found throughout the European Mediterranean zone from Spain to Greece. This tuberous plant is found in fields and on arid, uncultivated land, both singly and in large communities. The robust stalk, 40 to 70 centimetres (16 to 28 inches) tall, carries a unilateral cluster of bright red to violet flowers about 4 or 5 centimetres (1·5 to 2·0 inches) in length. They are supported by narrow lanceolate cover leaves. Nearer the base three to five broader long leaves enclose the stem. The gladiolus flowers from April to June.

35 The lizards have preserved the original type of the reptile more accurately than any other family, both in appearance and in their whole character. They still represent the standard form of the reptile body without having developed in any one particular direction. On the contrary, they have developed their potentialities in so many different ways simultaneously that they may be regarded as the most highly developed group of reptiles. The most impressive and also the most colourful European lizard is the jewelled lacerta *(Lacerta lepida)*, native in the southern part of our continent—in the Iberian peninsula, in the south of France, and in Liguria. It reaches an average length of 50 centimetres (20 inches), but much larger individuals are often encountered. Its slender tail alone accounts for about two-thirds of its total length. The rest of the body is squat and very powerfully built. Like all lizards, this 'small dragon' loves heat and will sun itself for hours on end in suitable spots. To do this, it frequently climbs on to bushes and trees. If alarmed, the lizard vanishes under flat stones or in hollow trees with the speed of lightning. If, however, its retreat is cut off it will face its enemy menacingly. Its powerful jaws and strong teeth enable it to inflict hard and painful bites. If cornered, it will attack even large dogs.
For food the jewelled lacerta hunts its smaller relations, as well as insects, mice, and young snakes. Occasionally

it also eats soft fruit. The female lays six to ten eggs in a parchment-like shell in the wood-mould of hollow tree-roots. After about two months, hatched by the warmth of the soil, the young lizards emerge.

36 Pipits are brown-streaked terrestrial birds; they run briskly and have long hind claws. The tawny pipit *(Anthus campestris)* shown in the picture is much larger and lighter in colouring than its closest relations, the tree pipit *(Anthus trivialis)*, the meadow pipit *(Anthus pratensis)*, the water pipit *(Anthus spinoletta)*, etc. It never approaches its nest directly; this is invariably well concealed by plants and situated in depressions in the ground. Returning often from a great distance, it always runs along under cover, and disappears in a salicornia bush or some similar shelter only after making sure that there is no danger. When leaving its nest the parent bird also first runs a few yards on the ground before flying off.

37 The family of the warblers *(Sylviidae)* embraces a large number of very lively, small insectivorous birds. Some of these birds build their elaborate nests among reeds and sedges, others on the ground or low above it. The spectacled warbler *(Sylvia conspicillata)* is a typical representative of the western Mediterranean region and one of the most common birds of the salicornia steppe in the Camargue. The male has a grey head and nape, with the remaining upperparts more or less reddish-brown. Its white throat contrasts strongly with its dark cheeks; its breast and belly have a touch of pink. The female, though similar, has a less bright colouring.
The bird builds its small, not too solid nest in the cover of thick salicornia bushes, the tops of which also serve it as a favourite look-out post. During the twelve or thirteen days which it takes for the chicks to hatch, the male and female take turns in sitting on the three to six eggs in the nest. At the slightest disturbance they will appear among the salicornia plants and utter a grating warning call. The young grow up very quickly. They leave the nest twelve or thirteen days after hatching out.

38 The seasonal marshes are flooded only from autumn to spring. These isolated stretches of low-lying ground fill during the autumnal rainy period. Their area, as a rule, is slight. Their average depth is 30 to 50 centimetres (12 to 20 inches). By the end of May, at the latest, they dry out completely and remain dry throughout the intervening period until the autumn.
Many of these stagnant waters are inhabited by large numbers of microscopic creatures such as water fleas *(Cladocera)*, Copepods *(Copepoda)*, and Ostracods *(Ostracoda)*. *Turbellaria* and freshwater pulmonates *(Basommatophora)* are also very numerous.

39-42 The principal feature of the central part of the delta—*i.e.,* those areas which on an average are about a metre above sea-level—is an extensive dry steppe with various groups of vegetation. In the lower-lying parts of this zone, the ones which in winter are normally under water, the shrublike *Salicornia fruticosa* predominates; from 30 to 60 centimetres (1 to 2 feet) high, it belongs, like *Arthrocnemum glaucum,* to the *Ranunculaceae.* The bare patches of ground, compared with the low-lying *sansouïre,* are very much fewer here; the salt content of the soil is far lower. The boundaries between the two types of glasswort named above are blurred. Both of them, depending on salinity, also occur intermingled. In the higher-lying dry areas we find patches of saladella *(Statice limonium* and *Statice virgata)* and extensive areas of grassland. Tamarisks *(Tamarix gallica)* and elms *(Ulmus campestris)* indicate the proximity of water-holes, pools, and lakes with only very slight salt content, or the presence of freshwater canals.

The fauna is richer than in the low-lying *sansouïre.* Especially in the grass and saladella steppes, where the effect of the salt is still slight, both vertebrates and invertebrates are strongly represented.
Plates 39 to 42 show the salicornia landscape of the central and upper Camargue through the changing seasons. Plate 39 (May) shows the water still standing several centimetres dep between the salicornia, which is sending up new shoots. The tamarisk bushes already bear their small scale-shaped leaves. Plate 40 (July) conveys the impression of the steppe in summer. The relatively few bare patches are covered by a fine white crust of salt. The finest colours are seen in the *sansouïre* in the late autumn following the heavy rains of

October and November (Plate 42, taken at the end of November). Again the water stands between the tall clumps of salicornia and in the ditches. The tamarisks have dropped their leaves and are now bare. Snowfalls as in Plate 41 (January) are rare in the Rhône delta and do not occur every year. In normal winters the conditions shown in Plate 42 continue largely unchanged. Only the strong colours pale gradually and, on those occasions when the temperature drops, a thin sheet of ice forms on the surface of the water.

43 The Etang du Fournelet in the south-eastern Camargue, just like the Etang de Vaccarès, belongs to a system of communicating brackish lakes. Together they cover large parts of the central and lower delta. Their salt content varies between annual averages of 5 and 16 grams per litre. Their shallowness, together with strong winds and high temperatures during the summer months, favour rapid evaporation and may result in total or partial drying up of the lakes. When that happens a marked rise in the salt content (up to 40 grams per litre and more) can be observed, especially in the central areas of the lakes.

44 The bull has left its unmistakable mark on popular custom and tradition in the Camargue and in Languedoc, the region west of the Lesser Rhône. The passionate interest shown by the people in this animal and the deep-rooted tradition reflected in the breeding of these magnificent black creatures, in the thrilling local contests, and in story and legend almost border on mythology. The origin and descent of this semi-wild primitive race of cattle has not been established beyond doubt. While several scientists see them as the direct descendants of the aurochs which became extinct in the seventeenth century, others describe the Camargue cattle as a later evolutionary form of races originally imported from Asia Minor or North Africa. Others still have compared the bones of the present-day Camargue cattle with certain prehistoric finds and established a striking agreement of certain features. Most probably the Camargue cattle represent a mixture of various Mediterranean races which developed into their present form through adjustment to their habitat on the one hand and as a result of human intervention on the other.

The Camargue cattle are relatively small. The body is long rather than tall, the head is small with a pointed mouth. The lyre- or crescent-shaped curved horns point upwards. Sometimes they are slightly recurved at the points. Their coat is thick and shiny, especially on the neck and on the forward part of the trunk. The animals run lightly and fast, suggesting stags. They live in herds whose composition, at least in the deliberately bred ones, is determined by man. Only a few choice bulls are left with the cows. In groups consisting exclusively of male animals the composition may change from day to day. Old bulls occasionally roam singly, outside the herd.
The distance within which these cattle will allow humans to approach before they retreat is about 50 metres if on foot and 5 to 10 metres if on horseback. Only very rarely is a man or a horse attacked. If this happens it is mostly by old solitary bulls which have lost their social position in the herd. Captured animals, on the other hand, or animals prevented from escaping, no matter whether bulls or cows, instantly and invariably attack humans. This characteristic is exploited in the arena, in the Provençal bull-fight during which small tassels, the *cocarde* and *glands*, are snatched from the bull's forehead and horns.

45 The wild boar *(Sus scrofa)* is one of the most common of the larger mammals in the Rhône delta. Its tracks, both in the form of broken reeds and footmarks, can be seen everywhere. Although a nocturnal animal by nature, the boar is not infrequently encountered in daytime, sometimes in small groups on cultivated land or in the open salicornia steppe. By breaking into the rice crops the animals cause heavy damage—not so much through feeding as by crushing immature plants and churning up the soil. Their daytime hideouts are in thick clumps of tamarisks and mock privet, as well as in large beds of reeds and bulrushes in the coastal areas. The wild boar often raises a large progeny. Not infrequently a powerful sow will give birth to five to eight young in a year. Larger litters are occasionally observed, smaller ones only exceptionally. The farrowing period is from March to May. But even in the summer, and occasionally well into the autumn, young piglets, striped yellow and brown, can be encountered. The sow looks after her young alone. The hogs live on their own outside the mating period.

46 In 1953 virtually the whole rabbit population of the Camargue was wiped out by myxomatosis, and during the subsequent years only a few individuals were observed. More recently, however, their numbers seemed to be recovering and growing again. The rabbit *(Oryctolagus cuniculus)*, which, unlike the much larger long-eared hare *(Lepus europaeus)*, is a sociable animal, builds its widely ramified warrens in the sandy soil. A dead-ended tunnel is softly upholstered by the female with her own pulled-out belly hair to serve as a nursery for the young. During spring and summer several litters are born, ranging from four to twelve young. The young rabbits are naked and blind at birth, whereas the young of the hare have a coat and can see. The rabbit's mode of life is predominantly nocturnal. But in remote quiet areas, such as are found in many parts of the Rhône delta, the animals may also be seen outside their warrens during daytime. But their activity then is usually confined to sunning themselves in the warm sand. Towards nightfall the whole company gradually emerges from hedges and shrubs to move out to graze on open land. In the event of danger the wild rabbit drums on the ground with its hindlegs, producing a clearly audible tattoo. To this all other rabbits in the neighbourhood react with heightened vigilance or flight.

47 The Camargue horse is an outstandingly lithe and exceptionally sturdy mount. Although, compared with other types of horses, it is not particularly fast, this is more than offset by its great endurance. Without the Camargue horse cattle-breeding would be unthinkable in the vast hostile plain of the Rhône delta with its numerous treacherous swamps and patches of salt mud.

Manadiers (the cattle-breeders) and *gardians* (the cowherds) depend very largely on their horses for rounding up their herds and pursuing escaped animals. The true Camargue horse is of medium size and stocky build. The strong, sinewy neck carries a large, broad head with short ears and a long, shaggy mane. Its short shoulders and laterally flattened thorax lend the foreparts of the animal a somewhat square appearance. The legs are muscular but well-shaped, with broad hooves. The majority of the foals have a black woolly coat at birth, but rust-coloured or dun young animals are occa-

sionally encountered. By their fourth year the colour changes to a light grey, which gets progressively paler until the horse's coat shows the final white or off-white of the adult. In the winter the horses' hair is particularly long and thick.

Scientific investigation of the origin and history of the Camargue horse has not—any more than in the case of the Camargue cattle—produced any certain or generally accepted results. Indeed, the theories diverge a good deal. One of many versions, and one which has quite a few points in its favour or at least cannot be ruled out entirely, suggests that the Camargue horse corresponds to the *Equus caballus robustus* (Nehring), the Central Asian steppe horse, one of the original prehistoric types. Needless to say, in view of the mingling of blood over the centuries, there can be no question of these horses being unchanged pure descendants. Unfortunately, the Camargue horse today is very much at risk —not in terms of survival of the herds but of survival of the type. In recent decades, and particularly since the end of the Second World War, there has been a good deal of cross-breeding, and this may lead to the loss of some of the typical features of the Camargue race.

48 The pratincole *(Glareola pratincola)* is rightly regarded as one of the most elegant and accomplished flyers among European birds. On long, pointed wings these lively graceful birds speed through the air above the sparsely grown plains of the Rhône delta. Their glassy-clear monosyllabic call, once heard, is never confused with that of any other bird. Apart from the Hungarian Puszta, the Camargue is the only Central European breeding ground of the pratincole. Outside this area it is found in the steppes of southern Spain, in the southern Balkans, and throughout Africa and the Far East. The birds return from their equatorial winter quarters towards mid-April and in the early summer establish their small-sized colonies to hatch their eggs—usually three, or more rarely two or only one, per nest. The protective colouring of these eggs is superb. Their irregular brown-black mottling completely breaks up their outline. Within the first few hours of their life the young chicks develop their flight reactions. In response to a parental warning call they immediately leave their

nests and hide under the nearest salicornia plant. There they are fed and sheltered under the parent birds' wings. The pratincole hunts its prey—insects of all kinds—in flight or, in the manner of plovers, on the ground. At the end of August, or certainly not later than in early September, it once more leaves the Camargue for more southerly regions.

49 The stone curlew *(Burhinus oedicnemus)* is distinguished in many ways from all other waders. About 40 centimetres (16 inches) long, this large, rather ungainly bird with its thick, round head and brilliantly yellow eyes is fond of wide-open spaces with sparse vegetation. Previously widespread in Central Europe also, it is now, owing the progressive cultivation of its former breeding grounds, found in appreciable numbers only on the waste lands of the south and the south-east. The stone curlew is a typical running bird which, as soon as it catches sight of a human, runs off furtively with head low and body hunched. Sometimes it flattens itself with head and belly on the ground and thus remains motionless. Thanks to the superb protective colouring of its streaked pale-brown and white plumage it can then be spotted only with difficulty. The size of its eyes betrays the true crepuscular and nocturnal bird. During the day it usually hides quietly, to become active towards nightfall, when it goes hunting for insects, snails, worms, mice, and lizards. After sunset its wailing call rings out over the steppe—starting low and finishing on a high fluting tone. The two parent birds share the task of sitting on the eggs during the twenty-seven-day hatching period. The chicks—usually two of them—leave the nest within hours of hatching and are kept under the parents' wings for a further two weeks. As a rule there is a second brood.

50 Nesting cliff of a bee-eater colony *(Merops apiaster)*. This section, approximately 5 by 8 metres (16 by 25 feet), of a large loess cliff, about 35 metres (120 feet) long and 10 metres (30 feet) high on average, conveys an idea of the density with which these colourful birds dig their nesting holes in suitable spots. In such large colonies it is usual for other bird species to profit from the available nesting facilities, and in this particular case the cliff regularly contained, in addition to the bee-eaters, also rollers *(Coracias garrulus)*, hoopoes *(Upupa epops)*, jackdaws *(Corvus monedula)*, and kestrels *(Falco tinnunculus)*.

51 The bee-eater *(Merops apiaster)*, the jewel of the Camargue bird world, shows a truly tropical brilliance of colour. It is a skilful flyer which hunts its food— beetles, dragonflies, butterflies, bees, wasps, and other exclusively flying insects—in the air and shows markedly gregarious habits. As a rule the breeding colonies consist of ten, twenty, thirty, or more pairs which spend the first two or three weeks in driving their nesting tunnels into banks and cliffs; these horizontal tunnels or tubes are between 1 and 1·8 metres (3 to 5 feet) long and at their far end enlarged to form a breeding chamber. Occasionally these tubes are also dug in the flat ground, in which case they lead obliquely downwards. A nest proper is not built. The five or six pure white and very thin-skinned eggs lie on the loose earth of the breeding chamber. The chicks hatch after about twenty-two days. At four and a half weeks old they leave the nesting tube but at first return to it for the night. They differ from the adult birds by their considerably less brilliant colours, with green predominating, as well as their dark (instead of ruby-red) iris and the absence of the adult bird's two 'tail spikes'.

The captured prey is invariably beaten against some hard surface such as a branch or post, etc., and kneaded over in the bill before being devoured. In this way the stinging mechanism of insects, which might be dangerous to the birds, is eliminated, although there is no actual 'drawing of the sting'. Indigestible chitinous parts are spewed out again. The bee-eater is a summer bird in Europe. It is common throughout the Mediterranean area and the Balkans, as far as Hungary. Now and then an occasional individual will lose its way to north of the Alps. It winters in tropical and southern Africa.

52 The mantises, the most common of which in Southern Europe is the praying mantis *(Mantis religiosa)*, are among the strangest of insects because of their striking shape, their interesting manner of hunting, and their odd resting position. This resting position is responsible for the creature's name. With its elongated prothorax and triangular head held upwards, and its forelegs, which

are developed into prehensorial instruments, peacefully folded, it does indeed give the impression of a harmless creature at prayer. But appearances are deceptive. The creature is lying in wait for its live prey which it will seize by pouncing from this position and for which there will be no escape from the spiked leg-sheaths. All mantises—there are about 1800 species—are predators —i.e., they are exclusively carnivorous. Most of them have superb camouflage colouring. The female of the European praying mantis, up to 7·5 centimetres (3 inches) long and heavier, is incapable of flight in spite of its wings; the smaller males, on the other hand, are capable of flight even though as a rule they do not fly very far. Nevertheless, this ability sometimes saves them from being devoured by the female immediately after copulation. But they do not always make use of their skill and are already being nibbled by the 'weaker sex' during the mating act and subsequently devoured.

The 'normal' diet of the praying mantis include flies, dragonflies, butterflies, locusts, and other medium-sized insects. On encountering possibly dangerous animals it often adopts an impressive menacing position with upper body almost vertically raised, wings opened wide, and abdomen curved upwards. This may so surprise an opponent that he may give up his intention and escape or at least give the mantis an opportunity for counter-attack.

53 A close relation of the praying mantis *(Mantis religiosa)* is the slightly smaller *Empusa pennata*. Its grotesquely helmeted head and, in the male insect, exceptionally long, feathered antennae are reminiscent of the strikingly shaped and coloured mantises of the tropics. In the European Mediterranean region the species shown in the plate occurs from May to July. The young generation hatches in September and winters in the larval state.

54 *Acrida mediterranea,* a short-horned grasshopper, is one of the very widespread family of locusts which comprises many thousands of species, including the feared migratory locust which periodically appears in vast numbers in various regions. The species illustrated is found regularly though not too frequently in South-ern Europe during the hot summer months. Particularly striking are its elongated conical head with its lanceolate antennae, flattened at their base, and its enormously long and narrow hind legs used for jumping. The males of a great many species of locusts produce a clearly audible 'song'. This chirping sound is produced by a rough chitinous strip on the thigh being rubbed against reinforced nerve studs on the forewing. This causes them to vibrate and emit a strong note.

55 As a rule it is only by chance that a stick insect sitting on a plant is discovered. Owing to its body structure, colouring, and behaviour its mimicry is so perfect that it is almost impossible to tell the insect from its natural environment. Most species—the majority of which inhabit the tropical regions—have an improbably thin head, body, and legs and look so fragile that one would think the slightest breath of wind would damage them. For hours these grasshoppers sit motionless on a leaf or on a stem, and even when they move they do so in very slow motion. A few tropical species reach a body length of up to 30 centimetres (12 inches). The species common in Southern Europe are considerably smaller. The female of the species shown in the plate *(Clonopsis gallica)* measures from 6·2 to 7 centimetres (about 2·5 inches). The smaller male—as with numerous other species, is exceedingly rare. Propagation of these insects is almost always by parthenogenesis. The females lay their eggs without fertilization by the male; from these eggs only females are hatched. Only after some twenty or more generations are male insects suddenly encountered again. All stick grasshoppers are herbivorous.

56 The false mantid *(Mantispa styriaca),* which belongs to the neuropterous insects, superficially resembles a small praying mantis *(Mantis religiosa)*. Its anterior legs are similarly developed into prehensorial instruments capable of being folded up like a penknife. The different development of the joint between hip and thigh, on the other hand, enables the false mantid to perform far more powerful stretching, flexing, and swinging movements than the praying mantis. The occurrence of the term *mantis* in the insect's name merely reflects its resemblance to a mantis proper and must not be taken to suggest kinship. The anterior wings of the false mantid

are membranous and transparent, revealing clear veining, whereas those of the praying mantis are much more sturdily constructed and serve as wing-cases covering the membranous posterior wings.

The false mantid is normally native to tropical and subtropical regions, but is exceptionally found also further to the north. As is the case with other neuropterous insects, the eggs of the false mantid, which measures 2·5 to 3·5 centimetres (1 to 1·4 inches), sit on long, thin stalks and are deposited in large numbers on the leaves and stalks of various plants. The larvae hatch in autumn, and winter without taking any food. In spring they seek out egg-cocoon-carrying wolf spiders, make their way into the cocoons, and inside turn first into a second larval form and then into the pupa. The pupa spends a first stage inside the egg-case of the spider, and a shorter second and mobile phase outside it. The fully grown false mantid is less aggressive than the praying mantis and feeds on smaller animals.

57 The saladella grassland *(Statice limonium* and *Statice virgata)* succeeds the salicornia steppe *(Salicornietum fruticosae)* in the higher-lying, drier, and less salty areas. The vegetation cover here is thicker and more varied, and as a rule covers the ground entirely. Various grasses and flowering plants occupy a dominant position—*Poa bulbosa, Carex chaetophylla, Obione portulacoides, Bellis annua, Inula viscosa,* as well as the mentioned *Statice limonium* and *Statice virgata.* On the highest ground, unaffected by salt, the dark-green bushes of mock privet *(Phillyrea angustifolia)* frequently form extensive thickets. Tamarisks *(Tamarix gallica)* and elm *(Ulmus campestris)* thrive wherever artificial freshwater ditches provide moisture through appreciable periods of the year. The fauna is represented by a great number of invertebrates as well as by vertebrates.

58 The family of shield bugs comprises a large number of species differing from each other greatly in colour, shape, and mode of life. Most of them are small—0·5 to 1·5 centimetres (0·2 to 0·6 inches). A few species, however, especially those in tropical regions, are considerably larger. An almost unlimited range of variations is encountered from plain brown or dull green ones

through strikingly brightly coloured and ornate ones to species with a metallic sheen. Some are broad and round, others narrow and long; some have a flat smooth surface and others an irregular one adorned with all kinds of excrescences. A few species are harmless plant-suckers, while others are downright predators. Others still are both simultaneously. Those which sting caterpillars and soft-skinned insects and suck them dry are useful allies of man in his struggle against plant pests, while others are pests themselves. All lay their eggs in groups on leaves or other parts of plants.

The eggs are barrel-shaped and, varying from one species to another, exhibit more or less strongly marked structures. Typical is a flat lid which is burst open by the hatching larva by means of a special organ. The shield bug in the picture, *Graphosoma semipunctatum,* measures 1·1 to 1·2 centimetres (just under half an inch). Together with a similarly coloured species, *Graphosoma italicum,* whose black stripes on the hood are not, however, broken, they are widespread in Southern Europe and are found on umbel-bearing plants.

59 The wasp species *Polistes gallicus,* which is native in Central and Southern Europe, belongs to the family of *Vespidae* or true wasps which includes all types from solitary to highly developed social wasps. *Polistes gallicus* is a medium-sized insect, 1·0 to 1·6 centimetres (0·4 to 0·6 inches) long, whose relatively small nest is made from a paper-like substance. The nests of all species of *Polistes* have open combs, without the protective membranes which are found on the nests of other similar insects, like the much-feared hornet *(Vespa crabro).* For that reason the nests are usually found in sheltered positions. After hibernation the young queen builds a nest in the spring and forms a colony. She lays her eggs, one in each cell, and some time later the larvae hatch out. These are fed with a chewed-up pulp of caterpillars and insects. The larvae thus live exclusively on a meat diet whereas the adult wasps feed chiefly on nectar and plant and fruit sap. Passing through a pupa stage, the larvae develop into sterile female workers which then help to enlarge the nest and look after the next wasp generation. During the summer months conditions in a wasp community are always such that only

sterile individuals—*i.e.,* female workers—can grow up. This is due, on the one hand, to the limited supply of food to the larvae and, on the other, to the fact that the worker wasps so stimulate the larvae that they give off certain body fluids. In the late summer more food is supplied but less or no saliva is then demanded. In consequence the larvae can develop into normal females capable of propagation. At the same time the queen lays unfertilized eggs from which the male insects develop. She then ceases laying eggs and the colony gradually perishes. Only the fertilized young females remain alive to ensure, as queens, the continuation of the species in the following year.

60 The pines *(Pinus spp.)* are the most widespread conifers in the western Mediterranean region. Occuring either as solid forest formations or, much more frequently, as individual trees or in small picturesque groups, their broad, usually umbrella-shaped, tops give the landscape its typically southern character. These conifers have been planted in Southern Europe since antiquity, for the sake of their seeds, the pine kernels. Since *Pinus pinea* (see plate) grows well even on sandy soil, it is particularly suitable for the afforestation of sand dunes. In the Rhône delta—the Great Camargue—the pines are a fairly rare feature. In the near-by Little Camargue, on the other hand, major patches of *Pinus pinea* are found on sandy soil.

61 The black-winged stilt *(Himantopus himantopus),* a graceful bird about 40 centimetres (16 inches) tall, breeds on the edge of rice paddies, marshes, and flooded lowlands. Its excessively long, pencil-thin legs, which in flight project unmistakably beyond the tail, are the typical characteristic of this wading bird. It reacts noisily and fearfully to all occurrences in its nesting area. With shrill wailing notes the members of a stilt colony will circle round any intruder approaching their nests, which are usually built on clumps of grass or piles of mud. Their shrill "kyip-kyip-kyip-kyip" causes an uproar throughout the neighbourhood.

When foraging, the stilt has a deliberate long-paced walk, with head and neck aimed towards the ground while the tail end of the body points obliquely upward.

Its long legs enable the bird to wade even in relatively deep water; moreover, it is quite a good swimmer. In the late summer the pairs with their fully fledged young unite to form major groups and formations. They are joined by arrivals from other regions which, together with many other species of wading birds, profit from the great wealth of food offered by the Camargue's marshes and lagoons. From early to mid-September they depart for their African winter quarters.

62 The European or green tree-frog *(Hyla arborea)* is the only amphibian frog in Europe which, thanks to small adhesive pads on its fingers and toes, is capable of climbing up smooth vertical surfaces. As a result, it is encountered not only in the water or on the ground, but regularly also high up among shrubs and on trees. The tropical rain forests harbour a large number of magnificently coloured relations of the European tree-frogs which, however, have become true tree-frogs and rarely if ever descend to the ground. The European tree-frog reaches a body length of 5 centimetres (2 inches). Its upperside, as a rule, is a beautiful leaf green, while its belly is whitish. A black line, often with a yellowish hem along the top, starting near the nose and running to behind the thigh (but confined to mouth and temples in *Hyla arborea meridionalis*), separates the two main colours. The upperside is subject to colour variations and may shade from light green into yellow or, on the other hand, through dark green and grey into brown.

From the end of March until June the European tree-frog is found chiefly by or in the water. That is also its mating time, when the male is particularly vociferous. The eggs are laid by the female in the form of small blobs of spawn which remain on the bottom of lakes and ponds until the tadpoles hatch out. In the course of about four months these develop into little tree-frogs, capable of changing over from an aquatic to a terrestrial existence. The diet of the European tree-frog consists of insects, their larvae, and worms.
In the late autumn the animals hide away in holes in the ground, under stones, or in other places of shelter in order to survive the winter in a deathlike rigour. The individual in the plate represents a rare colour variant of the sub-species *Hyla arborea meridionalis* which in

the Camargue takes the place of the Central European race *Hyla arborea arborea*. These animals do not change their colour but always keep their pale-blue coat.

63 Numerous freshwater marshes, together with their damp shore regions, provide the habitat of a variegated flora and fauna. These marshes have their highest water-level in winter. But even then it rarely exceeds 100 to 120 centimetres (40 to 48 inches) at the deepest points. From March onward the level usually begins to drop. The extent to which these marshes dry out during the summer depends on the incidence of rainfall and some-times also on the artificial influx of fresh water from rice paddies and irrigation canals. The salt content of the water increases with progressive evaporation, but does not exceed relatively low values even when the marshes dry out completely.

64-65 The Mediterranean marsh regions are of great importance for the migration and wintering of duck. Though not particularly suitable as breeding grounds because of their regular drying out during the summer months, they provide superb living conditions for hundreds of thousands of duck of various species during the winter. In the Camargue alone some 150,000 to 200,000 such duck are regular winter visitors. In open ponds, in flooded rice paddies and vineyards, and in brackish lakes they all find their favourite food such as grain, tubers, etc.

The largest contingents are provided by the teal *(Anas crecca,* Plate 65), the smallest European species of duck, and by the mallard *(Anas platyrhynchos),* with about 50,000 individuals each. The next most numerous are the wigeon *(Anas penelope),* with 20,000 to 25,000 individuals, pintail *(Anas acuta),* pochard *(Aythya ferina),* and shoveller *(Spatula clypeata,* Plate 64), whose male is altogether one of the most magnificent drakes —with black and white upperparts, a brilliant green head with yellow eyes, white chest, and rust-coloured belly and flanks. Populations of some 5000 individuals each, on average, are provided by the tufted duck *(Aythya fuligula),* gadwall *(Anas strepera),* and red-crested pochard *(Netta rufina).* Other species represented are scaup *(Aythya marila),* goldeneye *(Bucephala clangula),* and, by the sea, eider *(Somateria mollissi-*

ma), velvet scoter *(Melanitta fusca),* and common sco-ter *(Melanitta nigra).* Whereas the surface-feeding duck (such as mallards, teals, and shovellers) chiefly in-habit open bulrush marshes and their flooded neigh-bourhood, the diving duck (such as pochard, red-crested pochard, and tufted duck) prefer the deeper lagoons and brackish lakes.

66 Teal *(Anas crecca),* see notes to Plates 64–65.

67 Skeleton of a tamarisk on the wintry shore of a fresh-water pool. The tamarisk *(Tamarix gallica)* is typical of the western Mediterranean region. As a shrub or tree, occasionally reaching a height of 5 to 6 metres (16 to 20 feet), it dominates certain stretches of the central and upper Rhône delta. Because of their sturdiness, ta-marisks are grown as shelter belts against the wind along rice paddies and vineyards. Blossom time is from June to August. The delicate pale pink blossoms form thick clusters 10 to 30 centimetres (4 to 12 inches) long.

68 The lapwing *(Vanellus vanellus)* is distinguished by live-ly, graceful movements and superb flying skill. The Ca-margue and the adjacent regions offer this attractive bird all that it can possibly wish for its mode of living—wide-open spaces, humid low-lying marshes, and artifi-cially irrigated farmland with a very great variety of food such as worms, snails, larvae of insects, etc.

The lapwings begin to lay their eggs as early as the end of March or the beginning of April. Their nests are fre-quently in damp meadows and fields, or on clumps of grass and bulrushes in the flooded lowlands. The four olive-green eggs, occasionally with irregular dark-brown dots, spots, and lines, are invariably so arranged by the parent bird that their pointed ends touch at the centre of the nest. Sitting on the eggs is chiefly the task of the female, while the male—identifiable by its longer crest and its usually iridescent back feathers—keeps watch near the nest. When faced with enemies—and these include man—the lapwing, presumably relying on its great flying skill, displays astonishing courage. It will hurl itself towards the enemy, pull up steeply in front of him, fling itself first towards one side and then to the other, literally turn head over tail and utter its loud and urgent cry of "kee-wi—kee-wi". The rapid flapping of wings and the air passing through its plumage during such mock attacks produce a clearly audible rushing and booming.

69 The whiskered tern *(Chlidonias hybrida)* builds a floating nest of bulrush stems and young reed shoots among the sedge beds of shallow ponds. As a rule several small, territorially limited groups join to form a colony. The nesting material is picked up in the bill and frequently carried to the nesting place over great distances. In the Camargue the birds profit from the presence of the *taureaux,* the black cattle, which leave behind them a trail of broken bulrushes whenever they wade through or graze in a marsh.

The position of the nest provides excellent protection for eggs and chicks against four-legged enemies. On the other hand, heavy losses in eggs and young birds are occasionally caused by violent mistral winds, the tall waves raised by them, or the premature drying up of the lakes. Total destruction of a colony is not a rare occurrence. Sometimes, according to how advanced the season is, a second attempt at breeding is made. The two parent birds take turns in sitting on the eggs during the twenty days or so. Almost before they are dry the chicks are capable of leaving the nesting platform and swim to the nearest patch of vegetation to hide there. The whiskered tern feeds on small frogs, dragonflies, and the aquatic larvae of various other insects. Only exceptionally is a small fish caught. The whiskered tern does not breed in the Camargue every year; whether it does or not depends on the weather, the waterlevel, and the height of the vegetation.

70 The shores of the inland lakes are frequently edged by thick belts of reeds, often well above a man's height. The depth of these belts is sometimes several hundred metres. It is in the shelter of these reed thickets that a great variety of bird species propagate each year.
The reeds *(Phragmites communis),* with many-noded lignifying stems reaching a height of 4 metres (13 feet), need fresh water. Major reed-beds therefore are found chiefly in the vicinity of the freshwater canals running into the inland lakes.

71 Seasonal marsh on the fringe of a freshwater lake—see Plate 38.

72 The magnificently patterned European pond tortoise *(Emys orbicularis)* lives in ponds, slow-flowing canals, and freshwater ditches of the upper Camargue. In large individuals, its dark, red-brown to black dorsal armour measures up to 36 centimetres (14 inches) along the curvature. The individual plates are all more or less decorated with numerous yellow dots and radial lines. The tortoise's head, tail, and legs likewise bear irregular yellow patches. The legs are well suited to running and swimming and can be fully retracted between back and belly armour, as can also its head and tail. The toes are linked by webs and equipped with strong claws.

During the day the pond tortoise likes sunning itself on land. But in bad weather and at night it keeps mainly to the water. There also it hunts snails, amphibians, the larvae of insects, and small fishes. Food caught on land, an earthworm for instance, is invariably dragged into the water and there consumed.
In the summer (from the end of May until the end of June) the females dig holes into the earth of the banks and there deposit eight to sixteen eggs. Hard ground is softened up by means of excrement fluid. When the eggs have been laid the animals again carefully close up the hole. The topmost layer of earth is pressed down more firmly than the lower layers. All this work is usually done in the course of a single night. Hatched by the warmth and moisture of the soil, the young fully developed tortoises emerge the following spring, as small copies of their parents. They are completely independent right from the first day. The pond tortoise spends the winter buried in mud. As with all variable-blooded creatures, its body temperature adjusts itself to any ambient temperature which results in an appropriately reduced energy expenditure for the organism. This is one of the reasons why tortoises live to such great age.

73 With his surface of about 60 square kilometres (23 square miles), the Etang de Vaccarès, situated at the centre of the Camargue, is the largest of the inland lakes which are linked with one another by fords. Before the cultivation of rice—which was vigorously

promoted especially after the Second World War—the lake used to dry out in parts during the summer. The salt content of the water rose very sharply, reaching values of 40 to 80 grams per litre. The large quantities of freshwater which are now being run into the Etang de Vaccarès from the neighbouring rice paddies have resulted in a stabilization of its level. Its mean salt content over the year now amounts to 6·5 to 8 grams per litre. The south-eastern shore of the lake is subject to considerable erosion. Especially during the winter and spring months, heavy mistral gales cause the banks to be heavily battered by the waves, so that shore defences have had to be constructed at several points.

74 The most original creature of the Camargue, in every sense of the word, is the crab-like Branchiopod *Triops cancriformis,* sometimes called a fairy shrimp. As soon as the rice paddies are flooded in early summer or after heavy rainfall, producing puddles and pools, many of stagnant waters are suddenly alive with strange shapes vigorously swimming about the water or digging in the mud. Even where there has been no water whatever for several months or even years previously, nothing but dry ground and dust, these creatures, which are close to the prototype of the crab, are suddenly encountered.

The body is covered by a broad dorsal shield or carapace, 3 to 4 centimetres (1·2 to 1·6 inches) long, which carries at its forward edge three whip-like pairs of antennae. Three eyes *(Triops*—the three-eyed)—*i.e.,* a small central eye and two large lateral eyes—are on the frontal side of the head shield. From a small, articulated abdomen project two long, thin, forked bristles. The underside of the creature reveals its numerous swimming legs with their leaf-shaped feet which serve both for propulsion and for breathing and filtering its food, consisting of zooplankton. These feet are in a continuous rapid rhythmical movement so that the human eye can scarcely discern them singly. From the underside it can also be seen that the antennae are extensions of the anterior pair of legs.

The sudden appearance of large numbers of fairy shrimps is due to the fact that the extraordinarily resistant eggs, embedded in the bottom of dried-out pools, remain viable even through several years of total drought. Indeed, in order to develop, they must pass through at least one dry period. The larvae hatch out within hours of the ground being soaked. After twenty-one moultings they reach sexual maturity within two or three weeks. Thus, even before the pools dry out again, the existence of a further generation is ensured.

75 The bearded tit *(Panurus biarmicus)* is a veritable clown among the birds of the Camargue. Its presence in reed-beds is betrayed by its distinctive ringing "tching-tching", uttered chiefly in flight. Birds climbing about in the thicket frequently utter a soft grating "tchirr". Bearded tits are acrobats in the reeds. Even during violent mistrals they approach the wind-lashed reed stems with great assurance. One of their most striking characteristics is their curiosity. If their interest has been aroused by anything—even by a human—they will often come up very close to inspect.

The bird's upperparts and tail are a beautiful tawny colour. Breast and belly show a reddish-grey colouring; the primaries are pale grey to off-white. The male has a striking pale ash-grey head with two wide black 'moustache' stripes. These are lacking in the female and juveniles. Unlike the reed-warblers, the bearded tit does not suspend its nest from reed stems but invariably builds it close to the surface of the water, on a base of last year's broken reeds. The young birds hatch out after about twelve days, and barely two weeks later leave the nest. For some time the family roves through the neighbourhood together. Gradually these excursions are extended far beyond the breeding grounds. The bearded tit is found chiefly in Eastern Europe, the south of Russia, and Asia Minor. In Western Europe it is found only sporadically.

76 The purple heron *(Ardea purpurea)* builds its platform-like nests in large reed thickets. Like most herons, it breeds in colonies. Occasionally, but rarely, a pair may build an isolated nest. The colonies in the Rhône delta usually number five to thirty breeding pairs. Under favourable conditions, however, colonies of up to seventy, eighty, or more pairs may be established. The old birds, which appear very dark when seen in flight, reveal at close quarters a wonderful shading of

colour. Back and wings are dark grey with a faint touch of purple. Elongated chestnut feathers droop from the mantle. The very long, thin neck is likewise chestnut-coloured and boldly striped with black and white. Crown and cap are bluish-grey to black. Long, powerful prehensile toes enable the purple heron to climb effortlessly through the reeds. Even the young birds, which are fully fledged about six weeks after hatching, possess this skill and conduct early excursions in the neighbourhood of the nest. They also very soon develop the ability to fish so that, at the age of two months, they are independent of the parent birds.

The 'changing of the guard' at the nest is a magnificent spectacle. The two birds circle each other on the rim of the nest, their splendid feathers held away from their bodies, jerking their necks up and down and occasionally clicking their bills. The purple herons feed principally on fish but also catch frogs, snakes, and aquatic larvae of beetles. At spots with an ample supply of food groups of herons numbering over one hundred individuals can often be observed in July and August.

77 During the hot, dry summer months large conglomerations of snails, sometimes numbering several hundred, can be seen on grasses, chervil plants, bushes, and posts. These snails, in what is known as æstivation, have thus taken refuge from the hot ground in order to escape desiccation and certain death. The tight clustering of so many individuals and the simultaneous sealing of their shells with a fast-hardening calcareous membrane slow down the rate of body-fluid evaporation. As a result, at least the snails at the centre of such a bunch stand a chance of surviving the dry season.

78 Except during spawning time, which is in April and May, the Spanish spadefoot toad (Pelobates cultripes) rarely shows itself in daytime. Only at night does it emerge from its natural or self-dug caves to engage in foraging. It is a typical nocturnal creature and a superb 'digger', capable of working its way into sand or mud with astonishing speed. In this it is exceedingly well served by the large, horny, sharp-edged spades on the undersides of its hind legs. Its upperside is yellow-brown or pale grey, sprinkled with a large number of

olive or dark-brown dots, single or continuous. Its belly is a dirty white, sometimes sprinkled grey-brown. The body looks squat; the head is short and markedly convex. The vertical pupils are a striking feature. In its movements the Spanish spadefoot toad is more like the frog than the toad proper. It is considerably faster, more agile, and altogether more active than the better-known common toad (Bufo bufo). Its food consists mainly of insects and nocturnal snails. When alarmed, it occasionally adopts a strange menacing posture and secretes from its glands a liquid smelling of garlic. But the smell of this secretion is only weak. The Spanish spadefoot toad is native to northwestern Morocco, Spain, and the south of France. A peculiar feature are its larvae (tadpoles), which are enormous in comparison with those of other frogs and toads.

79 No other species of owl can be observed so frequently in southern Europe as the little owl (Athene noctua). This is due partly to the fact that, unlike most other owls, it does not shun daylight but on the contrary is frequently seen sitting on overhead wires, poles, blocks of stone, etc., in bright sunlight, hunting for insects and small vertebrates, and also to the fact that, generally speaking, it is not too shy of man. Frequently the bird can be observed sitting on top of road signs, allowing the cars to race past it. Unfortunately this habit has cost the lives of many little owls when at night, blinded by headlights, they have flown straight into the beam and have been struck by the vehicles. It is incredible that to this day so many people should regard this harmless and amiable bird as a harbinger of death, just because of its call and because it appears outside lighted windows at night catching insects. The ancient Greeks, much more appropriately, dedicated the little owl to the goddess Athene, the goddess of wisdom, and it has thus become the symbol of knowledge.

In hollow trees, in cliffs, in cracks in walls, in rifts in the ground and under rocks the female of the little owl sits on its three to seven pure white roundish eggs for twenty-eight days. The young birds, still wearing their downy plumage, leave the protection of their home at night and climb out to meet their parents returning to them with food.

80 The bite of the tarantula, which belongs to the family of wolf spiders, has always been regarded as dangerous and was thought to lead to a form of insanity that was curable only by furious dancing. This belief is reflected in the south Italian *tarantella* dance. In fact, its bite though painful is not in the least dangerous. This spider, 3 to 5 centimetres (1·2 to 2 inches) long, fawn-coloured with dark stripes on the abdomen and a black belly, lives in holes in the ground which it leaves chiefly at night to hunt for insects by running and leaping. It will also eat less vigorous individuals of its own kind. But the tarantula will show up outside its hole even during daytime. Occasionally it will sun itself, the forward part of its body projecting from the entrance. The moment its prey gets near the tarantula jerks out from its hole and kills it with a poisonous bite from its strong clawlike mandibles. The entrance to its hole is invariably camouflaged with short, dry blades of grass, small pebbles or crumbled soil, and some gossamer threads. During periods of great heat or rain the spider occasionally withdraws to its den for some time, in which case it seals off the entrance with cobwebs.

In the late summer the adult females carry about with them, attached to their abdomen, an egg cocoon which they defend furiously. In early September the young spiders hatch out and immediately climb on to their mother's back. There they spend seven months, until April of the following year, without taking any food, patiently carried about by the female. Only after this prolonged period do they leave their mobile nursery and start out on an independent life.
The picture shows a female of the species *Lycosa narbonensis*.

81 East of the Greater Rhône, in the triangle formed by Arles, Port-St-Louis, and Miramas, lie the stone deserts of the Crau. They represent the former alluvial area of the Durance, a river originating in the Massif des Hautes-Alpes. Before this river became a tributary of the Rhône it used to force its way through the Pertuis de Lamanon, a valley cut through the Alpilles, and empty directly into the Mediterranean. In its delta, the present-day Crau, the river deposited its detritus. In

places this stone deposit is up to 15 metres (50 feet) deep. The northern and eastern parts of this area of altogether 50,000 hectares (123,550 acres) have been turned into agricultural land by means of widely ramified canal systems. Pastures, vineyards, and olive groves produce good yields. In the central and southern parts, on the other hand, all one meets is flocks of sheep which roam through the monotonous landscape in winter and spring, feeding on the sparse vegetation. In some of the marginal areas various typical plants of the Mediterranean Garrigue have established themselves. These include Evergreen oak and Kermes oak *(Quercus ilex* and *Quercus coccifera)*, Spanish broom *(Spartium junceum)*, and rock-roses *(Cistus spp.)*. The presence of a few species of breeding birds which are rare in Central Europe makes the Crau particularly interesting to the ornithologist.

82 Above the steppes of the Rhône delta, and in particular over the stony desert of the Crau, a small, slim bird of prey, almost snow-white in certain lights, can be seen hunting regularly. Without even the slightest beating of its narrow, pointed wings it glides along close to the ground. This is the male of Montagu's harrier *(Circus pygargus)*, attempting to induce insects and small birds to fly up from the ground so it can seize them in the air. The female is built a little more sturdily, and its upperparts have a dark-brown colouring, while breast and belly shade into yellow with marked yellow-brown streaks. In flight, moreover, a white rump patch can be seen. This feature is shared also by the somewhat larger hen harrier *(Circus cyaneus)* and the pallid harrier *(Circus macrourus)*, which is less often observed in Europe.

Montagu's harrier lives sociably. In favourable hunting and nesting grounds several pairs frequently nest close together. The bird does not build a nest proper, the eggs being laid on trampled-down blades of grass and sedge stems. A particular feature about the bird's care of its young is that the female searches for chicks which have moved away from the nesting place and carries them back in her bill (this was observed at the nest in the picture by Dr. O. von Frisch, the zoologist, in 1966 and recorded on film).

83 A few miles north-east of Arles rise the limestone rocks of the Alpilles. They form, on the one hand, the northern boundary of the Crau, and on the other a transition from the vast monotonous delta landscape of the Camargue to the fertile regions of Provence. The hills rise to an average height of 300 to 400 metres (1000 to 1300 feet). Their steep slopes are heavily eroded. The valleys and flat slopes, on the other hand, are profusely covered with the evergreen bush forest of the Garrigue. Evergreen oak *(Quercus ilex)*, Kermes oak *(Quercus coccifera)*, common furze *(Ulex europaeus)*, and localized patches of Aleppo pines *(Pinus halepensis)* are the dominant trees. Rock-roses *(Cistus spp.)* and Spanish broom *(Spartium junceum)* lend the scene a bright touch of colour in spring.

84 In the areas adjoining the Camargue to the north and east—the hot, bush-grown Garrigue and the stony Crau—scorpions *(Euscorpius italicus)* are quite common. Predominantly nocturnal predators, they live hidden under tree bark, under stones, in cracks in walls, in the ground, etc. At first sight their pincers, which are converted mandibular antennae, as well as their backwards and sideways movement, are strongly reminiscent of crabs —except that the crabs' pincers are transformed anterior walking legs. The scorpion's 'tail', consisting of six narrow segments with the last link inflated like a vesicle, terminates in a needle-sharp curved sting which can be turned in all directions. Into it run the ducts from two poison glands whose secretion serves the paralysis or killing of its prey (insects, spiders and woodlice). The scorpion seizes these with its pincers, brings its flexible tail forward over its back, and thrusts the sting into the underside of the prey.

Scorpions do not get on too well with each other. After mating, which is often preceded by a prolonged prelude, the male is frequently killed and eaten up by the female. The young scorpions, about twenty to thirty at a time, are born alive and are carried about on their mother's back until their first moulting—*i.e.*, for many days and sometimes weeks.

The sting of the scorpion *(Euscorpius flavicaudis)*, which is about 4 centimetres (1·5 inches) long, is not in the least dangerous. It may be compared with a wasp or bee sting and merely produces skin irritation and local pain. Very much more painful but likewise not fatal, is the sting of the larger, usually yellowish-brown, scorpion of southern France, *Buthus occitanus*. Among the tropical scorpion species, on the other hand, there are some very much more dangerous animals whose sting may be lethal even to adults. In those cases death is usually due to paralysis of the respiratory centre.

85 The southern smooth snake *(Coronella girondica)*, which reaches a length of 60 to 70 centimetres (24 to 28 inches) when fully grown, is a rather lively snake and one that is relatively quick to bite. The basic colouring of its upperparts is a light or a dark shade of yellowish or greyish brown. There is usually a touch of red in it. The black band which runs from the rear end of the eye to the corner of the mouth usually continues along the side of the neck. The nape patch frequently has the shape of a horseshoe with its ends pointing forward. Definitely a crepuscular reptile, the southern smooth snake is rarely found lying in the sun. It hunts lizards, small rodents, and young birds which are killed by encircling and crushing.

This attractive snake is native to the Iberian peninsula, the south of France, and the south Tyrol, as well as parts of Italy and north-west Africa.

86 The viperine water snake *(Natrix maura)* is a short, slender snake with a clearly defined head. It loves the water and its vicinity. The colouring of its upperparts varies considerably, as does also the pattern of dark patches on its back. The colouring ranges, according to the age and habitat of the snake, from pale grey-brown or olive-green to yellowish or brown, and occasionally reddish. The variable patterning not infrequently shows a zigzag band, lending the viperine snake a deceptive similarity to the common adder *(Vipera berus)*. But its round pupils make it possible to distinguish it instantly from the adder. The females reach a length of nearly 100 centimetres (40 inches), while the males measure a mere 85 centimetres (36 inches). When pursued, the viperine snake whenever possible makes for water and submerges. If seized, it hisses and discharges its stench glands in the root of its tail; it never bites.

Its prey—frogs, fishes, earthworms, and occasionally toads and newts—are swallowed alive. In this it is helped by the exceptional mobility of jaw structure which it shares with all snakes. The bone parts of this structure are not rigid but linked with each other by joints, and capable therefore of lateral or frontal displacement.

87 The Montpellier snake *(Malpolon monspessulanus)*, one of the largest snakes in Europe, reaches a length of over 200 centimetres (80 inches). Its body is like a long cylinder and its head does not stand out from it to any marked degree. This snake is native to the whole Mediterranean zone. Unfortunately, the numbers of this fine reptile have been dropping unmistakably in the Camargue, due largely, it is thought, to the countless victims claimed by present-day road traffic.

The basic colour of the Montpellier snake varies from pale sandy or grey-brown (especially in the case of young animals—see plate) through olive-green to black. Its prey, which is killed by poison, consists of rats, small rabbits, young birds, and lizards. Occasionally it also devours small snakes. In spite of the presence of venom glands the bite of the Montpellier snake is not dangerous to humans. The injecting teeth are located far back in the upper jaw so they do not become effective in a quick bite.

88 The ladder snake *(Elaphe scalaris)*. This exceedingly temperamental snake, measuring about 150 centimetres (60 inches) when fully grown, inhabits the higher-lying dry regions of the Rhône delta. It is also found in the dunes. It is one of the most powerful European snakes and hunts mainly mice, lizards, and occasionally small birds. The basic colour of its upperparts varies from pale grey or grey-brown in young animals to reddish-brown or reddish-yellow in the adult (see plate). The young ladder snake has a black-brown forked band on the upper side of its head, with broad stripes running down the side through the eyes. Starting at the nape, a series of dark cross-shaped patches extends down the centre of its back as far as the point of its tail. In between and alongside a second string of lesser patches may be seen, with occasionally a third and a fourth line alongside or underneath. These disappear with increasing age until only two clearly visible longitudinal bands remain. The original ladder pattern is lost.

89 The caterpillar of the spurge hawk moth *(Celerio euphorbiae)* displays several characteristics common to all hawk moth caterpillars—large size and striking colouring. Many, moreover, are capable of adopting a rather strange menacing posture by more or less pronouncedly erecting the head and anterior body. Sometimes the head is also bent back under the large thorax. As a result of this, and also of the eye patches carried by certain species on the thorax, the front part of the caterpillar then looks like that of a much larger animal. The 'horn' carried by many hawk moth caterpillars at the tail end serves no particular function and appears to be merely an ornament.

The hawk moths differ from other moths in both body shape and mode of living. Their average wing span ranges from 6 to 10 centimetres (2·4 to 4 inches) and in the largest species may reach 20 centimetres (nearly 8 inches). The forewings are of a strikingly elongated, narrow, and usually pointed shape. The hindwings are relatively small. The body is streamlined. This, in conjuction with the rapid wing beat produced by powerful muscles, makes possible the arrow-swift flight of these creatures. Owing to the peculiar shape of their long, spirally coiled proboscis many species of hawk moth play an important part in the pollination of flowering plants whose anthers are located deep inside the flower together with the nectaries. The pollen adhering to the upper surface of the proboscis is carried by the hawk moth to the next flower and there brushed on its stigma. In this way pollination is accomplished, unintentionally but systematically. Only few species of hawk moth fly in daytime. Most of them come to life only at dusk and during the night.

90 The ant-lion *Palpares libelluloides,* belonging to the family *Myrmeleonidae,* is an insect with a wing span of 11 to 12 centimetres (4·3 to 4·7 inches). Its flight is slow and awkward and is invariably confined to short distances. In daytime the insects are quiescent and stay in hiding. Not till the early evening or the night do they come out to tumble from plant to plant. Their predatory larvae resemble those of another ant-lion, *Myrme-*

leon formicaria, both in appearance and mode of living. The larvae are flat and broad and, according to species, grow to a length of 3 centimetres (1·2 inches). Unlike the larvae of *Myrmeleon formicaria*—in fact, the name ant-lion belongs more properly to the larvae than to the perfect insect—they do not dig conical pitfalls in the loose soil but lurk for their prey in the sand, only slightly camouflaged. They are capable of very agile forward and backward movement and seize any prey that gets near them—ants and other insects. The prey is held in the suction claws and stung. A digestive fluid is injected into the body of the prey, and when it has dissolved the food it is sucked back again. This process, known as external digestion, is met with also in spiders and the larvae of various beetles. The structure of the insect's internal organs does not enable it to digest its food internally.

91-93 *Saturnia pyri,* the largest European moth, and no doubt one of the most beautiful, is a close relation of the Emperor moth *(Saturnia pavonia),* one of the largest English moths. It belongs to the family *Saturniidae* which comprises the largest moths in terms of wing area. Their bodies, as a rule, are covered with a woolly fur and their wings are heavily scaled. The antennae of the males are broadly feathered. Many species, including *Saturnia pyri,* carry large coloured eyespots, especially on the hindwings. The male insects are strong, though somewhat cumbersome, flyers. The thicker-bodied females are less mobile. *Saturnia pyri* is common throughout southern Central Europe. Its mating flights, made famous by the classical experiments of J. H. Fabre, the French entomologist (1823–1915), can be readily observed. Fabre tried to solve the mystery of why a large number of males would, within a short time, seek out his newly hatched captive females, and how they managed to find their way to them over a great distance. He did not exclude the possibility that the males might be attracted by a scent emitted by the females. More recent experiments have largely confirmed this assumption. The female allure substances trigger off reconnaissance flights by the males, in the course of which, guided by the heightened intensity of the scent, they eventually find the female. Whether any additional guidance systems are used in this connection remains to be est-

ablished. The large green or greenish-yellow caterpillars of *Saturnia pyri* are covered with blue tubercles bearing long, spiky lashes (Plate 91). Before pupation they spin dense durable cocoons. Their front part is shaped like a funnel trap, preventing the ingress of predatory insects but permitting the later hatching of the moth. These elaborately spun structures are usually attached near the bottoms of tree-trunks or to stones.

94 About 20,000 species of orchid are distributed over nearly the whole globe. Their wealth of form and colour is most striking in tropical and sub-tropical regions. The species native to Central and Southern Europe, being adapted to their less luxuriant surroundings, are of more modest appearance than their cousins from the regions of steamy heat. Even so, their flowers with their delicate shapes and detailed patterning are of great beauty.

The genus *Ophris,* to which the bee orchid *(Ophris apifera)* in the picture belongs, is distributed throughout Europe, Western Asia, and North Africa in about thirty species. It is marked by its great variability of colour, lip form and design, and shape of sepals. The plant attains a height of eight to twenty inches. Its flowers measure 2·5 to 2·8 centimetres (1·0 to 1·1 inches). A few leaves surround the stem at its base, others, progressively smaller, continue up the stem, the upper ones supporting the flowers.

95 The singing cicadas are generally regarded as the insects able to emit the most powerful sound. This is produced by means of a unique and exceedingly complex apparatus. To simplify a little, it consists of four small indentations situated on the underside of the body and covered with two ear-like lobes, with one membrane, or drum, each inside them, a powerful muscle on the second segment of the hind legs, a large air space inside the insect's body, and two membranes acting as amplifiers on the front and rear sides of the indentations. This muscle sets the membranes vibrating. The vibrations thus produced reach the amplifier membranes through the cavity, and these give the note its strong volume. The lobes mentioned above serve the regulation of the swelling and dying away of the note. The

singing insects, as a rule, are males. Only in a few species do the females also produce sounds. The principal distribution area of the singing cicadas are the tropics. There, too, the largest species are found, such as *Pomponia imperatoria,* native to the Malayan archipelago, with a wingspan of 18 centimetres (7·2 inches). By comparison the five species found in Central Europe are real pygmies. The biggest of them, *Cicada plebeja,* measures 4·5 to 5 centimetres (1·8 to 2·0 inches). *Cicadetta montana* reproduced here measures 2·3 to 2·8 centimetres (0·9 to 1·1 inches).

The transparent wings of the singing cicadas are folded, when the insect is at rest, in a roof shape over the abdomen and invariably project beyond it. The cicadas feed on plant juices which they ingest by means of their suction apparatus.

96 In classical antiquity the Rhône delta was formed by several arms of the river. Their courses can still be traced when one flies over the Camargue, by depressions in the ground, pools, and lagoons. In the seventh century B.C., at the time of the settlement of the Camargue by the Phocaeans (Greeks from Asia Minor) and later, when the coastal areas had been conquered by the Romans, the major river courses were navigable far into the interior of the country. Through the centuries the waters of the Rhône continued to hollow out new river-beds and to flood formerly fertile land. The last great flood was shortly before the French Revolution, when the river forged its two present estuary arms, which, of course, have since been regulated.

The big eastern arm, the Greater Rhône, carries nine-tenths of the total water from the river fork north of Arles; without any major change of direction it runs into the sea at the Gulf of Fos. The Lesser Rhône first makes a wide detour to the west, and then, after many twists and changes of direction, empties into the Gulf of Beauduc west of Les Saintes-Maries-de-la-Mer. Both arms of the river, but especially the Greater Rhône, are lined over long stretches with thick strips of deciduous trees. In several places these assume the form of damp riparian forests over a hundred yards deep. The tall vegetation is provided chiefly by white poplar *(Populus alba),* elm *(Ulmus campestris),* ash *(Fraxinus oxyphylla),* and willow *(Salix alba),* while the undergrowth is provided by privet *(Ligustrum vulgare),* dogwood *(Cornus sanguinea),* and hawthorn *(Crataegus spp.).*

97 One of the most frequently encountered birds in the Rhône delta, and certainly one of the most striking, is the graceful little egret *(Egretta garzetta),* with its snow-white plumage. The birds can be seen stalking through freshwater ponds and rice paddies, along irrigation canals, brackish lakes, and the lagoons near the sea, or else skimming close above the surface of the water. Their hunting grounds are frequently a great distance away from the breeding colonies. These are often shared with the night heron and the much less common Squacco heron *(Nycticorax nycticorax* and *Ardeola ralloides).* The nests—in large colonies there may be as many as thirty to fifty in a single tree—are usually built from just a few twigs. Not infrequently the pale-blue eggs can be seen from below through the base of the nest, and sometimes a single incautious movement of the bird settling down may cause an egg to tumble out.

The young herons are skilful climbers. Even before they are capable of flight they will leave their nest to spend the day among the near-by branches. But they always return to the nest for feeding. In summer the adult birds have a very long, drooping crest and greatly elongated scapulars, forming a hazy, drooping cloak. The black legs with yellowish-green feet are typical of the little egret and are particularly conspicuous in flight.

98 The nest of the penduline tit *(Remiz pendulinus)* is a real masterpiece. With indefatigable energy the bird weaves a dense, pliable, and very soft suspended pouch from plant fibres and animal wool. The nest building work is almost exclusively started by the male. During his work he sings vigorously in order to attract the attention of any female in the vicinity. When a pair have come together the nest is then completed by their joint efforts. Frequently, but by no means always, the pouch is fitted with a long projecting entrance tube.

Both sexes have the same colouring, though the female's colours are a little less bright. During the breeding season the back of the birds is chestnut, while head and throat are a striking greyish-white with a broad black patch across the face, reaching as far as the ears. Breast and belly are buffish-white. The eggs, between five and eight, are pure white and are hatched by the female alone. Often a male will mate with a second and occasionally with a third female, without, however, taking any part in the bringing up of the young. The principal distribution areas of the penduline tit are Italy, Eastern Europe, and parts of Asia. In Western Europe it appears only sporadically.

99 Persistent cold spells, extremely hot and dry summers, or a marked change in the salinity of the ground water frequently result in the dying off of entire patches of deciduous trees. The bizarre bare skeletons of their trunks and branches will tower skywards from the low vegetation for dozens of years until, rotten and decayed, they crumble into mould.

100 A species of reptile only rarely found in the Camargue and the adjacent areas is the seps *(Chalcides chalcides striatus)*, which belongs to the family of skinks. Skinks are widespread, in numerous species, chiefly in Africa and Asia. The seps resembles a blindworm *(Anguis fragilis)* in size and shape, but on closer inspection its four minute leg stumps with their three short toes each are immediately seen. The toes bear scarcely perceptible claws. This reptile, in fact, is a splendid example of morphological development. As a transitional form between the limbed and the limbless reptiles it is living testimony to the infinitely slow but continually active evolutionary process. Several species of skinks still possess fully developed legs, while others show greatly shortened ones. Other species still reveal such a degree of atrophy that the limbs are totally absent. The seps hardly uses its residual limbs for locomotion; indeed, it presses them flat against the body while making its way by snaking. But it still uses them in the resting position. The seps shown in the picture is decorated with nine to thirteen brownish or blackish longitudinal bands and is native to southern France and the Iberian Peninsula.

(For the success of this photograph the authors are indebted to Dr.O. von Frisch, Brunswick.)

101 After the flamingo, the rarest and most valuable animal species of the Rhône delta is the beaver *(Castor fiber)*. At one time the beavers' lodges and dams were part of the landscape of European river valleys. But ill-considered and short-sighted hunting, practised until quite recently and indeed to this day, so decimated the beaver population that the species was brought to the verge of extinction. Nowadays this largest European rodent survives only in southern Norway, in the southern reaches of the Rhône, on the middle Elbe, in northern Poland and in a few parts of Russia. Even there, their numbers have been greatly reduced.

Various countries, such as Sweden, Finland, Switzerland, and Austria, are now endeavouring to resettle the beaver. It is thought that in the Camargue their number has very recently been increasing again on the banks of the Rhône and the islands in the river, but owing to the animals' circumspect and purely nocturnal way of life observation is usually difficult.

In the Rhône delta the beavers only rarely build the kind of lodges from branches and boughs cemented with mud which their cousins in Northern Europe are so fond of constructing. Along the Rhône the beavers instead dig holes into the earth of the steep banks with entrances about 40 to 50 centimetres (16 to 20 inches) below the surface of the water. From these lodges a fresh-air chimney is occasionally driven upwards into the open. This can be several metres long and is sometimes covered with branches and boughs; it is found chiefly at beavers' lodges where young animals are raised. As, however, the beaver requires only a very little oxygen such a chimney is by no means universal. In order to reach their feeding grounds by swimming, and in order to float their food reserves (branches and twigs of soft woods) to the vicinity of their lodges, the animals regularly build small dams to back up the water. The damage caused by their felling of trees (principally young willows and poplars) is exceedingly slight and usually negligible.

Beavers are exclusively herbivorous and never eat fish. They spend the major part of their lives in the water. They swim and dive superbly, submerging sometimes for up to ten minutes, but on land move rather slowly and awkwardly. As a danger signal they beat the water with their broad, flattened, scaly tail just before diving.

102 Whereas in Central Europe the hoopoe *(Upupa epops)*, a strikingly coloured black, white, and orange-brown bird, is rather rare, it belongs to the most common species in Southern Europe. In the Camargue it is almost ubiquitous in open woodlands and parkland. Even in the neighbourhood of human habitation its far-carrying mating call of "hoo-poo-poo-hoo-poo-poo" can be heard in spring and its young seen a few weeks later. It nests generally in old woodpecker holes or hollow trees, but its eggs, usually five to seven, are found also in holes in the ground, among piles of stones, in sandy or loamy banks, in sheep pens, and in old implement sheds. The stuffy, rather unpleasant smell which sometimes emanates from the hoopoe's nesting place is due not, as is often assumed, to the nest being fouled, but to the fact that the young birds secrete a malodorous fluid from their rump glands to ward off unwelcome intruders and enemies. During the breeding period the female also possesses this means of defence.

The hoopoe forages almost entirely on the ground. It runs along, nodding its head and frequently erecting its head tufts, chasing insects and their larvae. Now and again it will eat also small animals such as young lizards. This bird is very fond of extensive sand and dust baths. The young leave the nest about twenty-five days after hatching. The family, however, keeps together for some time while the parent birds teach their offspring the art of catching their prey.

103 With a body length of 19 centimetres (7·5 inches) the Scops owl *(Otus scops)* is only very slightly larger than the smallest European owl, the pygmy owl *(Glaucidium passerinum)*. Its body has a slim appearance, with a tapered shape; the small, round head with its not always conspicuous ear tufts is remarkably flexible. Whenever the bird believes itself to be in danger it ruffles its feathers, including the ones on its head and its face, and puffs itself up to almost twice its size. Combined with a simultaneous slow-motion rocking of its whole body, this behaviour is particularly impressive.

The preferred habitat of the Scops owl is in thick patches of deciduous woodland with old, rotten, and hollow tree-trunks. It does not fear human proximity and is frequently found nesting in gardens and parks near human habitations. Its food consists chiefly of insects, and it therefore finds a rich supply of its prey outside lit windows at night when beetles and moths are attracted there in great numbers. Unfortunately, this amiable bird appears to be progressively displaced in the Camargue by the increasing number of noisy jackdaws. Its mournful ocarina-like note is nowadays heard far less frequently than was the case a few years ago.

104 Green deciduous trees always indicate the presence of fresh water. For that reason they are found, apart from along the two arms of the Rhône, only in the central and upper Camargue, along irrigation canals and near human habitation. Here they provide welcome shade during the hot summer, a shade that is very rare in the rest of the delta.

105 The night heron *(Nycticorax nycticorax)*, as its name suggests, does not become truly active until nightfall. Except during breeding time, when it is busy also during the day, this short-legged, squat heron, rather plump in comparison with the little egret *(Egretta garzetta)*, leads a secret sort of life. Not until twilight does it fly out to find its prey among the rice paddies and on the edges of pools and irrigation ditches. It is then that its hoarse call is heard. In flight it has a stumpy, owl-like silhouette. Like the little egret, the night heron nests in colonies, in thickets and deciduous or coniferous trees, such as pines. It usually nests in association with the little egret, the boundaries of the nesting areas of the two species not being clearly delineated. The nests of little egrets and night herons are often closely interspersed, without the two species interfering with each other's breeding. On the other hand, pure colonies of night herons are sometimes found in small clumps of bushes, especially among tamarisks and elms on the edge of marshes. The night heron feeds chiefly on crustaceans, insects, amphibians, reptiles, and other small vertebrates. Fish, because of the bird's preferred hunting ground, less frequently form part of its diet. In big mixed colonies the night herons often collect the food dropped or vomited on to the ground by the young birds. Nor is it unprecedented for them to go occasionally for a little egret chick.

The night herons arrive in the Camargue from their African winter quarters at about the end of March or the beginning of April. Their departure is between the end of September and early October.

106 The roller (*Coracias garrulus*), a 30-centimetre (12-inch) bird resembling a jay, is distributed chiefly throughout Southern and Eastern Europe, throughout Asia as far as 80°E and throughout North Africa. A migratory bird, the roller leaves its European breeding grounds during the second half of the year in order to winter in southern and eastern Africa. Its closest relations live in the tropics. At the start of the mating period the males perform splendid nuptial display flights, frequently tumbling over several times in the air. The roller's vivid blue wings with black borders and violet-coloured wing-coverts are particularly well observed during these performances which are invariably accompanied by shrill notes of "gray-ray-ray-ray". The roller likes open steppe-like country with a few clumps of trees and some individual trees. There it will sit at points of vantage, such as treetops, poles, electric wires, etc., hunting dragonflies, cicadas, grasshoppers, and other large insects. These it catches both in flight and on the ground. The powerful bird also catches small vertebrates such as mice and lizards.

Its nest, as a rule rather untidily built of the roots and stems of plants, is found in hollow trees, or in holes in banks or walls. Favourite breeding places are major patches of woodlands with clearings inside. Sandpits in open country likewise often serve as nesting places. Frequently the roller associates with bee-eaters, widening the latter's nesting holes to suit its own larger body. In this case small colonies consisting of several pairs are occasionally established. Near its nest the bird is exceedingly cautious and timid, and after a disturbance will not return to it for a very long time, and then only after performing astonishing deception manœuvres. The normal voice of the roller is a corvine "kr-r-r-ak" or a disyllabic "krak-ak". When excited or alarmed it utters a hard, drawn-out "kray".

List of Vertebrates of the Camargue

The list below is designed to inform the reader about the species of vertebrates that can be observed in the Camargue. The list of fish, amphibians, reptiles, and mammals includes only those species which are found in the Camargue itself; the list of birds, on the other hand, also includes those species which are seen not in the delta area proper but outside it, over a radius of about 100 kilometres (sixty miles). For most of these, a note on their habitat is appended, as well as, in the case of migratory birds, the months of their passage or stay in the Camargue.

The list is intended as an aid to visitors to the Camargue and makes no claim to scientific completeness. For that reason also no reference is made to sources. Species which were formerly encountered in the Camargue but have not been confirmed over the past few decades are not included. Species illustrated in this book are marked with an asterisk (*).

Fish *Pisces*

RAYS *Rayidae*

Spotted ray *Raia montagui*. Caught along the *graus*, the links between sea and lagoons.

STURGEON *Acipenseridae*

Sturgeon *Acipenser sturio*. Occasionally caught in the Rhône and along the *graus*.

CARP *Cyprinidae*

Carp *Cyprinus carpio*. The most common fish in the fresh-water pools; also found in slightly brackish water.
Tench *Tinca tinca*. Widespread in fresh water.
Barbel *Barbus barbus*. Infrequent in fresh water.
Gudgeon *Gobio gobio*. Widespread in fresh water.
Bream *Abramis brama*. Common in fresh water and in slightly brackish water.
Bleak *Alburnus alburnus*. Widespread in fresh water.
Rudd *Scardinius erythrophthalmus*. Common in fresh water.
Roach *Leuciscus rutilus*. Common in fresh water.
Chub *Squalius cephalus*. Fairly common in fresh water.
Nose-carp *Chondrostoma nasus*. Common in fresh water.

CATFISH *Siluridae*

Catfish *Ameiurus nebulosus*. Very common in fresh and brackish water. Imported from America.

HERRING *Clupeidae*

Pilchard *Clupea pilchardus*. Occasionally enters brackish water from the sea.

Twaite shad *Alosa finta*. Along the *graus*.
Anchovy *Engraulis encrasicholus*. Along the *graus*.

SALMON *Salmonidae*

Sea trout or salmon trout *Salmo trutta*. Travels down the Rhône to the sea.

PIKE *Esocidae*

Pike *Esox lucius*. Widespread in fresh water.

CYPRINODONTS *Cyprinodontidae*

Common gambusia or mosquito fish *Gambusia affinis*. Very common in fresh and brackish water. Introduced from America to control larvae of mosquitoes.

SKIPPERS *Scombresocidae*

Garfish *Belone belone*. Enters brackish lakes from the sea.

EELS *Anguillidae*

Eel *Anguilla anguilla*. Very common in all fresh, brackish, and salt-water lakes in the Camargue. Most important commercial catch.

STICKLEBACKS *Gasterosteidae*

Stickleback *Gasterosteus aculeatus*. Common in fresh and brackish water.

SYNGNATHIDS *Syngnathidae*

Sea-horse *Hippocampus spp*. Infrequent in brackish lakes.
Pipe-fish *Syngnathus abaster*. Widespread in brackish lakes.
Great pipe-fish *Syngnathus acus*. Along the *graus*.

ATHERINIDS *Atherinidae*

Sand-smelt *Atherina mochon*. Very common in brackish lakes.

GREY MULLET *Mugilidae*

Grey mullet *Mugil cephalus*. Common in all Camargue waters except pure fresh water.
Thin-lipped grey mullet *Mugil capito*. Common in brackish water.
Golden grey mullet *Mugil auratus*. Common in brackish lakes.

SEA BREAM *Sparidae*

Annular gilt head *Diplodus annularis*. Enters the *graus* from the sea.
Sea bream *Diplodus sargus*. Enters the *graus* from the sea.
Gilt head *Chrysophrys aurata*. Widespread in brackish lakes, which it enters from the sea.

RED MULLET *Mullidae*

Red mullet *Mullus barbatus*. Enters the *graus* from the sea.

PERCH *Percidae*

Perch *Perca fluviatilis*. Widespread, but less common in fresh water.
Sea bass *Morone labrax*. Common in brackish lakes, which it enters from the sea.
Pike-perch *Lucioperca lucioperca*. Common in fresh water. Originally from the Danube basin.

FRESH-WATER SUN-FISH *Centrarchidae*

Pumpkin-seed sun-fish *Eupomotis gibbosus*. Common in fresh water. Introduced from America.

WRASSE *Labridae*

Corkwing wrasse *Grenilabrus melops*. Enters the *graus* from the sea.

GOBIES *Gobiidae*

Transparent goby *Aphia minuta*. Enters the *graus* from the sea.
Gobius lota. Common in brackish water.

GURNARDS *Triglidae*

Sapphirine gurnard *Trigla hirundo*. Enters the *graus* from the sea.

WEEVERS *Trachinidae*

Lesser weever *Trachinus vipera*. Enters the *graus* from the sea.

BLENNIES *Blenniidae*

Blenny *Blennius sanguinoletus*. Enters the *graus* from the sea.

MACKEREL *Scombridae*

Mackerel *Scomber scombrus*. Enters the *graus* and the lower reaches of the Rhône from the sea.

FLOUNDERS *Pleuronectidae*

Sole *Dicologlossa cuneata*. Enters the brackish lakes.
Turbot *Scophthalmus maximus*. Enters the brackish lakes from the sea.
Brill *Scophthalmus rhombus*. Enters the *graus* from the sea.
Flounder *Flesus flesus*. Common in brackish lakes, even with very low salt content.
Sole *Solea vulgaris*. Common in brackish lakes.

GADIDS *Gadidae*

Burbot *Lota lota*. Infrequent in fresh water.

Amphibians *Amphibia*

SALAMANDERS *Salamandridae*

Palmate newt *Triturus h. helveticus*. Near slow-flowing canals and fresh-water pools.

SPADEFOOT TOADS *Pelobatidae*

Parsley frog or spotted mud-frog *Pelodytes punctatus*. By lakes, ditches, and fresh-water pools.
*Spanish spadefoot toad *Pelobates cultripes*. Widespread by fresh-water pools.

TOADS *Bufonidae*

Natterjack or running toad *Bufo calamita*. Prefers sandy soil and is regularly found among dunes.

TREE FROGS *Hylidae*

*European or green tree frog *Hyla arborea meridionalis*. Very common in the most varied habitats: near ditches, in reed-beds on the edges of lakes, in damp meadows, in gardens, etc.; in summer in trees and shrubs.

TRUE FROGS *Ranidae*

Edible frog *Rana esculenta*. Common near still and muddy fresh-water marshes.
Marsh frog or laughing frog *Rana ridibunda perezi*. More commonly found as a pond frog, advances into brackish-water areas.

Reptiles *Reptilia*

AQUATIC TORTOISES *Emidae*

*European pond tortoise *Emys orbicularis*. By stagnant or slow-flowing fresh water.
Caspian terrapin *Clemmys caspica*. By stagnant or slow-flowing fresh water.

SKINKS *Scincidae*

*Seps *Chalcides chalcides striatus*. Predominantly on dry grassland.

LIZARDS *Lacertidae*

*Jewelled lacerta *Lacerta lepida*. Not very common in the Camargue, but common in adjacent areas.
Green lizard *Lacerta viridis*. Common, mainly in bushes and thickets along the fresh-water canals.
Wall lizard *Lacerta muralis*. Very common and widespread.

SANDRACERS *Psammodromus*

Spanish sandracer *Psammodromus hispanicus*. Common among coastal dunes.

SNAKES *Colubridae*

Grass or ringed snake *Natrix natrix*. Common and widespread, especially near stagnant and running fresh water.
*Viperine water snake *Natrix maura*. Common, especially near stagnant and running fresh water.

*Ladder snake *Elaphe scalaris.* Common and widespread; prefers dry sunny spots.

*Southern smooth snake *Coronella girondica.* Rare; chiefly in dry spots.

*Montpellier snake *Malpolon monspessulanus.* Fairly common in dry sunny places, but also likes water.

Birds *Aves*

DIVERS *Colymbidae*

Black-throated diver *Gavia arctica.* Occasionally on the sea.

Great northern diver *Gavia immer.* Exceptionally on the sea.

Red-throated diver *Gavia stellata.* Fairly regularly on the sea in winter.

GREBES *Podicipidae*

Great crested grebe *Podiceps cristatus.* Breeds fairly commonly in fresh water. Several hundred in the Camargue throughout the year.

Red-necked grebe *Podiceps griseigena.* Occasionally in winter and spring; chiefly on the sea.

Horned or Slavonian grebe *Podiceps auritus.* Rare; on the sea.

Black-necked grebe *Podiceps nigricollis.* Regular, but rather few individuals in fresh and brackish water from August to February.

Little grebe *Podiceps ruficollis.* Commonly breeds in fresh water. At least a few hundred in the Camargue throughout the year.

PETRELS AND SHEARWATERS *Procellariidae*

Storm petrel *Hydrobates pelagicus.* A few breeding on the islands south of Marseilles. Occasionally on the sea off the Camargue.

Manx shearwater *Puffinus puffinus.* A few breeding on the islands south of Marseilles. Occasionally on the sea off the Camargue.

Cory's shearwater *Puffinus diomedea.* A few breeding on the islands south of Marseilles. Occasionally on the sea off the Camargue.

GANNETS *Sulidae*

Gannet *Sula bassana.* A small number regularly along the Camargue coast. In autumn sometimes hundreds.

CORMORANTS *Phalacrocoracidae*

Cormorant *Phalacrocorax carbo.* Common from August/September to March/April on Etang de Vaccarès, in low ponds and on the sea; about 1000 wintering.

Shag *Phalacrocorax aristotelis.* Occasionally in autumn and spring.

HERONS AND BITTERNS *Ardeidae*

Heron *Ardea cinerea.* Occasionally breeds. Very numerous (several hundreds) chiefly from late June to September. Smaller number wintering. Near fresh, salt, and brackish water.

*Purple heron *Ardea purpurea.* Common. Mid-March to September. Over 1000 pairs in reed-beds.

Great white heron *Egretta alba.* Occasionally, chiefly October to January.

*Little egret *Egretta garzetta.* Common. March to October. Several thousand pairs breeding in deciduous and coniferous forests, in association with night herons. Several hundreds stay the winter.

Squacco heron *Ardeola ralloides.* Rare. April to September. Fresh-water marshes and rice paddies. Several dozen pairs in little egret and night heron colonies.

Cattle egret or buff-backed heron *Ardeola ibis.* Rare. April to September. Fresh-water marshes. One breeding pair in 1957, 1958 and 1968 Increasing.

*Night heron *Nycticorax nycticorax.* Common. Late March to September/October. More than 1000 pairs breeding in colonies, usually allied with little egrets.

Little bittern *Ixobrychus minutus.* Fairly common. April to September. Nests chiefly in small reed-beds.

Bittern *Botaurus stellaris.* In limited numbers in large reed-beds throughout the year. Its call heard from January to early May.

STORKS *Ciconiidae*

White stork *Ciconia ciconia.* Regularly in small numbers from July to October, on grassland and in fresh-water marshes. Occasionally in winter and spring.

Black stork *Ciconia nigra.* Almost regularly, individual birds in August and September; rare in October, November, April, May. Near fresh-water marshes.

SPOONBILLS AND IBISES *Plataleidae*

Spoonbill *Platalea leucorodia.* Occasionally from April to October. Near fresh-water or brackish marshes.

Glossy ibis *Plegadis falcinellus.* Occasionally from April to June, rarely from August to October. Near fresh-water or brackish marshes.

FLAMINGOS *Phoenicopteridae*

*Flamingo *Phoenicopterus ruber.* Common throughout the year; often more than 10,000 near brackish and salt water, from spring until summer. Usually 4000 to 5000 pairs nesting.

SWANS, GEESE, DUCKS, AND MERGANSERS *Anatidae*

Mute swan *Cygnus olor.* A few birds occasionally in winter.

Whooper swan *Cygnus cygnus.* A few birds occasionally in winter.

Bewick's swan *Cygnus bewickii.* A few birds occasionally in winter.

Greylag goose *Anser anser.* Small numbers fairly regularly in winter.

White-fronted goose *Anser albifrons.* Very rare in winter.

Bean goose *Anser fabalis.* Small numbers fairly regularly in winter.

Pink-footed goose *Anser brachyrhynchus.* Very rare.

Shelduck *Tadorna tadorna.* Regular breeder in brackish and salt water. About 100 individuals.

Ruddy shelduck *Tadorna ferruginea.* Exceptionally.

Mallard *Anas platyrhynchos.* Commonly breeding. Up to 50,000 individuals in winter. In brackish and fresh water.

*Teal *Anas crecca.* Common from August to April. More than 50,000 individuals wintering. In brackish and fresh water.

Marbled teal *Anas angustirostris.* Exceptionally in August/September.

Blue-winged teal *Anas discors.* Exceptionally.

Garganey *Anas querquedula*. Thousands in March/April and August/September. Winters very rarely; breeds in small numbers.

Gadwall *Anas strepera*. Breeds in small numbers. Up to 10,000 individuals in winter, chiefly in fresh water.

Wigeon *Anas penelope*. Common from September to March/April. In winter about 20,000 individuals, chiefly in brackish water.

Pintail *Anas acuta*. Breeds exceptionally. Common from October to April; up to 10,000 individuals in December, in brackish water.

*Shoveller *Spatula clypeata*. Breeds occasionally. Common from September to April. Sometimes over 10,000 individuals. In fresh and brackish water.

Red-crested pochard *Netta rufina*. Breeds commonly. Numerous throughout the year except in late summer; 5000 to 8000 individuals in November, chiefly in fresh water.

Pochard *Aythya ferina*. Common from September to April; more than 10,000 individuals in early winter, chiefly in fresh water.

Tufted duck *Aythya fuligula*. Common from October to April; more than 5000 individuals in early winter, chiefly in fresh water.

Ferruginous duck or white-eyed pochard *Aythya nyroca*. Occasionally or regularly in small numbers, chiefly in early winter.

Scaup *Aythya marila*. Regularly in small numbers during winter; fresh water and sea.

Goldeneye *Bucephala clangula*. Regularly in small numbers in winter; Rhône and brackish water.

Long-tailed duck *Clangula hyemalis*. Occasionally on the sea in winter.

Velvet scoter *Melanitta fusca*. Regularly in small numbers on the sea during winter.

Common scoter *Melanitta nigra*. Regularly in small numbers on the sea during winter.

Eider *Somateria mollissima*. Regularly in small numbers on the sea throughout the year.

Goosander *Mergus merganser*. Very rare in winter.

Red-breasted merganser *Mergus serrator*. Regularly in winter until April, in small numbers; brackish water.

Smew *Mergus albellus*. Occasionally in winter.

VULTURES *Aegypiidae*

Egyptian vulture *Neophron percnopterus*. A few pairs breeding in the Alpilles and in neighbouring massifs. Regularly visits the Camargue from March to October.

Griffon vulture *Gyps fulvus*. Exceptional.

EAGLES, BUZZARDS, HAWKS, KITES, HARRIERS, AND FALCONS *Falconidae*

Golden eagle *Aquila chrysaëtos*. A few breeding in Alpine foothills and Massif Central. Occasionally in the Camargue in winter.

Spotted eagle *Aquila clanga*. Regularly a few during winter.

Bonelli's eagle *Hieraëtus fasciatus*. A few pairs breeding in neighbouring massifs. Fairly regular visitor to the Camargue.

Buzzard *Buteo buteo*. Does not breed in the Camargue. Common from October to April.

Rough-legged buzzard *Buteo lagopus*. Occasionally in winter.

Sparrow hawk *Accipiter nisus*. Breeds along the Rhône; frequent visitor to the Camargue.

Goshawk *Accipiter gentilis*. Breeds in the neighbourhood. Occasional visitor to the Camargue.

Kite *Milvus milvus*. Regularly but in limited numbers in autumn, winter, and spring.

Black kite *Milvus migrans*. Breeds commonly. Stays from mid-March to September.

White-tailed eagle *Haliaëtus albicilla*. Occasionally in winter.

Honey buzzard *Pernis apivorus*. On migration; April/May and August/October; sometimes in large numbers.

Marsh harrier *Circus aeruginosus*. Common breeder and resident. Hundreds in the Camargue throughout the year.

Hen harrier *Circus cyaneus*. Regularly but in small numbers in autumn, winter and spring.

*Montagu's harrier *Circus pygargus*. Breeds regularly; not numerous in the Camargue, more common in the Crau from spring until autumn.

Short-toed eagle *Circaëtus gallicus*. Breeds regularly in the neighbourhood. Regularly in the Camargue in small numbers from March to October.

Osprey *Pandion haliaëtus*. Regularly on migration in small numbers, in March/April and September/October. Sometimes also in summer.

Peregrine *Falco peregrinus*. Regularly in small numbers from July to March; occasionally from April to June.

Hobby *Falco subbuteo*. Breeds regularly in small numbers in the pinewoods of the dunes. April to October.

Eleonora's falcon *Falco eleonorae*. Exceptionally.

Merlin *Falco columbarius*. Winters regularly in small numbers.

Red-footed falcon *Falco vespertinus*. Occasionally in April/May.

Lesser kestrel *Falco naumanni*. Breeds regularly in Provence; often in small colonies. Spring until autumn.

Kestrel *Falco tinnunculus*. Breeds commonly. Hundreds in the Camargue throughout the year.

PHEASANT, PARTRIDGE, AND QUAIL *Phasianidae*

*Red-legged partridge *Alectoris rufa*. Breeds regularly in the higher-lying parts of the Camargue and even more so in the hinterland.

Quail *Coturnix coturnix*. Breeds regularly in the hinterland and probably in the upper Camargue. Regularly on migration from April to October.

Pheasant *Phasianus colchicus*. Breeds fairly commonly. Introduced.

CRANES *Gruidae*

Crane *Grus grus*. Occasionally, October to March.

RAILS *Rallidae*

Water rail *Rallus aquaticus*. Commonly breeds in freshwater marshes; numerous throughout the year.

Spotted crake *Porzana porzana*. Breeds regularly but in smaller numbers in reedbeds.

Baillon's crake *Porzana pusilla*. As *Porzana porzana* but rarer.

Little crake *Porzana parva*. As *Porzana pusilla*.

Corncrake *Crex crex.* Occasional visitor to the Camargue; April/May and September/October.

Purple gallinule *Porphyrio porphyrio.* Seen in the Camargue from 1930 to 1940 and in 1969

Moorhen *Gallinula chloropus.* Commonly breeds in fresh-water marshes. Numerous throughout the year.

Coot *Fulica atra.* Breeds commonly in fresh-water marshes. Numerous throughout the year.

BUSTARDS *Otididae*

Little bustard *Otis tetrax.* Breeds and winters regularly in the Crau and in the Costières du Gard. Occasionally appears in the Camargue in winter.

OYSTERCATCHERS *Haematopodidae*

Oystercatcher *Haematopus ostralegus.* Breeds regularly in small numbers in brackish and salt-water pools. A few birds winter.

PLOVERS *Charadriidae*

*Lapwing *Vanellus vanellus.* Breeds commonly; very numerous in winter.

Ringed plover *Charadrius hiaticula.* Common on migration, late February to May and July to November. Perhaps breeds occasionally. Winters occasionally.

Little ringed plover *Charadrius dubius.* Common bird of passage; July to September and late February to April. Breeds occasionally.

*Kentish plover *Charadrius alexandrinus.* Breeds commonly on shores of brackish and salt-water pools and on saline soil. Numerous in autumn from August to November.

Grey plover *Pluvialis squatarola.* Frequently in passage between August and May; limited numbers in winter. Occasionally stays summer.

Golden plover *Pluvialis apricaria.* Common during winter, sometimes in hundreds together with lapwings and starlings; especially in the Crau and in the grasslands of the Camargue.

Dotterel *Eudromias morinellus.* Occasionally in March/April and August to November.

Turnstone *Arenaria interpres.* Regularly in limited numbers on migration and during the winter. Brackish and salt-water pools.

SNIPES, CURLEWS, GODWITS, AND SANDPIPERS *Scolopacidae*

Snipe *Capella gallinago.* Common from August to April; thousands in August and September. Fresh-water marshes.

Great snipe *Capella media.* Very rare from autumn to spring.

Jack snipe *Lymnocryptes minimus.* Regularly in small numbers from autumn to April. Fresh-water marshes, often in puddles near trees.

Woodcock *Scolopax rusticola.* Regularly in small numbers from autumn to spring. In deciduous trees and bushes.

Curlew *Numenius arquata.* Common from autumn to spring; occasionally in summer.

Whimbrel *Numenius phaeopus.* Frequently on passage from July to September and in April/May. Brackish and salt-water pools and seashore. Occasionally in summer.

Black-tailed godwit *Limosa limosa.* Common from February to May and July to October. Occasionally in winter and summer. Fresh and brackish water.

Bar-tailed godwit *Limosa lapponica.* Regularly in small numbers on migration and in winter. Salt water and seashore.

Green sandpiper *Tringa ochropus.* Common from July to October and March to May; not numerous in winter and only occasionally in summer. Fresh water.

Wood sandpiper *Tringa glareola.* Very numerous in July to October, common March to May, occasionally in winter and in summer. Fresh-water marshes and rice paddies.

Redshank *Tringa totanus.* A small number breeding regularly. Very numerous from July to November, less numerous in winter and spring. Chiefly near brackish water.

Spotted redshank *Tringa erythropus.* Common but in small flights, from August to May. Fresh and brackish water.

Greenshank *Tringa nebularia.* Common but in small flights, from July to November and April/May.

Marsh sandpiper *Tringa stagnatilis.* Regularly but in small numbers, July to September and April/May. Fresh and brackish water.

Common sandpiper *Tringa hypoleucos.* Common July to October and April/May, occasionally in winter. Fresh and brackish water.

Terek sandpiper *Tringa terek.* Exceptionally.

Knot *Calidris canutus.* Regularly but in small numbers, from April to June and in autumn. Brackish and salt water.

Little stint *Calidris minuta.* Common August to November and February to May; winters in limited numbers. Fresh and brackish water.

Temminck's stint *Calidris temminckii.* Common but in small flights, July to September and April/May; chiefly in fresh water.

Dunlin *Calidris alpina.* Very numerous October/November and February/March; major flights wintering. Brackish and salt water.

Curlew sandpiper *Calidris ferruginea.* Regular on migration in spring and autumn, usually in small flights, but often very numerous in late July and August; chiefly brackish and salt water.

Sanderling *Calidris alba.* Regularly but usually in rather small numbers, July to March, important passage April-May. Brackish and salt water.

Pectoral sandpiper *Calidris melanotos.* Exceptionally.

Broad-billed sandpiper *Limicola falcinellus.* Occasionally during autumn or spring migration.

Ruff *Philomachus pugnax.* Very numerous on migration, late February to early May and late July to September. Occasionally in winter; chiefly brackish water.

AVOCETS AND STILTS *Recurvirostridae*

*Avocet *Recurvirostra avosetta.* Several hundreds of pairs nesting. Fairly common in the Camargue throughout the year; a limited number wintering. Brackish and salt water.

*Black-winged stilt *Himantopus himantopus.* Breeds commonly in widely fluctuating numbers; April to September. Chiefly fresh water but also brackish water.

PHALAROPES *Phalaropodidae*

Grey phalarope *Phalaropus fulicarius.* Exceptionally.

Red-necked phalarope. *Phalaropus lobatus.* Regularly in small numbers; brackish water.

STONE CURLEWS *Burhinidae*

*Stone curlew *Burhinus oedicnemus.* Commonly breeds in the Crau. Fairly common on dry grassland and among salicornia in the Camargue; March to October. Winters in the Crau.

PRATINCOLES AND COURSERS *Glareolidae*

*Pratincole *Glareola pratincola.* Breeds regularly in small groups among the salicornia and in the Crau. April to September.

SKUAS *Stercorariidae*

Arctic skua *Stercorarius parasiticus.* Regularly in small numbers. Autumn and spring.
Great skua *Stercorarius skua.* Exceptionally.
Pomarine skua *Stercorarius pomarinus.* Exceptionally.

GULLS AND TERNS *Laridae*

Great black-backed gull *Larus marinus.* Occasionally in winter.
Lesser black-backed gull *Larus fuscus.* Regularly in small numbers from October to April. Brackish water.
*Herring gull *Larus argentatus.* Hundreds of pairs breeding. Common throughout the year.
Common gull *Larus canus.* Regularly in small numbers from August to late March. Brackish water and sea.
*Slender-billed gull *Larus genei.* One or two pairs regularly breeding among the black-headed gulls. May to August.
Mediterranean black-headed gull *Larus melanocephalus.* Individual pairs occasionally breeding among the black-headed gulls. Regularly on migration and in small numbers in winter; chiefly on seashore.
Little gull *Larus minutus.* Regularly on migration in relatively small numbers, chiefly in April and May. Occasionally stays the summer.
*Black-headed gull *Larus ridibundus.* Thousands of pairs breeding. Very numerous throughout the year.
Kittiwake *Rissa tridactyla.* Occasionally on the sea.
Black tern *Chlidonias niger.* Very numerous on migration, April to May and July to October. Sometimes stays the summer. Rice paddies, fresh, brackish, and salt water.
White-winged black tern *Chlidonias leucopterus.* Regularly in limited numbers; late April and May, occasionally until July.
*Whiskered tern *Chlidonias hybrida.* Breeds commonly; April to September. Fresh-water marshes.
*Gull-billed tern *Gelochelidon nilotica.* Breeds regularly; a few hundred pairs from April to September, on small islands in brackish lakes. Forages in fresh water, in meadows, and in dunes.
Caspian tern *Hydroprogne caspia.* Regularly in limited numbers on migration. April to May and August to November. Occasionally in summer; brackish water and sea.
Common tern *Sterna hirundo.* Breeds very commonly on the small islands in the brackish lakes; forages chiefly over the sea. March to September.

Roseate tern *Sterna dougallii.* Individual pairs breeding occasionally in common tern colonies.
*Little tern *Sterna albifrons.* Breeds commonly on the small islands in the brackish lakes. April to September.
*Sandwich tern *Sterna sandvicensis.* Breeds fairly commonly on the small islands in the brackish lakes; forages chiefly over the sea. Winters regularly.
Lesser crested tern *Sterna bengalensis.* Exceptionally.

AUKS *Alcidae*

Razorbill *Alca torda.* Regularly, usually in limited numbers, on the sea, mainly in winter.
Guillemot *Uria aalge.* Exceptionally; on the sea.
Puffin *Fratercula arctica.* Exceptionally; on the sea.

SANDGROUSE *Pteroclidae*

Pin-tailed sandgrouse *Pterocles alchata.* About a hundred pairs breeding in the Crau.

DOVES *Columbidae*

Stock dove *Columba oenas.* Fairly common from September to March.
Wood pigeon or ring dove *Columba palumbus.* Common from September to May, chiefly from October to November.
Turtle dove *Streptopelia turtur.* Breeds commonly, chiefly in brambles. Late April to October.
Collared turtle dove *Streptopelia decaocto.* Exceptionally.

CUCKOOS *Cuculidae*

Cuckoo *Cuculus canorus.* Common from April to September.
Great spotted cuckoo *Clamator glandarius.* Regularly and fairly commonly in pinewoods, olive groves, and woodlands in the hinterland; less common in the Camargue. Winters exceptionally. March to September.

OWLS *Strigidae*

Barn owl *Tyto alba.* Fairly common breeder and resident near human habitations.
*Scops owl *Otus scops.* Commonly breeds in parks, woodlands, etc. April to October.
Eagle owl *Bubo bubo.* A few pairs breeding in the Alpilles and other mountains of the hinterland.
*Little owl *Athene noctua.* Common breeder and resident.
Tawny owl *Strix aluco.* Common breeder and resident.
Long-eared owl *Asio otus.* Breeds regularly in small numbers. Fairly numerous in winter.
Short-eared owl *Asio flammeus.* Fairly regularly sporadic individuals on migration.
Tengmalm's owl *Aegolius funereus.* Exceptionally in the Camargue. Nests on Mont Ventoux.

NIGHTJARS *Caprimulgidae*

Nightjar *Caprimulgus europaeus*. Breeds in the hinterland and perhaps locally in the Camargue itself. Regularly on migration, April to May and August to September.

SWIFTS *Apodidae*

Swift *Apus apus*. Breeds in villages; hunts over the Camargue, often in large numbers. April to September.
Pallid swift *Apus pallidus*. Occasionally in the Camargue; has bred at Aigues-Mortes. April to October.
Alpine swift *Apus melba*. Breeds in the hinterland (Pont du Gard, Cevennes, perhaps also Alpilles). A few birds of passage regularly in the Camargue, March/April and August/September.

KINGFISHERS *Alcedinidae*

Kingfisher *Alcedo atthis*. A few pairs breeding. Common from late June to October, in small numbers during the rest of the year.

BEE-EATERS *Meropidae*

*****Bee-eater** *Merops apiaster*. Breeds commonly; late April to mid-September.

ROLLERS *Coraciidae*

*****Roller** *Coracias garrulus*. Breeds commonly in the hinterland; less common in the Camargue, where the species is confined to the higher ground (dry grassland). Late April to September.

HOOPOES *Upupidae*

*****Hoopoe** *Upupa epops*. Breeds commonly. Late February to early October.

WOODPECKERS *Picidae*

Green woodpecker *Picus viridis*. Common breeder and resident in all thickets.

Great spotted woodpecker *Dendrocopus major*. Infrequent breeder and resident in the wooded parts of the Camargue.
Lesser spotted woodpecker *Dendrocopus minor*. Breeds infrequently in the woodlands along the banks of the Rhône.
Wryneck *Jynx torquilla*. Common on migration, late March to early May and August to October. Occasionally winters.

LARKS *Alaudidae*

Calandra lark *Melanocorypha calandra*. Local breeder and resident in the Crau and Costière. Absent from the Camargue.
Short-toed lark *Calandrella brachydactyla*. Breeds very commonly in the Crau; fairly common in some salicornia patches in the Camargue. April to October.
Crested lark *Galerida cristata*. Common breeder and resident in the higher zones of the Camargue and in parts of the hinterland.
Wood lark *Lullula arborea*. Breeds commonly in the hinterland, the Alpilles, the Cevennes, etc. Regularly on migration in the Camargue.

Skylark *Alauda arvensis*. Very common breeder and resident.
Shore lark *Eremophila alpestris*. Exceptionally.

SWALLOWS *Hirundinidae*

Swallow *Hirundo rustica*. Breeds very commonly. Late February to early November.
Red-rumped swallow *Hirundo daurica*. At times unintentional visitor.
House martin *Delichon urbica*. Breeds commonly. Late February to early November.
Sand martin *Riparia riparia*. Breeds in neighbourhood (e. g. Durance) and occasionally in the Camargue itself. Very common on migration, March to May and chiefly August to September.
Crag martin *Ptyonoprogne rupestris*. Breeds and winters in the hinterland; occasionally in the Camargue.

ORIOLES *Oriolidae*

Golden oriole *Oriolus oriolus*. Breeds commonly in parks and deciduous woodlands. Late April to September.

CROWS *Corvidae*

Raven *Corvus corax*. Breeder and resident in Massif Central, the foothills of the Alps and in lesser mountains of the hinterland.
Carrion crow *Corvus corone*. Breeder and resident in the woodlands along the rivers; local in the Camargue.
Rook *Corvus frugilegus*. Exceptionally.
Jackdaw *Corvus monedula*. Very common breeder and resident chiefly near human habitations.
Magpie *Pica pica*. Very common breeder and resident.
Jay *Garrulus glandarius*. Breeder and resident in the hinterland and in the woodlands along the banks of the Rhône.
Chough *Pyrrhocorax pyrrhocorax*. Breeder and resident in the mountains of the hinterland (Cevennes, etc.).

TITS *Paridae*

Great tit *Parus major*. Breeds commonly and stays the whole year. Particularly numerous from October to November.
Blue tit *Parus caeruleus*. Common, but numbers fluctuating widely from year to year; September to March. Particulary numerous from October to November.
Coal tit *Parus ater*. Irregularly. In some years small invasions in October.
Crested tit *Parus cristatus*. Occasionally penetrates to the Camargue.
Long-tailed tit *Aegithalos caudatus*. Fairly common breeder and resident in deciduous woodlands.
*****Penduline tit** *Remiz pendulinus*. Breeds commonly in deciduous trees, March to June. A few birds stay in the Camargue for the rest of the year. Numbers fluctuate.
*****Bearded tit** *Panurus biarmicus*. Common breeder and resident in reed-beds.

NUTHATCHES *Sittidae*

Nuthatch *Sitta europaea*. Breeder and resident in the mountainous hinterland. Absent from the Camargue.

CREEPERS *Certhiidae*

Short-toed tree creeper *Certhia brachydactyla*. Breeder and resident in the woodlands along the banks of the Rhône and in the hinterland.
Wall creeper *Tichodroma muraria*. Small numbers regularly arrive in the Alpilles in winter. Exceptionally in the Camargue.

WRENS *Troglodytidae*

Wren *Troglodytes troglodytes*. Common on migration, October to November and March to early April. Small numbers wintering.

DIPPERS *Cinclidae*

Dipper *Cinclus cinclus*. Breeder and resident in the Massif Central and in the foothills of the Alps. Absent from the Camargue.

THRUSHES *Turdidae*

Mistle thrush *Turdus viscivorus*. Breeds in small numbers in the hinterland. Regularly in the Camargue from October to April and, indeed, fairly common in October and from February to April.
Fieldfare *Turdus pilaris*. Fairly common from November to March.
Song thrush *Turdus philomelos*. Nests in the mountainous hinterland; very common on migration, October to November and February to April. Small numbers wintering.
Redwing *Turdus iliacus*. Common from mid-October to March.
Ring ouzel *Turdus torquatus*. Regularly in small numbers on migration, September to October and late March to April, chiefly in the dunes.
Blackbird *Turdus merula*. Breeds locally in the woodlands along the banks of the Rhône and in the hinterland. Very common from October to March.
Rock thrush *Monticola saxatilis*. Breeds in the foothills of the Alps and in the Massif Central. Regular migration through the Camargue, in small numbers, mid-April to mid-May.
Blue rock thrush *Monticola solitarius*. Breeder and resident in the Alpilles; exceptionally in the Camargue.
Wheatear *Oenanthe oenanthe*. Very common on migration, late March to early April and mid-April to October.
Black-eared wheatear *Oenanthe hispanica*. Breeds regularly in the Crau, in Bas-Languedoc and in Basse-Provence. Small numbers passing through the Camargue, chiefly mid-April to May.
Pied wheatear *Oenanthe leucura*. Exceptionally.
Stonechat *Saxicola torquata*. Breeds in the hinterland. Fairly common in the Camargue from late September to early March, particularly from October to November.
Whinchat *Saxicola rubetra*. Breeds in the hinterland. Common on migration in the Camargue, late April to May and mid-August to early October.
Redstart *Phoenicurus phoenicurus*. Breeds in the hinterland. Very common in the Camargue on migration from mid-March to May and August to October.
Black redstart *Phoenicurus ochrurus*. Breeds in the hinterland. Common in the Camargue on migration from late February to April and mid-October to November. A limited number wintering.

Nightingale *Luscinia megarhynchos*. Breeds very commonly, chiefly in brambles and deciduous thickets. April to September.
Bluethroat *Luscinia svecica*. Common on migration, March to early April and especially mid-August to early October. Occasionally wintering.
Robin *Erithacus rubecula*. Breeds in the hinterland. Very common in the Camargue from mid-September to April, especially on its autumn and spring migrations.

WARBLERS *Sylviidae*

Cetti's warbler *Cettia cetti*. Common breeder and resident in deciduous thickets. After cold winters occasionally absent for several years.
Grasshopper warbler *Locustella naevia*. Regularly on migration in small numbers.
Savi's warbler *Locustella luscinioides*. Regularly breeds in small numbers in reedbeds. Late March to September.
Moustached warbler *Lusciniola melanopogon*. Commonly breeds among reeds and bulrushes.
Great reed warbler *Acrocephalus arundinaceus*. Commonly breeds in reedbeds, April to mid-October.
Reed warbler *Acrocephalus scirpaceus*. Breeds very commonly in reedbeds from late April to October.
Marsh warbler *Acrocephalus palustris*. Exceptionally.
Sedge warbler *Acrocephalus schoenobaenus*. Fairly common on migration from August to mid-October; less common in spring (April).
Aquatic warbler *Acrocephalus paludicola*. Regular on migration in small numbers, at least in autumn (August to October).
Melodious warbler *Hippolais polyglotta*. Breeds very commonly in gardens and patches of woodland. Late April to September.
Icterine warbler *Hippolais icterina*. On migration in small numbers. Late April to May and late August to September.
Olivaceous warbler *Hippolais pallida*. Exceptionally.
Orphean warbler *Sylvia hortensis*. Breeds in the neighbourhood; fairly common in the Camargue on migration, late April and particularly mid-July to mid-October.
Garden warbler *Sylvia borin*. Very common on migration, late April to mid-June and mid-August to mid-October.
Blackcap *Sylvia atricapilla*. Breeds commonly. Very numerous on migration in March and September to November; a limited number wintering.
Whitethroat *Sylvia communis*. Breeds commonly. Very numerous on migration, April to May and August to early October.
Lesser whitethroat *Sylvia curruca*. Occasionally on migration.
Sardinian warbler *Sylvia melanocephala*. Fairly common on migration, also resident, chiefly in evergreen shrubs.
Subalpine warbler *Sylvia cantillans*. Commonly breeds in hard-leaf thickets of the hinterland. Common in the salicornia steppes of the Camargue from autumn to early spring.
***Spectacled warbler** *Sylvia conspicillata*. Commonly breeds in the salicornia steppes of the Camargue. Late March to September. Winters occasionally.

Dartford warbler *Sylvia undata*. Commonly breeds in hard-leaf thickets of the hinterland. Common in the Camargue on migration, late March to May and July to September.
Rufous warbler *Cercotrichas galactotes*. Exceptionally.
Fan-tailed warbler *Cisticola juncidis*. Common breeder and resident along ditches and in dry pastures in the farmed parts of the Camargue. After cold winters may be absent for several years.
Chiffchaff *Phylloscopus collybita*. Breeds in the hinterland. Very common in the Camargue on migration in March and from mid-September to November. Often wintering in considerable numbers.
Willow warbler *Phylloscopus trochilus*. Very common on migration, mid-March to May and late July to October.
Wood warbler *Phylloscopus sibilatrix*. Common on migration, especially April/May, less common mid-July to September.
Bonelli's warbler *Phylloscopus bonelli*. Breeds in the hinterland. Common on migration, mid-April to May and especially July to September.
Yellow-browed warbler *Phylloscopus inornatus*. Exceptionally.
Radde's bush warbler *Phylloscopus schwarzi*. Exceptionally.

GOLDCRESTS *Regulidae*

Goldcrest *Regulus regulus*. Common on migration, October to late November. A small number staying the winter until April.
Firecrest *Regulus ignicapillus*. Breeds in the hinterland. Common in the Camargue, late August to early December. A small number staying the winter until April.

FLYCATCHERS *Muscicapidae*

Spotted flycatcher *Muscicapa striata*. Breeds fairly commonly. Numerous on migration, mid-April to May and August to October.
Pied flycatcher *Ficedula hypoleuca*. Very common on migration April to May and August to October.
Collared flycatcher *Ficedula albicollis*. Occasionally on migration, April to May.
Red-breasted flycatcher *Ficedula parva*. Occasionally on migration.

ACCENTORS *Prunellidae*

Dunnock or hedge sparrow *Prunella modularis*. Breeds in the hinterland. Common on migration, March to mid-April and October to November. A small number wintering.
Alpine accentor *Prunella collaris*. Occasionally on migration.

PIPITS AND WAGTAILS *Motacillidae*

*Tawny pipit *Anthus campestris*. Breeds fairly commonly at definite spots in the dunes and on dry grassland. Mid-April to October.
Tree pipit *Anthus trivialis*. Common on migration, April to mid-May and especially September to October.
Meadow pipit *Anthus pratensis*. Very common from October to March.
Water pipit *Anthus spinoletta*. Very common from mid-October to March.
White wagtail *Motacilla alba*. Breeds in the hinterland. Common from September to November and mid-February to March. A small number wintering.

Grey wagtail *Motacilla cinerea*. Breeds in the hinterland. Common in the Camargue chiefly from September to November. A small number wintering and on migration in spring (March to April).
Blue-headed wagtail *Motacilla flava*. Commonly breeds in the salicornia steppes; numerous on migration. Late March to October.

WAXWINGS *Bombycillidae*

Waxwing *Bombycilla garrulus*. Occasionally penetrates to the hills of the hinterland but never as far as the Camargue.

SHRIKES *Laniidae*

Great grey shrike *Lanius excubitor*. Breeds in limited numbers in evergreen thickets, chiefly in the Crau; also winters.
Lesser grey shrike *Lanius minor*. Breeds in limited numbers near cultivated land, chiefly in the Crau. April to September.
Woodchat shrike *Lanius senator*. Breeds in limited numbers in cultivated zones. Very numerous on migration, April to May and particularly July to September.
Red-backed shrike *Lanius collurio*. Breeds in the hinterland. Fairly common on migration, late April to May and mid-July to late September.

STARLINGS *Sturnidae*

Starling *Sturnus vulgaris*. Breeds irregularly and locally. Very numerous from mid-September to early April, particularly in October.
Rose-coloured starling *Sturnus roseus*. Exceptionally.

FINCHES AND BUNTINGS *Fringillidae*

Hawfinch *Coccothraustes coccothraustes*. Breeds in the hinterland. Small numbers fairly regularly in the Camargue from October to April.
Greenfinch *Carduelis chloris*. Limited numbers breeding, on migration, and wintering.
Goldfinch *Carduelis carduelis*. Very common breeder and resident.
Siskin *Carduelis spinus*. Fairly regular visitor, usually in small numbers, from late September to March.
Linnet *Carduelis cannabina*. Common breeder and resident on cultivated land, dikes, and dunes.
Twite *Carduelis flavirostris*. Exceptionally.
Redpoll *Carduelis flammea*. Occasional winter visitor.
Citril finch *Carduelis citrinella*. Occasional winter visitor in the hinterland.
Serin *Serinus serinus*. Breeds locally in the Camargue, commonly in adjacent areas. Winters fairly commonly.
Bullfinch *Pyrrhula pyrrhula*. Occasional autumn and winter visitor.
Crossbill *Loxia curvirostra*. Casual summer and autumn visitor, sometimes in large numbers.
Chaffinch *Fringilla coelebs*. Rarely breeds in the Camargue. Very numerous from October to early April.
Brambling *Fringilla montifringilla*. Regularly, in widely fluctuating numbers, from mid-October to mid-March.
Corn bunting *Emberiza calandra*. Common breeder and resident in the cultivated zones and on dry grassland.

Yellowhammer *Emberiza citrinella*. Regularly, but not in large numbers, from autumn to spring.
Black-headed bunting *Emberiza melanocephala*. Exceptionally.
Cirl bunting *Emberiza cirlus*. Breeds in the hinterland. Common in the Camargue from mid-October to March.
Ortolan bunting *Emberiza hortulana*. Breeds in adjacent regions. Regular visitor, occasionally in very large numbers, to the Camargue, particularly from mid-April to late May and mid-August to late September.
Rock bunting *Emberiza cia*. Fairly regularly, in small numbers, October to mid-April.
Little bunting *Emberiza pusilla*. Occasional winter visitor.
Reed bunting *Emberiza schoeniclus*. Commonly breeds on the edge of reed-beds. Winters in very large numbers.
Snow bunting *Plectrophenax nivalis*. Occasional winter visitor.

SPARROWS AND SNOW FINCHES *Passeridae*

House sparrow *Passer domesticus*. Very common breeder and resident; often far from human habitations.
Spanish sparrow *Passer hispaniolensis*. Exceptionally.
Tree sparrow *Passer montanus*. Common breeder and resident. Very common from autumn to spring.
Rock sparrow *Petronia petronia*. Breeds locally in the hinterland.

Mammals *Mammalia*

HEDGEHOGS *Erinaceidae*

Hedgehog *Erinaceus europaeus*. Common nocturnal and crepuscular animal near human habitations.

SHREWS *Soricidae*

Water shrew *Neomys fodiens*. Lives on the banks of the Rhône and of fresh-water lakes, but seems to be totally absent from the lower half of the delta.
Savi's pygmy shrew *Suncus etruscus*. In bushes and hedges. Remains very often found in the excrement of the barn owl *(Tyto alba)*.
Lesser white-toothed shrew *Crocidura suaveolens*. In open habitats in the Camargue, including the salt steppes.
Common European white-toothed shrew *Crocidura russula*. In sheltered habitats—*e.g.,* shrubs and thickets.

MOLES *Talpidae*

Mole *Talpa europaea*. In fields, meadows, and thickets; can live only in moist ground.

HORSESHOE BATS *Rhinolophidae*

Greater horseshoe bat *Rhinolophus ferrum-equinum*. Repeatedly caught in the Camargue and observed hunting.

VESPERTILIONID BATS *Vespertilionidae*

Large mouse-eared bat *Myotis myotis*. Repeatedly caught in the Camargue; remains found in excrement of birds of prey.

Pipistrelle *Pipistrellus pipistrellus*. Repeatedly caught in the Camargue.
Nathusius' pipistrelle *Pipistrellus nathusii*. Similar to *Pipistrellus pipistrellus;* almost regularly caught in the Camargue. The small bats which are observed in the delta at dusk in the summer belong mainly to this species.
Serotine *Vespertilio serotinus*. Has been caught in the Camargue.

HARES AND RABBITS *Leporidae*

***Rabbit** *Oryctolagus cuniculus*. Nocturnal and crepuscular; numbers again increasing in spite of myxomatosis. Often also observed in daytime. Lives colonially. Warrens found in dry, loose, or sandy soil in open habitats.
Hare *Lepus europaeus*. Although far less common than the rabbit, regularly observed in fields, meadows, and thickets. The two species do not get on together in the same area, the hare invariably being the one that withdraws.

BEAVERS *Castoridae*

***Beaver** *Castor fiber*. Lives along the two arms of the Rhône, in the delta proper, and particularly north of Arles. More common than often assumed, but only active at night.

COYPUS *Myocastoridae*

Coypu *Myocastor coypus*. South American rodent introduced to various European countries for fur farming and partly gone wild again. Regularly observed in the fresh-water marshes of the Camargue during the past two years. Feeds on aquatic vegetation. Diurnal animal; excellent swimmer and diver.

SQUIRRELS *Sciuridae*

Red squirrel *Sciurus vulgaris*. Rarely in the deciduous woodlands along the two arms of the Rhône in the Camargue.

DORMICE *Gliridae*

Garden dormouse *Eliomys quercinus*. Fairly common; fond of settling in magpie nests.

VOLES *Microtidae*

Water vole *Arvicola amphibius*. Lives on the banks of the Rhône and fresh-water lakes; often observed in daytime.
Mediterranean pine vole *Pitymis duodecimcostatus*. Predominantly underground in fields and meadows, particularly in damp spots near river courses, lakes, and pools.
Short-tailed field vole *Microtus agrestis*. Chiefly in thickets and hedges, and on the edges of marshes.

MICE AND RATS *Muridae*

Harvest mouse *Micromys minutus*. Prefers open and dry areas or dried-out reed marshes.
Wood mouse *Apodemus sylvaticus*. Prefers thickets and bushes, but also frequent on open ground and well into the salt steppes.

Black rat *Rattus rattus*. Predominantly in buildings, but also in holes in the ground. Only occasionally observed in the Camargue and far less common than the brown rat.

Brown rat *Rattus norvegicus*. Very common. Lives in earth holes and in buildings, frequently also on the edge of water, especially reedy marshes.

House mouse *Mus musculus*. Very common throughout the Camargue, even in the salt steppes, the dunes, and the islands in the brackish lakes.

DOGS *Canidae*

Fox *Vulpes vulpes*. Its holes are found in the Camargue chiefly on high-lying, dry, barely saline grassland with *Statice limonium* and bushes of *Phillyrea angustifolia*. Often also close to deciduous woodlands and human habitations.

MARTENS *Mustelidae*

Badger *Meles meles*. Fairly common in the same habitats as the fox.

Weasel *Mustela nivalis*. Widespread, chiefly in the upper half of the delta in zones with high-lying grassland with bushes and small thickets along the fresh-water canals.

Polecat *Mustela putorius*. Infrequent in marshy areas with *Phragmites communis* and *Typha angustifolia*. Feeds largely on frogs and fishes; excellent swimmer and diver.

Otter *Lutra lutra*. Very rare, possibly extinct. Used to be observed on both arms of the Rhône and by lakes, ponds, and marshes.

PIGS *Suidae*

***Wild boar** *Sus scrofa*. Common; during the day hides in damp thickets and bushes, in reed-beds, etc., Often roams far in search of food; its tracks are found even among the dunes by the sea.

As for aquatic mammals, mention will be made here only of the common dolphin, *Delphinus delphis*. There is always a chance of other species of dolphins and certain species of whale approaching the coast; in the winter of 1963, for instance, a rorqual, *Balaenoptera physalus*, was stranded near Les Saintes-Maries-de-la-Mer.